METHUEN'S MONOGRAPHS ON BIOLOGICAL SUBJECTS

General Editor: KENNETH MELLANBY, C.B.E.

THE CHEMISTRY OF PLANT PROCESSES

THE CHEMISTRY
OF PLANT PROCESSES

C. P. Whittingham, Ph.D.

Professor of Botany at
Queen Mary College, London

METHUEN & CO LTD

11 NEW FETTER LANE · LONDON E.C.4

First published in 1964
© C. P. Whittingham, 1964
Printed in Great Britain by Butler & Tanner Ltd
The Selwood Printing Works, Frome and London

203917

Preface

This book attempts to introduce students who have some basic knowledge in the physical sciences to problems in plant metabolism. No distinction is made between the contributions from plant physiology and plant biochemistry since both disciplines are necessary for an understanding of a plant process.

It is assumed that the reader has some previous acquaintance with the problems of plant function in their most elementary aspects. This book attempts to present concisely a broad survey of plant physiology and biochemistry suitable for university students. Some detail has been omitted and no attempt has been made to include all the latest work in this rapidly expanding subject. Rather, an attempt has been made to provide a framework to prepare the reader for the study of original papers in those aspects of special interest to him.

I am grateful to a number of colleagues who have helped in preventing more errors than remain.

C. P. W.

January 1964

5

Contents

PART ONE: CELLULAR METABOLISM

1 The development of experimental botany   *page* 11
2 Cellular structure and function   17
3 Enzymes   25
4 Fermentation and respiration   36
5 Energetics of respiration and biological syntheses   63
6 Photosynthesis   73
7 Nitrogen metabolism   104

PART TWO: PLANT PROCESSES

8 Osmotic relations of the individual cell   117
9 Water relations of the whole plant   134
10 Translocation   151
11 Growth   160

APPENDIX:

The chemistry of the constituents of living organisms   183

REFERENCES   195

INDEX   205

List of Plates

1 Late telophase in barley root tip *facing page* 16

2 Spadix of *Arum maculatum* 17

3 Section of leaf of *Nicotania tobacum* 32

4 Chloroplasts in palisade leaf cells of *Vicia faba* 33

5 Open stoma of *Cyclamen persicum* before and after puncture of one guard cell 144

PART ONE

Cellular Metabolism

CHAPTER ONE

The Development
of Experimental Botany

Man's first interest in plants arose from his search for food, for fuel, and for fibre. He soon discovered that many plants had marked effects on his physiological functions, and consequently the earliest botanists, the Greeks, were primarily interested in the classification of plants in accordance with their medicinal properties. During the early Renaissance a considerable number of writings were produced, but few of these were based on personal observation, many being copies and even copies of copies of the early Greek writers such as Dioscorides. At that time botanists were either medical men or apothecaries. In 1538 William Turner commented that 'as yet there was no English herbal but one full of cacographies and the universal naming of herbs'. Later he himself wrote a herbal largely intended for the use of apothecaries and it was shortly followed by that of Gerard. These pioneers in the study of British plants led up to the work of Ray. Ray personally observed almost all the plants listed in his Catalogue and was the first to distinguish and limit the number of species, noting that most herbalists 'mistake many accidents for notes of specific distinction'. He attempted to set up criteria which might be used to distinguish species and to formulate a system of classification. The detailed study of specific differences was pursued throughout the following century and culminated in the investigations of Linnaeus. The flora replaced the pharmacopoeia, the herbarium the physic garden, and the microscope the hand lens. But a fuller understanding of the nature of species came only after Darwin had formulated the concept of evolution. This resulted in an intensive and more purposeful pursuit of new facts which has continued until the present day. A practical system of plant classification is a first essential of all botanical research.

Prior to the nineteenth century, botany was not wholly or indeed mainly concerned with an answer to the question 'What plant is this?' That question must be answered, but the reasons why one answer is to be preferred to another are largely pragmatic. Other questions first asked by Aristotle and Theophastrus were: 'How does this plant grow, how does it feed, and how does it reproduce?' Satisfactory answers to these questions must be based on experiments. These had been carried out from the earliest times, not by the apothecaries who collected plants, but by chemists, who sought to explain all the phenomena in the world around them, including the process of life itself.

As early as the seventeenth century the Belgian chemist J. B. van Helmont planted a willow branch weighing 5 lb in a pot containing 300 lb of dry soil. Nothing was added to the pot but water, and at the end of five years the willow tree weighed 164 lb; yet the soil had decreased in weight by merely 2 oz. Van Helmont concluded that the tree had not gained its weight from the soil but rather from the water added. This simple experiment initiated the overthrow of the classical view of Aristotle, that plants derive their nourishment from the soil.

In the next century Stephen Hales, perpetual curate of Teddington and a serious student of Ray's work, began a series of experiments on plants which remain the basis of many exercises used in teaching today. Hales writes:

On June 29th I set a well-rooted plant of peppermint in a glass cistern full of earth and then poured in as much water as it would contain; over this glass cistern I placed an inverted glass. At the same time also I placed in this same manner another inverted glass of equal size with the former but without any plant under it . . . the water in the two inverted glasses rose and fell, as it was affected either by the different weight of the atmosphere or by the dilation or contraction of the air inside [that is, with pressure and temperature]. But the water in the vessel in which the peppermint stood rose so much above the surface of the water in the other vessel that one seventh part of the air must have been reduced to the fixed state, by being imbibed into the substance of the plant. . . . We may reasonably conclude that the one great use of leaves is to perform in some measure the same office for the support of vegetable life that the lungs of animals do for the support of animal life; plants very probably drawing through their leaves some part of their nourishment from the air.

Hales entered Bennett College, Cambridge, now called Corpus Christi College, in the year that Boyle died, 1696. He was aware of Boyle's work concerning the expansion of gases and indeed, had he not made allowance for the physical properties of gases in his experiment, he would have been misled in attributing the results solely to the biological material. He was prevented from pursuing the problem further by the lack of chemical knowledge, and another fifty years passed before Joseph Black first distinguished an individual 'air', namely 'fixed air' or carbon dioxide. Prior to this, individual gases had not been characterized. In 1777 Priestley wrote:

Van Helmont and other chemists who succeeded him were acquainted with the property of some vapours to suffocate and extinguish flames and of others to be ignited. But they had no idea that the substances (if indeed they knew that they were substances and not merely properties and affectations of bodies which produced these effects) were capable of being separately exhibited in the form of a predominantly elastic vapour . . . any more than the thing which constitutes smell.

Oxygen was discovered by Priestley and shortly afterwards shown by him to be produced by green plants. Unfortunately in his later years he became disturbed by his inability to repeat his earlier experiments and partly doubted the significance of his findings. Subsequently, Ingenhousz demonstrated the reasons for Priestley's difficulty. He showed that plants produce oxygen only when illuminated, whereas in darkness they behave just like animals, consuming oxygen and producing carbon dioxide.

By the beginning of the nineteenth century the two major activities of living green plants were recognized; on the one hand respiration – the oxidation of foodstuffs in the dark and an activity shared with the animals – and on the other, the production of foodstuffs from carbon dioxide in the light – called photosynthesis – a process peculiar to plants. Animals were dependent on plants, firstly for their food supply and secondly for the maintenance of an oxygen supply to the earth's atmosphere. Dutrochet (the discoverer of osmosis) realized in 1837 that only cells which contained chlorophyll could assimilate carbon dioxide in the light.

There are three main approaches to the problems of plant metabolism and function. The first, the quantitative study of some response of the living plant to its environment, is represented by the work of van Helmont. The full understanding of the influence of the environment on plant growth had to await further development in other branches of science. Two centuries passed before it became possible to determine the influence on plant growth of individual chemical elements, and this work led in the nineteenth and early twentieth centuries to the use of fertilizers as an important part of agricultural practice. Even in the present century further work has shown that certain rare chemical elements, previously thought of as unlikely to influence plant growth because of their trace concentrations in ordinary soils, are nevertheless essential for the growth of various crop plants. Such investigations of plant growth have been largely empirical.

A second experimental approach is to investigate the chemical nature of characteristic constituents of the plant. The ambition of the early herbalist was to isolate and purify the 'effective principles' of plants. This has now been achieved in certain cases, and once the chemical structure of a plant constituent is known its eventual synthesis outside the plant becomes a possibility. After isolation of a substance a search for related derivatives can be undertaken and new compounds discovered which may prove yet more powerful in their physiological action. Recent striking examples include the development of new and more effective antibiotics and herbicides. The remaining question to be answered is: by what means does the organism manufacture these substances from the simpler chemical compounds which constitute its food? This is the science of plant biochemistry. It requires a knowledge of the chemistry of the organic molecules which make up the plant, a brief summary of which will be found in the Appendix. The reactions which are concerned in the synthesis and interconversion of plant constituents are discussed in the first part of this book.

The third approach to the study of plants considers the structure of the plant with reference to its function. An understanding of the chemistry of the plant constituents alone will not be sufficient since we cannot consider the plant simply as a large and somewhat unusually shaped test-tube. Certain examples of the limitation of physiological potentialities by morphological structure are well known. For example, the seeds of *Robinia* take an unusually long time to germinate because of the hardness of the seed coat. If the seed coat is weakened by scraping with a knife, by treatment with acid or even by boiling for a few minutes, germination takes place rapidly. Such considerations also arise at the cellular and subcellular level. The first observations of plant anatomy were made by the earliest users of the microscope, Robert Hooke, Malpighi, Grew, and Leeuwenhoek in the years between 1660 and 1700. Their ideas remained undeveloped until the middle of the nineteenth century. From that time onwards the discovery of new preparatory techniques, and more recently of new types of microscope, have allowed rapid advances in our knowledge of the structure of plants. The relationship between structure and function at the cellular level will be discussed further in the next chapter. The complex relationships which arise at the multicellular level are fundamental to an understanding

14

of the physiology of the whole plant and are considered in the second part of the book.

Thus, an understanding of plant metabolism involves more than the elucidation of the chemical nature of the compounds concerned. The problem for the biologist is that of co-ordinating the data obtained by the plant physiologist studying the whole plant, by the plant biochemist studying plant extracts, and by the morphologist and anatomist studying plant structure, in an attempt to obtain an insight into the working of the plant as a functional unit. At the present time we are far from attaining this end *in toto*. Nevertheless, comparative studies of the biochemistry of a number of metabolic processes such as photosynthesis, respiration, and nitrogen metabolism in a wide range of organisms indicate a remarkable similarity in the types of chemical compound and reaction mechanisms concerned. In general, the cleavage of a larger molecule can be achieved by mixing suitable chemicals outside the plant, whereas synthesis is often only possible in the presence of plant structures. This point is discussed further in Chapter 5. At the present time the biologist is becoming increasingly aware of the significance of structure in the biochemical mechanisms of living organisms; and with the development of new techniques for the study of structure and function a new understanding of the essential principles of biological synthesis and function becomes probable in the immediate future.

GENERAL REFERENCES

(*a*) *Historical*

J. PRIESTLEY (1774–7) *Experiments and Observations on Different Kinds of Air*. J. Johnson

S. HALES (1727) *Vegetable Staticks*. Innys & Woodward

J. SACHS (1890) *History of Botany from 1530 to 1860*. Engl. trs. O.U.P.

J. R. GREEN (1909) *History of Botany from 1860 to 1900*. O.U.P.

A. E. CLARK-KENNEDY (1929) *Stephen Hales*. C.U.P.

H. S. REED (1949) *J. Ingenhousz*. Chron. Bot. Co.

J. S. GILMOUR (1944) *British Botanists*. Collins

(*b*) *General*
The reader who has no previous knowledge of the subject will find an excellent introduction in *The Principles of Plant Physiology* (1952) by J. BONNER and W. GALSTON, publ. W. H. Freeman.

Reviews of recent work are to be found in *The Annual Review of Plant Physiology*, publ. Annual Reviews Inc., since 1950, and in *The Encyclopaedia of Plant Physiology*, ed. W. Ruhland, publ. Springer (from 1949).

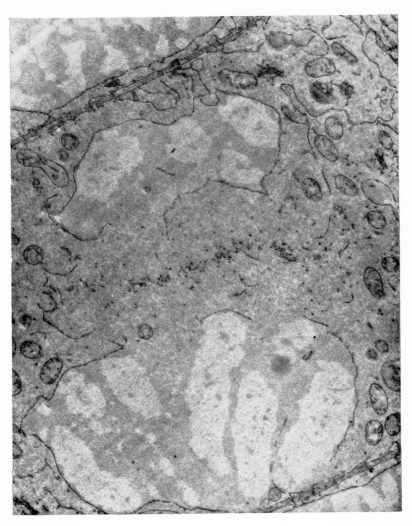

Plate 1. An electron micrograph showing late telophase in barley root tip. Droplets are present across the region where a new cell wall is to be formed. Many mitochondria are present, showing internal structures. The preparation was stained with $KMnO_4$, which does not stain the chromosomal material which appears white. $\times$ 25,200. (Dr B. E. Juniper, Botany School, Oxford, unpublished)

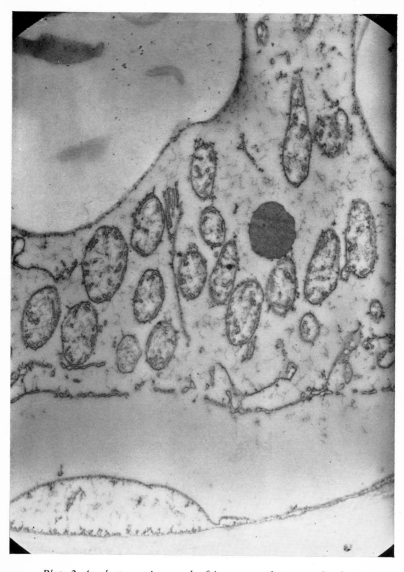

Plate 2. An electron micrograph of Arum maculatum *spadix showing mitochondria. Membrane structures in the cytoplasm are presumed to be endoplasmic reticulum. The material was fixed in OsO_4 and embedded in methacrylate.* × *50,000. (N. W. Simon and J. A. Chapman, Manchester University[138])*

CHAPTER TWO

Cellular Structure and Function

The seed is the resting stage of the higher plant. After a period of dormancy it will germinate, provided that water and oxygen are supplied and the seed is at a suitable temperature. From the seedling the mature plant differentiates into root, shoot, and leaves – the principal organs of the vegetative plant. These various tissues arise by differentiation from a common cell type, and become more or less adapted to special functions. Very early studies showed that the tissues of a plant were composed of individual units, and the generalization was made that the basic unit of the plant was the cell. The study of the relationship between structure and function in the individual cell is therefore an essential preliminary to an understanding of the functioning of the plant as a whole.

Cell Structure

The determination of the structure of cells has been carried out mainly with the help of optical and X-ray methods. These include studies of stained sections using the ordinary light microscope, of living material by the phase contrast microscope, and of dried sections by the electron microscope. The phase contrast microscope is especially valuable in permitting observation of the motion of living cell constituents.

The main features of the electron microscope are the same as those of a light microscope except that electric and magnetic fields are used to focus the electron beam. In practice, the use of electrons allows a resolving power of up to 10 or 20 Å (i.e. 1 or 2 mμ).* After fixation and staining, specimens are prepared by impregnating the plant tissue with synthetic resins. These must be cut very finely and the ultramicrotome (which uses a glass knife as cutting edge) has been developed to cut sections of impregnated tissue of the order of 10 mμ thick. Since electrons produce no visual sensation, the image is recorded on a fluorescent screen or a photographic film.

* 1 Å = 10^{-8} cm. 1 mμ = 10^{-7} cm.

Material to be studied microscopically is generally fixed and usually stained. Various methods of fixation have been developed in an attempt to preserve the structure as close as possible to that in the living state. The type of dye to be used is determined by the chemical composition of the structure under investigation. For example, the nucleus requires basic dyes such as haematoxylin whilst the cytoplasm requires acid dyes such as eosin. A combination of the two may be used to bring out the characteristics of both the nucleus and the cytoplasm.

A TYPICAL CELL

We shall consider the main structures of a plant cell, though not all of these are necessarily present in any particular cell.

Protoplasm is the term used for the cell substance as a whole, including the nucleus; cytoplasm designates the material of the cell other than the nucleus. The contents of a living cell constitute a unit of protoplasm known as the protoplast.

Cell wall

Development

The cell wall begins to be formed at the end of cell division (telophase) as a result of the condensation of droplets of material which form a platelet (see Plate 1). The nature of the changes taking place is not fully understood, but the resulting structure is the *middle lamella* which forms the boundary between two adjacent cells. It is isotropic and largely consists of pectin. In meristematic regions the divided cells have a deposition on the middle lamella called the primary cell wall and consisting largely of cellulose.* During this deposition, expansion of the cell takes place with the formation of a conspicuous vacuole. Thereafter a secondary wall (often exhibiting three principal layers, a thin inner and outer layer and a middle layer) is deposited on the primary wall. In the formation of this secondary wall the cell may become impregnated with lignin, which is deposited both in the secondary and also in the primary wall. Under other conditions suberin or cutin may be deposited in the secondary wall on which it forms a superficial layer. Essentially, the secondary wall is a relatively rigid structure capable of only limited further expansion. Pits occur in the cell wall, generally opposite each other in adjacent cells, constituting pit pairs; regions which have no primary wall but only

* The chemistry of the main components of the cell wall is briefly summarized in the Appendix.

18

middle lamella, the primary pit fields, have *plasmodesmata* which penetrate the middle lamella, giving continuity of protoplasm between adjacent cells.

The layers of the cell wall are clearly distinguished by their differing chemical composition,[116] but they also differ in physical structure. This can be studied by the microscope with visible light, preferably polarized, by the use of X-rays,[122] and by the electron microscope.[112] In the primary wall (at least of higher plants) the microfibrils tend to be arranged in criss-cross array, in general transversely orientated to the longitudinal cell axis.[135] The diameter of the microfibrils is of the order of 100 to 300 Å, as are the spaces between them, resulting in a porous structure. This favours cell expansion longitudinally rather than laterally. In the secondary wall the microfibrils tend to lie approximately parallel to one another in any given part of a layer, those of the middle and outer layers being generally orientated more longitudinally whilst those of the inner layers maintain their transverse orientation. There is not entire agreement concerning the results from X-rays and the electron microscope, and there may be some variation between structures in different plants.[123]

Growth

Two methods of growth have been suggested – intussusception and apposition. Intussusception involves the opening up of the existing structure with the introduction of new material amongst that already present. Apposition is the superficial deposition of new material on to the existing material. During the process of cell expansion there is a considerable increase in cell wall material so that in spite of the increased surface area the thickness of the wall is maintained constant. Thus the growth of the primary wall probably involves both intussusception and apposition, whereas the secondary wall probably increases in thickness largely by apposition.

Membranes

Studies with the electron microscope show that there are two membranes of the order of 100 Å thick bounding the cytoplasm, one on the outside of the protoplast, the other between the vacuole and the cytoplasm.[108] The outer membrane, the *plasmalemma*, is more readily seen in plasmolysed cells, but it is generally believed to be present also in turgid cells. It can be dissected from the protoplasm of isolated beet tissue. It is believed to be permeable to certain ions and small molecules as demonstrated by the rapid attainment of equilibrium between cytoplasm and external solutions. The vacuolar membrane

19

or *tonoplast* is permeable to water but is relatively impermeable to other molecules. It retains within the vacuole a solution of inorganic salts and organic molecules such as acids or sugars. Both membranes appear in the electron microscope as complex structures consisting of an inner and outer region of material which densely stains with osmium with a less densely staining region in between.

Vacuole
The vacuole contains an aqueous solution. It is regarded by some as a place where the plant accumulates the end products of metabolism. In meristematic cells the vacuoles are numerous and small; as the cell develops these vacuoles increase in size and coalesce, resulting in cell elongation.[31] The mature cell has a single large vacuole.

Cytoplasm
Cytoplasm contains a number of polymeric molecules such as proteins and polysaccharides together with the corresponding monomeric forms such as the amino acids and sugars.* The cytoplasm is a colloidal solution and is assumed to have a rigid structure by virtue of cross linking between the polypeptide chains of the proteins. Adjacent polypeptide chains may form cross linkages, for example, by reaction between adjacent acidic and basic groups or by oxidation of adjacent —SH groups with the formation of an S—S link. Physical forces also operate to form points of attachment between polar groups forming hydrogen or water bridges.

The elasticity of cytoplasm is shown during plasmolysis when the cytoplasm may be drawn out into long threads (Hecht's threads). The viscosity of cytoplasm is large compared with aqueous solutions and increases under pressure. Also cytoplasm when forced to flow becomes birefringent. These facts suggest that cytoplasm contains randomly orientated long chain molecules which may become more closely aligned under applied forces. Studies with the electron microscope of the cytoplasm of animal cells have shown two distinct phases: (i) a continuous membrane system, the *endoplasmic reticulum*, which connects together the cell membranes, nuclear membrane, and other inclusions; and (ii) a relatively structureless matrix which fills the space between the membranes of the reticulum. Attached to the membranes of the reticulum are small densely staining spheres, which are rich in ribonucleic acid (RNA)† and are the *ribosomes*.[129] So far relatively few observations have been made with plant cells but there is evidence for the existence in some mature plant cells of

* See the Appendix for a brief discussion of their chemical structure.
† See the Appendix for a brief discussion of the chemical structure.

20

membranes corresponding to at least part of the endoplasmic reticulum[12] (see Plate 2). This structure is less well developed in meristematic cells. The structure of the membranes of the endoplasmic reticulum is probably essentially similar to that of the plasmalemma and the tonoplast.

Organelles – the living inclusions

A number of specific particulate bodies within the protoplasm include the nucleus, which will not be dealt with in detail, the mitochondria, and the chloroplasts. The *mitochondria* have a boundary membrane (75 Å thick) which is seen in the electron microscope after staining to be a double layer (see Plate 2). The inner of the two layers is folded to form intrusions into the interior, thus giving an internal membrane system amongst an otherwise granular matrix.[118] In chemical composition the mitochondria are rich in protein and phospholipid and also contain nucleic acid (RNA).

The *chloroplasts* also have a double-layered bounding membrane approximately 150 Å thick. Two types of internal structure are found. In algae and in the starch sheath of maize the internal membranes or lamella extend throughout the plastid, whereas in mesophyll cells from higher plants the lamellae show regions of close alignment, interspersed with regions of fewer membranes which are not closely aligned (see Plate 4). The ordered regions are the *grana* and the less ordered the *stroma*. The lamellae of the stroma are continuous with those of the grana, but in the grana they may bifurcate and are greater in number than in the stroma.[57] Chlorophyll is believed to be orientated on the lamella surfaces so that it is more concentrated in the grana than in the stroma.[71]

Cell Metabolism*

An understanding of the metabolism of the cell can be approached from two viewpoints. Firstly we can try to understand the chemical structure of the constituents of the cell and how they are made and broken down. This constitutes the biochemistry of the cell. On the other hand, we may inquire as to how far the physical structure of the cell influences the chemical reactions taking place, and this is included in the study of biophysics. Food materials enter through the cell wall and certain of the membranes which must have a certain permeability for these substances. Within the cell the substance moves either by

* This part of the chapter presupposes material in later chapters and may be left until a second reading.

diffusion or convection until it arrives at a place where reaction occurs. A complete description of metabolism involves a knowledge of where the reactions take place, together with the rates of these reactions and the rates of transport of substances through the cell. If the cell were a homogeneous system one might be able to infer what the intermediate steps were simply from observations on the rates at which substances are assimilated and excreted. But the complex structure of the cell described in the first part of the chapter makes any such approach too simple.

REACTION OF ISOLATED CELL CONSTITUENTS

At the sub-cellular level there is heterogeneity within the cell owing to the presence of particulate bodies including the mitochondria and chloroplasts. Again, at the molecular level there may be spatial separation due to the formation of molecular aggregates. The study of function cannot ignore this structural complexity.

One question which arises is whether there are reaction steps in metabolism which cannot take place in the absence of specialized structures. A number of enzymes have been isolated from higher plants and most have been shown to be capable of acting *in vitro* in the absence of gross structure. In fact, quite complicated reaction sequences have been built up with simple mixtures of isolated enzymes. For example, all the steps of the carbon cycle (which operates in photosynthesis) can be carried out *in vitro* either individually or in combination. With a mixture of as many as nine enzymes, Racker[126] was able to demonstrate *in vitro* the formation of a sugar from carbon dioxide. By contrast, the necessity for structure to order a reaction sequence can be seen with reference to the oxidative processes of respiration. The enzymes concerned are known to be largely localized in the mitochondrion. The internal membranes can be separated from the contents of the mitochondria, and it is then found that whilst the contents can still catalyse oxidative reactions the phosphorylation reactions which normally accompany these are absent. It may be concluded that a membrane structure is necessary for the transfer to phosphate compounds of some of the energy which would be otherwise liberated in oxidation. No mixture of isolated enzymes has yet been shown to be capable of transferring free energy from one chemical form to another with high efficiency. Similarly, the detailed internal structure of the chloroplast is generally believed to be essential for photosynthesis in which light energy is converted into a chemical form. It may be that wherever efficient energy conversion takes place in a living organism it requires an ordered structure.

Even when the structure is not apparent at the microscopic level it may still exist and control metabolism. When the structure of the cell is broken down by grinding or by poisoning, reactions can take place which do not occur under natural conditions. For example, when potato or apple tissue is bruised, a brown colour is developed due to polyphenol oxidase activity. Both the enzyme and substrate are present in the tissue, but they do not normally react whilst the structure of the living cell is maintained. Other evidence of localization has been obtained in experiments in which a radioactive isotope is fed to a plant. Its incorporation into a particular compound may be rapid at first, after which it may continue for a considerable time at a slower rate. The initial incorporation and the second slower phase may result from separate reaction mechanisms. The simplest case arises when there is known to be a barrier to free movement between two parts of the cell containing the same constituent. For example, that fraction of the compound within the cytoplasm might be expected to equilibrate with substances fed from outside more rapidly than that in the vacuole. Compounds which equilibrate amongst themselves relatively rapidly are regarded as belonging to a single metabolic 'pool'. For example, when carbon 14 is fed to a photosynthetic organism the ribulose-diphosphate becomes radioactive and its level of radioactivity soon stabilizes. It is regarded as being in a single pool with the carbon dioxide. On the other hand, phosphoglyceric acid shows a rapid increase in radioactivity followed by a gradual slower increase. It may, therefore, exist in at least two pools, one more, and one less, active. In some cases the radioactivity in a compound may reach a steady value but nevertheless have a specific activity considerably smaller than that of the fed radioactive metabolite. In this case the substance is considered to exist in both an active pool and a totally inaccessible or inactive pool.

The existence of separate pools of metabolic activity indicates a degree of isolation between enzymes and their potential substrates. By these means the physical structure of the cell determines which, of all the potential reactions, will actually take place and the organization may be such that certain reactions take place faster and more efficiently *in vivo* than *in vitro*.

GENERAL REFERENCES

J. BRACHET (1957) *Biochemical Cytology.* Academic Press

A. FREY-WYSSLING (1948) *Submicroscopic Morphology of Protoplasm and its Derivatives.* Elsevier

R. D. PRESTON (1952) *The Molecular Architecture of Plant Cell Walls.* Wiley

CHAPTER THREE

Enzymes

The catalysts in living cells which facilitate the metabolic reactions
are called enzymes. All enzymes are proteins or their derivatives and
vary in molecular weight from 10,000 up to 500,000. Amylase is an
example of an enzyme which is a simple protein. A number of enzymes have been isolated and obtained in a crystalline form, and the
enzymic activity has been shown to increase per weight of preparation as the protein is purified. Other enzymes are derivatives of
protein formed by combination with some other group such as a
metal. Enzymes containing a wide range of metals including iron,
copper, zinc, molybdenum, manganese, and magnesium are known.
In other cases the protein is combined with a larger group which
may be organic in nature, e.g. flavin.

Euler distinguished two parts of an enzyme. He referred to the
protein part, characterized as heat labile and colloidal, as the
apoenzyme; and to the heat stable and dialysable part as the *coenzyme*. The whole enzyme, i.e. apo + coenzyme, he called the holo-
enzyme. This terminology is useful when the enzyme can be isolated
in two separate parts – a heat labile portion and a heat stable portion.
But frequently an enzyme is obtained as a single protein derivative
which, although it may consist of two parts, does not freely dissociate.
Then the usual terminology refers to that part of the molecule with
which the substrate combines as the active or prosthetic group and
to the larger residue of the molecule which is proteinaceous as an
activating group. Model catalysts have been made which show that
the catalytic property may reside in and be characteristic of a small
part of the whole molecule. However, catalytic activity can be enhanced and often given a greater degree of specificity by being
associated with a larger molecule. For example, iron as iron filings
will catalyse the dissociation of hydrogen peroxide into water and
oxygen at a rate of 10^{-5} mole/sec; combined in organic form as
haem the rate is 10^{-2} mole/sec, whilst when the haem is complexed
with a protein to form the enzyme catalase the rate is 10^5 mole/sec,

all at 0 °C. In other cases it has been shown that part of the protein can be removed from native enzymes without loss of activity.

One may attempt to classify enzymes according to the various reactions catalysed by them. One category, 'splitters', catalyse the breaking of bonds, frequently the hydrolysis of molecules. These include hydrolases such as proteases, lipases and invertase, amylase, and maltase. Other enzymes, 'transferases', are concerned in the transfer of a group from one molecule to another, e.g. the transaminases (Chapter 7) or phosphoglucomutase (Fig. 4.1); 'adders' catalyse the addition of one molecule to another, e.g. aspartase, which catalyses the addition of ammonia to fumarate to form aspartate. Finally there is the group of oxidation-reduction enzymes which are concerned with the transfer of hydrogen or of electrons from one molecule to another, causing the oxidation of one and the reduction of the other.

Enzymes are characterized in their catalytic properties by their specificity. Some enzymes are specific to a particular molecule such as the enzyme aspartase (see previous paragraph). Others are specific to a type of linkage only, such as the α-glucosidases which will hydrolyse all compounds containing an α-linked glucose. Invertase catalyses both hydrolysis of sucrose and of raffinose which have the same linkage, i.e. the enzyme is a β-fructofuranosidase. Lipases hydrolyse fat molecules without regard to the nature of the fatty acid in the fat. The peptidases represent an intermediate class, being specific to a particular link, the peptide link, but requiring also a particular type of grouping in its immediate proximity. For example, the carboxy-peptidases can attack only a peptide link which has a carboxyl group in the vicinity and the amino-peptidases only a peptide link which has an amino group in the vicinity (see Chapter 7). In an oxidation-reduction reaction the specificity of the enzyme may refer to both the reagents, i.e. both the substance oxidized and that reduced. Certain of the dehydrogenases will transfer hydrogen from substrates for which they are characteristic to coenzyme I (diphosphopyridine nucleotide or nicotinamide adenine dinucleotide) and not to coenzyme II (triphosphopyridine nucleotide or nicotinamide adenine dinucleotide phosphate); other of the dehydrogenases are specific to coenzyme II and will not transfer hydrogen to coenzyme I (see Chapter 4).

Enzymes permit reactions to take place in living organisms which otherwise would not take place at an appreciable rate at ordinary temperatures and may thereby exert a directive effect on the meta-

26

bolism of the cell. For example, by accelerating certain pathways to a greater extent than others they may virtually direct the metabolism along one of two possible routes. The control of the metabolism of the cell is dependent on the degree of spatial localization of enzymes. Certain enzymes (e.g. cytochrome oxidase) are confined to the mitochondrion; others are confined to the chloroplast. Thus it is possible for reactions to be taking place in the mitochondria which are in effect the opposite of reactions which may be taking place simultaneously in the chloroplasts. In general, a broad distinction can be made between the so-called soluble enzymes which are readily extracted from the cell and the particulate enzymes that are believed to be localized on various particles which cannot themselves be rendered soluble.

Many enzymes are regularly present in a particular species of living organism, and indeed some are almost universal. When invertase is present in an organism it is always present. It has therefore been referred to as a *constitutive enzyme*. This is to distinguish it from an *adaptive or induced enzyme* which is apparent only when its particular substrate (or a near analogue) – the inducer – is available to the organism.[110] In the absence of the appropriate substrate the enzyme is present in very small amounts, but after addition of the inducer the enzyme appears in the organism after a short lag period of a few minutes called the 'adaptation' period. In almost all cases removal of the inducer results in cessation of further enzyme synthesis.

THE MECHANISM OF ENZYME CATALYSIS

Like inorganic catalysts, enzymes accelerate reactions but do not affect the position of equilibrium (see Fig. 3.1). They have been described as acting as a lubricator. It is not always possible to recover an enzyme from the reaction mixture unchanged at the end of the reaction, but an essential feature is that it should not affect the final equilibrium mixture, i.e. it does not affect the free energy of the reaction. Enzymes accelerate a reaction by lowering the energy of activation and thus act in a similar way to an increase in temperature, namely, by increasing the proportion of colliding molecules which react. Michaelis and Menten[104] first postulated that enzymes were able to act as catalysts because they combined with their substrates – essentially the same principle as Oswald's law of chemical catalysis. They suggested that the energy 'hump', which must be overcome for reaction to take place (i.e. the activation energy), was lower for the enzyme-substrate complex than for the free substrate in the absence of enzyme. The enzyme-substrate complex breaks down to give products and free enzyme. From this hypothesis they deduced the relationship between the rate of an enzyme catalysed reaction and the concentration of substrate.

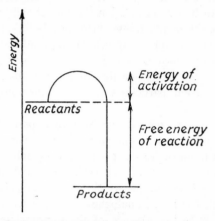

Fig. 3.1. Only those molecules of reactant with energy in excess of the average energy can react: the excess energy required is called the activation energy. The smaller the activation energy the greater will be the number of reacting molecules. The activation energy is not related to the free energy change of the reaction which is the difference in energy content between reactants and products

The enzyme-catalysed reaction may be represented in the following way:[23]

$$E_f + S \underset{k_2}{\overset{k_1}{\rightleftharpoons}} E_s \overset{k_3}{\rightharpoonup} E_f + \text{products}$$

where (S) represents the concentration of total substrate

(E) represents the concentration of total enzyme

(E_s) represents the concentration of enzyme combined with substrate

(E_f) represents the concentration of free enzyme

and k_1, k_2, and k_3 are reaction velocity constants.

Then $(E) = (E_s) + (E_f)$

Applying the Law of Mass Action:

Rate of formation of $E_s = k_1(E_f)(S)$ (provided $S \gg E$ so that $E_s \ll S$)

28

Rate of breakdown of $E_s = k_2(E_s) + k_3(E_s)$

Then at the steady state (when rate of formation of E_s equals rate of breakdown)

$$k_1(E_f)(S) = (k_2 + k_3)(E_s)$$

but

$$(E_f) = (E) - (E_s)$$

$$\therefore k_1[(E) - (E_s)]S = (k_2 + k_3)(E_s)$$

whence,

$$(E_s) = \frac{k_1(E)(S)}{k_1(S) + k_2 + k_3} = \frac{(E)(S)}{(S) + \dfrac{k_2 + k_3}{k_1}}$$

Hence the rate of breakdown of E_s to give products, R, is given by

$$R = k_3(E_s) = \frac{k_3(E)(S)}{(S) + \dfrac{k_2 + k_3}{k_1}}$$

The constant $\dfrac{k_2 + k_3}{k_1}$ is called the Michaelis constant for the enzyme (k_m). It is a characteristic of the enzyme which may be used for identification.

Thus

$$R = \frac{k_3(E)(S)}{(S) + k_m} \tag{1}$$

When (S) becomes very large $\dfrac{(S)}{(S) + k_m}$ approaches unity and the maximal rate of the reaction (R_∞) will be given by $k_3.(E)$.

Hence,

$$R = \frac{R_\infty(S)}{(S) + k_m}$$

When $(S) = k_m$, then $R = \dfrac{k_3 E}{2} = \dfrac{R_\infty}{2}$ and hence k_m can be defined as that concentration of the substrate which gives half the maximal rate.

R_∞ and k_m can be estimated from the relationship between R and (S) (see Fig. 3.2), but if only a limited number of experimental points is available greater accuracy can be achieved by transforming the R/S relation to a linear form, e.g. by plotting $1/S$ against $1/R$ (Fig. 3.3). From equation (1), taking reciprocals:

$$\frac{1}{R} = \frac{1}{k_3(E)} + \frac{k_m}{k_3(E)(S)}$$

29

When $\dfrac{1}{S} = 0, \quad \dfrac{1}{R} = \dfrac{1}{k_3(E)}$ (intercept on vertical axis)

When $\dfrac{1}{R} = 0, \quad \dfrac{1}{S} = \dfrac{-1}{k_m}$ (intercept on horizontal axis)

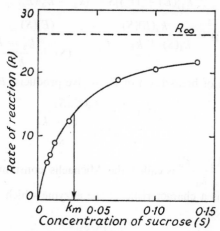

Fig. 3.2. *The rate of hydrolysis of sucrose catalysed by invertase plotted against sucrose concentration. The values of R_∞ and k_m are deduced from Fig. 3.3. (After W. Kuhn[87])*

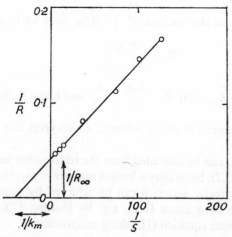

Fig. 3.3. *The reciprocal of the rate of the hydrolysis of sucrose catalysed by invertase plotted against the reciprocal sucrose concentration (data of Fig. 3.2)*

30

From these two intercepts the maximal rate and the Michaelis constant can be calculated.[94]

It will be noticed that in the reciprocal plots undue weight may be given to the rates determined at low substrate concentrations, i.e. those most liable to error. The plot between R/S and R (which can also be shown to be linear) is less liable to errors introduced by undue weighting. In this case the intercepts on the vertical and horizontal axes are respectively:

$$\frac{k_3(E)}{k_m} \quad \text{and} \quad (k_3 E).$$

These relationships, deduced theoretically, can be tested experimentally for a number of enzyme reactions *in vitro*. It has been found that the relationship between R and S provides a satisfactory fit for many enzyme catalysed reactions provided that 'initial' rates of reaction are used, i.e. the rate of the reaction extrapolated to zero time. Moreover, the same type of relationship can be observed *in vivo* between the rate of certain physiological processes and the substrate concentration, e.g. between the rate of oxygen uptake in respiration in yeast and the oxygen partial pressure or between the rate of acidification in *Crassulacean* plants and carbon dioxide concentration. Since the value of k_m is independent of enzyme concentration it can be deduced that an enzyme which has been shown to have a higher k_m (i.e. a lower affinity for the substrate) *in vitro* than that observed for the physiological process cannot be the primary enzyme operating *in vivo*. For example, it is improbable that malic enzyme (which catalyses the carboxylation of pyruvic acid to malic acid) is responsible for acidification in *Kalanchöe* since it shows a lower affinity *in vitro* than that observed for the process *in vivo*. Further complications may have to be considered. An apparent lowering of an enzyme affinity *in vivo* can result from the presence of a finite diffusion path between the external source of substrate and enzyme, an example of which is discussed with reference to photosynthesis in Chapter 6.

The maximum rate, R_∞, can be alternatively expressed as a turn over number (T.O.N.), i.e. the number of moles of substrate reacting/mole enzyme/minute. Its value may be of significance in determining the importance of an enzyme *in vivo*. For example, in yeast cells it has been shown that the concentration of cytochrome is such that working at its maximal rate it could account for the whole of the oxygen uptake in respiration.

Britten Chance[33] has made observations of the formation of the enzyme substrate complex by a method independent of the study of the overall rate of reaction. Chance studied the oxidation of phenols by hydrogen peroxide catalysed by the enzyme peroxidase. This enzyme has a characteristic absorption spectrum in the visible part of the spectrum. He found that addition of one of the substrates of the reaction, hydrogen peroxide, to the peroxidase preparation produced a marked change in absorption spectrum of the mixture, suggesting that the peroxide had combined with the peroxidase. When a phenol such as guaiacum was added the spectrum reverted in part to its original form, showing that after reaction had taken place between guaiacum and the hydrogen peroxide-enzyme complex, the enzyme had reverted to its original form. In fact, Chance found several complexes of peroxidase, including one with one molecule of peroxide, and another with one hundred molecules of peroxide. By studying the kinetics of the formation of the complex spectroscopically he was able to show that the complex of one molecule of each reagent gave kinetics consistent with those which could be deduced from the kinetics of the overall reaction. Thus in this case the formation of an enzyme-substrate complex has been demonstrated spectroscopically.

The Michaelis–Menten mechanism also offers an interpretation of the effect of change of pH on enzyme catalysis. Since enzymes are proteins they can exist as positively or negatively charged or neutral molecules. As the pH is varied the proportion of each type of molecule will vary. The kinetics of many enzyme catalysed reactions are consistent with a dissociation of certain hydrogen ions of the protein molecule (presumably those near to the active group), resulting in a complex with the substrate which is unable to give rise to products.* This phenomenon has been most intensively investigated with invertase in the alkaline range of pH. The effect of increasing alkalinity is a reversible one, and the rate changes in a way consistent with the view that only the uncharged substrate-complex gives rise to products. Under acid or extreme alkaline conditions the enzyme is denatured and satisfactory results cannot be obtained. In other reactions the ionization of the substrate as well as the enzyme may also affect the rate of reaction.

Furthermore, the Michaelis–Menten hypothesis leads one to expect two types of substance which would interfere with enzyme catalysis.

* The optimal pH for catalysis will coincide with the I.E.P. of the enzyme only if *all* ionizations affect the reactivity of the enzyme substrate complex.

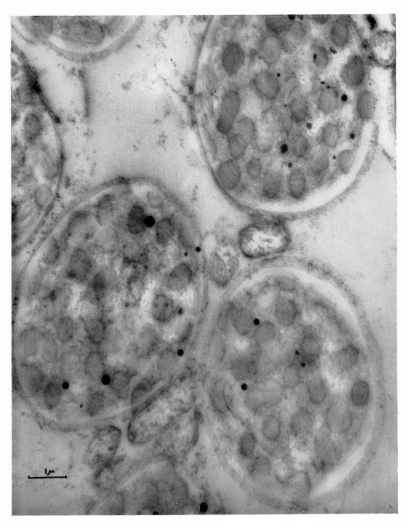

Plate 3. A section from a leaf of Nicotiana tobacum *showing three chloroplasts and several mitochondria.* × *18,000. (After G. E. Palade*[118]*)*

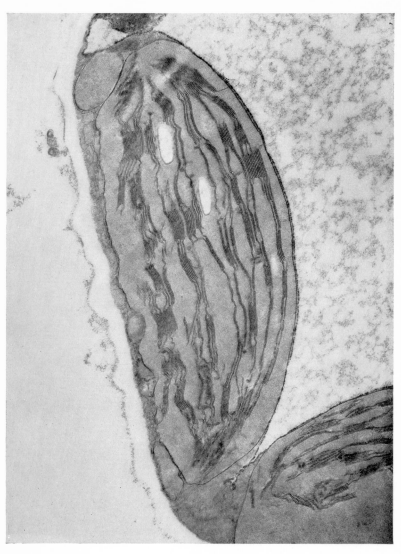

Plate 4. The structure of the chloroplast in palisade leaf cells of Vicia faba *showing the grana where the lamellae are closely aligned and the stroma. Fixation with* $KMnO_4$. × *40,000.* (*A. D. Greenwood, Botany Department, Imperial College, London, unpublished*)

First those substances which combine with the enzyme in the same way as the substrate but cannot themselves give rise to products. In this case the degree of inhibition is less the greater the substrate concentration since substrate and inhibitor compete for combination with the enzyme. For example, β-glucose inhibits invertase increasingly as the concentration of sucrose is lowered. This is referred to as a *competitive inhibition*. Other substances, e.g. mercury salts in the case of invertase, inhibit the catalysis of the reaction, but the degree of inhibition is independent of the concentration of substrate. These compounds are presumed to impair the activity of the enzyme-

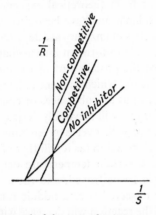

*Fig. 3.4. The reciprocal of the rate of an enzyme catalysed reaction plotted against the reciprocal of the substrate concentration in the presence of a non-competitive or competitive inhibition. A competitive inhibitor increases k_m but does not alter R_∞; a non-competitive inhibitor does **not** alter k_m but reduces R_∞*

substrate complex by combination at some point other than where the substrate combines and are referred to as *non-competitive* inhibitors. Both types of inhibition have been widely observed. They are most easily characterized by their influence on the relationship between the reciprocal of the rate of the catalysed reaction and the reciprocal of the substrate concentration (Fig. 3.4).

The study of the kinetics of enzyme reactions under a wide range of conditions has led to the view that the Michaelis–Menten hypothesis enables correct prediction of enzyme kinetics.[60] A number of exceptional cases have been observed where there is an apparent departure from expectation: for example, the hydrolysis of fatty acid esters such as ethyl butyrate by certain esterases shows a rate of catalysis which at first increases and subsequently decreases as the concentration of substrate is increased. A satisfactory explanation has been given of this anomaly since the kinetics indicate that either one or two molecules of substrate can combine with the enzyme but that the complex formed between the enzyme and two molecules of the substrate cannot give rise to products. Again, at high concentrations of sucrose the catalytic activity of invertase is impaired. This is believed to be due to the higher osmotic pressure resulting at higher sucrose concentrations causing changes in the enzyme molecule which prevent its effective combination with the substrate. In all cases when deviations from theoretical expectation have been observed, reasonable explanations have been provided.

The catalytic properties of enzymes are dependent on two features: (i) that the enzyme is able to form an intermediate complex with the substrate and (ii) that the protein part of the molecule is preserved in its native state. Factors which prevent either of these conditions will destroy catalysis. Thus all substances or conditions which cause denaturation of an enzyme will inevitably destroy its catalytic ability. Increase in temperature will, over a given range, increase the rate of an enzyme catalysed reaction (as it will that of any other chemical reaction), but above a certain temperature denaturation will take place, the enzyme will be destroyed, and the catalytic activity lost. Both effects may be observed over a middle range. At higher temperatures the rate of the reaction will decrease with time owing to the progressive denaturation of the enzyme; hence the effect of temperature on the rate of catalysis can be properly deduced only from the effect on the initial rate. Otherwise an apparent optimum temperature will be observed which will be a function of the time taken to measure the reaction.

GENERAL REFERENCES

M. DIXON and E. C. WEBB (1958) *The Enzymes*. Longmans

J. B. NIELANDS and P. K. STUMPF (1958) *Outline of Enzyme Chemistry*. 2nd edition. Wiley

J. B. SUMNER and K. MYRBACK (eds) (1950–2) *The Enzymes*. (2 vols.) Academic Press

TABLE 3.1

The following abbreviations are used throughout:

	ADP	adenosine diphosphate
	ATP	adenosine triphosphate
NAD = CoI=DPN		diphosphopyridine nucleotide; nicotinamide adenine dinucleotide
NADH$_2$ = CoIH$_2$=DPNH$_2$		reduced diphosphopyridine nucleotide
NADP = CoII=TPN		triphosphopyridine nucleotide; adenine dinucleotide phosphate
NADPH$_2$ = CoIIH$_2$=TPNH$_2$		reduced triphosphopyridine nucleotide
	DNA	deoxyribonucleic acid
	DNP	dinitrophenol
	FAD	flavin adenine dinucleotide
	FMN	flavin mononucleotide
	GDP	guanosine diphosphate
	GMP	guanosine monophosphate
	GTP	guanosine triphosphate
	IAA	3-indoleacetic acid
	P$_i$	inorganic phosphate (H$_3$PO$_4$)
	P	phosphate (H$_2$PO$_3$)
	PGA	3-phosphoglyceric acid
	PP	pyrophosphate
	RDP	ribulose diphosphate
	RNA	ribonucleic acid
	TP	triosephosphate (3-phosphoglyceraldehyde)
	UDP	uridinediphosphate
	UTP	uridinetriphosphate

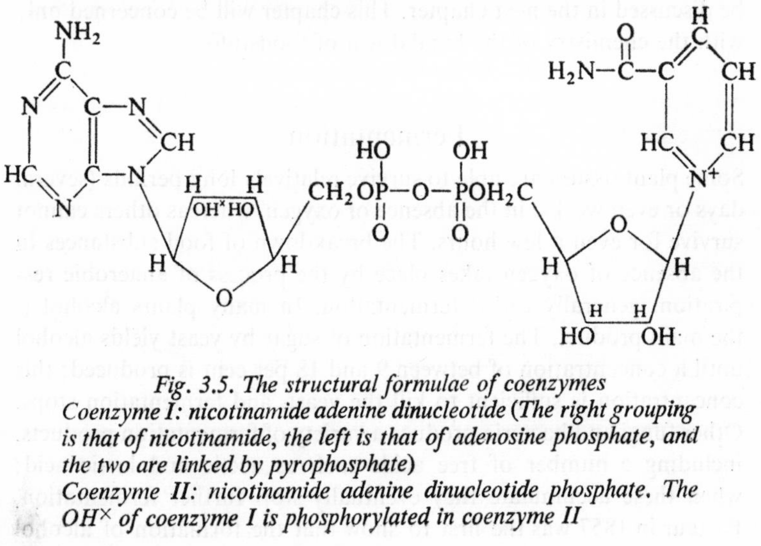

Fig. 3.5. The structural formulae of coenzymes
Coenzyme I: nicotinamide adenine dinucleotide (The right grouping is that of nicotinamide, the left is that of adenosine phosphate, and the two are linked by pyrophosphate)
Coenzyme II: nicotinamide adenine dinucleotide phosphate. The OH$^\times$ of coenzyme I is phosphorylated in coenzyme II

CHAPTER FOUR

Fermentation and Respiration

In the following chapters we shall consider the operation of a number of enzymes in reaction sequences.

Enzymes were first systematically investigated in a study of the chemistry of fermentation, a process of considerable economic importance. Early studies showed that a complex sequence of reaction steps was concerned and the isolation of the intermediates and of the enzymes catalysing their interconversion occupied biochemists for some forty years. Their work is the subject of this chapter.

During this period it began to be realized that some reactions were important to living organisms primarily because they were energy-yielding. Some took the view that this was the *essential* feature of respiration and defined the process in this way. The manner in which the energy obtained from the oxidation of foodstuffs is utilized for the synthesis of other complex substances required for growth will be discussed in the next chapter. This chapter will be concerned only with the chemistry of the breakdown of foodstuffs.

Fermentation

Some plant tissues are able to survive relatively long periods (several days or even weeks) in the absence of oxygen, whereas others cannot survive for even a few hours. The breakdown of food substances in the absence of oxygen takes place by the process of anaerobic respiration, generally called fermentation. In many plants alcohol is the main product. The fermentation of sugar by yeast yields alcohol until a concentration of between 9 and 18 per cent is produced; this concentration is sufficient to kill the yeast, and fermentation stops. Other fungi and bacteria produce a variety of fermentation products, including a number of free acids such as acetic and lactic acid; when these accumulate they eventually stop further fermentation. Pasteur in 1857 was the first to show that the formation of alcohol depended on the presence of living yeast cells, and he referred to fermentation as life without air. Subsequently many chemists sought to investigate the mechanism whereby alcohol was formed from sugar.

FERMENTATION IN YEAST

Von Bayer in 1880 considered that lactic acid probably gave rise to alcohol by the loss of carbon dioxide, a suggestion based on the structural similarity of the two molecules. Little real advance was made until 1897, when Buchner and Buchner showed that a juice could be expressed from yeast which fermented added sugar about twenty times slower than the whole cells from which it had been obtained. However, when lactic acid was added to the expressed yeast juice no fermentation resulted. In 1911 Neubauer and Fromherz suggested that pyruvic acid might be an important intermediate. They showed that when yeast was fed with pyruvic acid, acetaldehyde and carbon dioxide were produced. Therefore they postulated that sugars gave rise to pyruvic acid, which broke down into acetaldehyde and carbon dioxide, the acetaldehyde in turn giving rise to alcohol. Later Fernbach and Schren showed that yeast fed with sugar in the presence of excess calcium carbonate accumulated pyruvic acid. Calcium carbonate kept the medium alkaline and it was found that pyruvic acid could only be fermented by yeast when the medium was acid. From feeding suspected intermediates it was thus possible to deduce a mechanism whereby alcohol could be formed from a three-carbon precursor.

The next problem to be considered was the derivation of the three-carbon compound from the sugar substrate. Yeast is able to ferment a number of sugars, including glucose, fructose, galactose and mannose* and therefore each of these sugars must be converted to a common intermediate before it is broken down further. A clue to this intermediate was obtained when Harden and Young investigated the conditions necessary for the continued fermentation of sugar by expressed yeast juice. They showed that the production of carbon dioxide from yeast juice ceased unless inorganic phosphate was continuously added to the reaction mixture. A mole of carbon dioxide was produced for each added mole of inorganic phosphate, the phosphate being converted to fructose 1 : 6-diphosphate. This indicated that phosphate was essential for the reaction and suggested that all sugars are first converted to a phosphorylated intermediate, now

* The structure of these sugars is shown in the Appendix.

37

known to be fructose 1: 6-diphosphate, before they are capable of being broken down further in fermentation. The reactions involved are shown in Fig. 4.1.

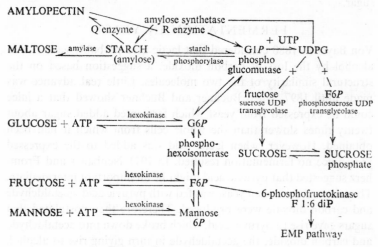

Fig. 4.1. Interconversion of sugars

TABLE 4.1a
Embden–Meyerhof–Parnas pathway

	Enzyme
1. Hexose+2ATP $\rightarrow$ Fructose-1 : 6-diphosphate+2ADP	Varies according to hexose
2. F-1: 6-diP $\rightarrow$ Triose P $\rightarrow$ + diOH acetone P	aldolase
3. Triose P $\rightleftharpoons$ diOH acetone phosphate	Triosephosphate isomerase
4. 2 Triose P+2P$_i$ $\rightarrow$ 2 diphosphoglyceric acid +2NAD (CoI) P$_1$P$_3$GA +2NADH$_2$ (CoIH$_2$)	Phosphoglyceraldehyde dehydrogenase
2P$_1$P$_3$GA+2ADP $\rightarrow$ 2ATP+2-phosphoglyceric acid P$_3$GA	Phosphoglycerate kinase
5. 2P$_3$GA+2P$_2$P$_3$GA $\rightleftharpoons$ 2P$_2$P$_3$GA+2P$_2$GA	Phosphoglyceromutase
6. 2P$_2$GA $\rightarrow$ 2 Phosphoenolpyruvate+2H$_2$O PEP	Enolase
7. 2PEP+2ADP $\rightarrow$ 2 Pyruvic acid+2ATP Pyr	Pyruvate phosphokinase
1–7. Hexose+2ADP+2P+2NAD $\rightarrow$ 2-Pyr+2ATP+2H$_2$O+2NADH$_2$	

Inhibitors
Iodoacetate inhibits reaction 4.
Fluoride inhibits reaction 6.
In the presence of bisulphite an addition compound is formed with acetaldehyde and the reoxidation of CoIH₂ by reaction with acetaldehyde is prevented; reoxidation can take place by reaction with diOH acetone phosphate to give glycerol phosphate and hence glycerol. This may also happen at the beginning of fermentation when little acetaldehyde has as yet been formed.

Reactions 2, 3, 4, 5, and 6 of the EMP pathway

Nielsen in 1933 showed that if sugar and phosphate were added to yeast juice in the presence of fluoride, phosphoglyceric acid accumulated during fermentation. Earlier, Pasteur had shown traces of glycerol amongst the fermentation products and Neuberg was able to show that the addition of bisulphite during yeast fermentation caused an accumulation of glycerol, implicating a derivative of glycerol as an intermediate. From the work of Embden, Meyerhof, Parnas, and others it was finally deduced that a hexose sugar was first converted to fructose-1:6-diphosphate which then broke into two three-carbon fragments, triose phosphate (glyceraldehyde-3-phosphate) and dihydroxyacetone phosphate. The triose phosphate was oxidized to phosphoglyceric acid and finally the phosphoglyceric acid gave rise to pyruvic acid and thence to alcohol. Thus the complete analysis of the reactions now referred to as the Embden–Meyerhof–Parnas (EMP) pathway resulted (i) from feeding suspected intermediates, (ii) from feeding a cofactor such as phosphate, and (iii) from the addition of a poison such as fluoride or a trapping agent like bisulphite. The complete reaction sequence is shown in Table 4.1a.

Coenzymes

The interconversion of the carbon intermediates in fermentation depends on the presence of appropriate enzymes and two coenzymes. The first coenzyme, cocarboxylase, now known to be pyrophosphothiamine, is concerned in the final step in which carbon dioxide is evolved from pyruvic acid. The other coenzyme, nicotinamide adenine dinucleotide or diphosphopyridine nucleotide (coenzyme I, NAD, formerly DPN), acts as an acceptor for the hydrogen which is removed from the carbon substrate during the process of oxidation of the sugar triose phosphate to phosphoglyceric acid. If the reaction is to continue the $NADH_2$ formed must be reoxidized. This is achieved in a number of ways in different types of fermentation (Table 4.1b). In the simplest process the pyruvic acid formed is

TABLE 4.1b

Fermentation

1. Pyruvic acid + $NADH_2$ (CoI H_2) →   Lactate
   $CH_3COCOOH$ Lactic acid + NAD   dehydrogenase

OR

1. Pyruvic acid → Acetaldehyde + CO_2 α-Carboxylase
   CH_3CHO +pyrophosphothiamine
                                     (co-carboxylase)

2. Acetaldehyde + $NADH_2$ →   Alcohol
   Ethyl alcohol + NAD   dehydrogenase
   CH_3CH_2OH

reduced to lactic acid by reaction with $NADH_2$. This is the reaction which occurs in animal muscle and also in a number of plants. Alternatively, the pyruvic acid can break down in the presence of carboxylase and cocarboxylase with the liberation of carbon dioxide and the formation of acetaldehyde. The acetaldehyde then reacts with the $NADH_2$ to form alcohol and oxidized coenzyme (NAD).

40

Phosphate balance

Warburg and Christian showed that the oxidation of triosephosphate to phosphoglyceric acid was the reaction which would take place only if inorganic phosphate was present. The reaction (reaction 4, Table 4.1a) takes place in three stages, involving first the oxidation of triose phosphate attached to the enzyme, then the uptake of inorganic phosphate to form diphosphoglyceric acid, and finally transfer of one phosphate from the diphosphoglyceric acid formed to adenine diphosphate (ADP) to form ATP.* ATP is consumed in the initial conversion of sugars to fructose-1: 6-diphosphate (reaction 1, Table 4.1a), but the phosphate added to the sugar molecule at this stage is returned in a subsequent step when phosphopyruvic acid is hydrolysed to pyruvic acid (reaction 7, Table 4.1a). These two reactions balance; hence the phosphate incorporated during the oxidation of triose results in a net consumption of phosphate and the formation of ATP as a reaction product. For each molecule of hexose fermented there is a net production of two molecules of ATP and a consumption of two molecules of inorganic phosphate. In yeast juice the ATP produced reacts with further sugar to produce fructose diphosphate as a final reaction product; in living plant cells ATP may be utilized in a variety of other ways including break-down by the enzyme ATPase which is generally present.

FERMENTATION IN HIGHER PLANTS

The essential mechanism of fermentation involves the conversion of substrate to a phosphorylated sugar, the cleavage of this into two three-carbon fragments and the subsequent oxidation of the triose sugar to an acid which is finally converted to pyruvic acid. This reaction sequence is common to various organisms including yeast, a number of higher plants, various bacteria, and animal muscle. In this process, in addition to the conversion of sugar to pyruvate and the uptake of the phosphate with the formation of adenosine triphosphate, there has also been an oxidation which results in the reduction of NAD to $NADH_2$.

In higher plant fermentation, the ratio, moles alcohol/moles carbon dioxide produced, is frequently less than one.[82] This indicates that carbon dioxide is produced by some mechanism other than the reactions which result in the formation of alcohol. Several explanations have been offered. The first is that acids other than lactic acid

---

* The chemical structure of ADP is shown in the Appendix.

are formed from pyruvic acid and then partially decarboxylated. Second, it has been suggested that acetaldehyde, or some derivative of acetaldehyde, may accumulate in the tissue so that carbon dioxide is produced from pyruvate without the subsequent formation of alcohol. This has not been demonstrated experimentally. A third possible supply of extra carbon dioxide may result from the accumulation of acids causing a change in the pH of the tissue with a consequent liberation of carbon dioxide from any bicarbonate present. Which of these alternatives is most likely has not yet been established.

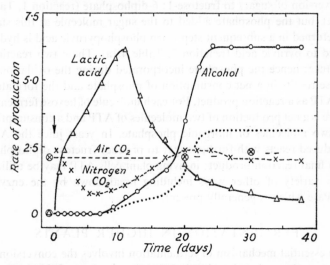

Fig. 4.2. The production of alcohol, carbon dioxide and lactic acid in fermentation of whole potato tubers. The dotted line (················) shows the production of carbon dioxide equivalent to the alcohol produced. (After J. Barker and A. F. El Saifi[5])

In many plant tissues there is the potentiality for two types of fermentation. For example, when potato tubers are placed in nitrogen, no alcohol is produced during the first few days but only lactic acid; later, after a considerable period, the fermentation changes to the formation of alcohol and carbon dioxide with relatively little further formation of lactic acid[5] (see Fig. 4.2). On the other hand, if the potato tissue is sliced and then placed under anaerobic conditions alcohol fermentation takes place from the very beginning. There are some variations according to the particular variety of potato. Lactic acid has been shown to be a product of fermentation in a number of germinating seeds and in some leaves and algae.

The rate of production of alcohol can be utilized to measure the rate of fermentation. In this way the inhibitory effect of oxygen on fermentation can be investigated. The minimum concentration of oxygen at which alcohol formation is totally suppressed is referred to as the *extinction point* and has been found to be of the order of 2 per cent for such tissue as apple fruits, rhododendron leaves, and germinating buckwheat seeds. In rice the value may be as high as 10 to 20 per cent. If the oxidative mechanism of respiration is poisoned (see later), for example, by the addition of cyanide, then fermentation may be induced under aerobic conditions at quite high concentrations of oxygen in all plants.

Inhibitor studies

Various inhibitors have been used to study fermentation. Iodoacetamide or iodoacetic acid primarily inhibit fermentation by preventing oxidation of triose phosphate to phosphoglyceric acid (reaction 4, Table 4.1a). This is shown by the accumulation of triose phosphate in the presence of relatively weak concentrations of iodoacetate. At higher concentrations other reactions in the sequence are also affected. If arsenate is added to yeast juice, the production of carbon dioxide takes place continuously; whereas it will be remembered that with a limited amount of phosphate present fermentation ceases after the production of an amount of carbon dioxide equivalent to that of the inorganic phosphate originally present. The diphosphoglyceric acid normally produced in the oxidation of triose is stable, and can only break down by reaction with adenosine diphosphate, whereas the phosphoarsenical glyceric acid derivative produced in the presence of arsenate hydrolyses rapidly into free arsenate and phosphoglyceric acid. Thus the arsenate is liberated for further reaction and is not accumulated in a stable end product as in the case of phosphate. Fluoride inhibits the enzyme enolase, and as mentioned previously its presence leads to an accumulation of phosphoglyceric acid.

Respiration

Respiration is the process of breakdown of complex organic substances in the presence of oxygen. First, the mechanism of production of carbon dioxide from carbohydrate will be considered. Second, the removal of hydrogen from carbon substrates and its eventual reaction with oxygen to form water will be discussed. Finally, a third aspect of respiratory metabolism involving the formation of phosphorylated derivatives will be considered.

THE CARBON METABOLISM
OF RESPIRATION

The formation of pyruvate

The initial sequence of reactions in the oxidation of carbohydrate are the same as those in the process of fermentation. Pfeffer originally regarded respiration as a further oxidation of the products of anaerobic metabolism. Kostychev suggested that in respiration some of the reactions of fermentation were bypassed. The latter view is known now to be correct since it has been established that only the reactions between fructose-1:6-diphosphate and pyruvate (EMP pathway) are common to respiration and fermentation.

Heard and James fed barley seedlings with hexose diphosphate and demonstrated an accumulation of phosphoglycerate. Neuberg and colleagues showed that pea and bean preparations could convert phosphoglycerate to pyruvate aerobically. In general, tissue homogenates of plant material fed with glucose and ATP will accumulate phosphoglyceric acid and in the presence of certain inhibitors an accumulation of pyruvate occurs, showing that these are intermediates common to the two processes. Inhibitors such as iodoacetate inhibit both fermentation and respiration and Turner showed that in carrot tissues the degree of inhibition of both processes was the same. There is little doubt that pyruvate is formed in the aerobic breakdown of carbohydrate.

There is an alternative method of glucose degradation.[56] Glucose-6-phosphate is oxidized to 6-phosphogluconate which is then oxidatively decarboxylated to form ribulose-5-phosphate. Two molecules of ribulose phosphate react in a sequence involving sedoheptulose phosphate and erythrose phosphate and ultimately reform glucose-6-phosphate. Thus a cyclic reaction system operates in which carbon dioxide is evolved from the carbon atom 1 of glucose (Table 4.2). The accompanying oxidation is associated with the reduction of nicotinamide adenine dinucleotide phosphate, formerly called triphosphopyridine nucleotide (NADP, coenzyme II, formerly TPN), and this may be its main significance for plant metabolism. With suitable enzymes to reoxidize the $NADPH_2$ a mechanism, referred to as the pentose phosphate pathway, is provided for the complete oxidation of glucose to carbon dioxide. Two important enzymes are concerned in the process, transketolase, which catalyses the transfer of —CHOH.CHO from a keto- to an aldo-sugar, and transaldolase, which catalyses the transfer of $CH_2.OH.CO.CHOH$— in

44

a similar way. These enzymes are of general importance because they permit interconversion of short chain and longer chain sugars.

The relative importance of the EMP and the pentose phosphate pathways has been investigated by feeding glucose radioactive in either the one or six carbon atom.[55] If the EMP path is operating, then the same production of labelled carbon dioxide should occur whether the one or six carbon atom is labelled. If the pentose shunt operates more radioactive carbon dioxide will be produced when the glucose is labelled in Cl than in C6. Such experiments have demonstrated that in mature plant tissues the pentose phosphate shunt may account for a considerable portion of the total carbon dioxide produced in respiration.[127] Its activity relative to the EMP path may be ultimately determined by the relative rates of reoxidation of $NADPH_2$ and $NADH_2$.

The Krebs cycle

The further oxidation of pyruvate in respiration is a complex process. Szent Gyorgi showed that the aerobic metabolism of slices of animal tissue was inhibited as a result of washing, but it could be restored by addition of a tissue extract. Heating the extract did not destroy its effectiveness and the necessary substances which it contained were found to be succinic, fumaric, malic, and oxaloacetic acids. All these acids were shown to be interconvertible within the tissue so that addition of any one sufficed. Krebs in 1937 showed that citric acid was equally effective. Szent Gyorgi had taken the view that the catalytic activity of these acids was related to the oxidoreduction reactions

TABLE 4.2

Pentose phosphate pathway

1. G6P+NADP (CoII)
   $\longrightarrow$ Gluconolactone 6P+$NADPH_2$ (CoIIH$_2$)   Phosphoglucone dehydrogenase

2. Gluconolactone 6P+H_2O $\longrightarrow$ Gluconate 6P   Gluconolactonase

3. Gluconate 6P+NADP $\longrightarrow$ CO_2+$NADPH_2$+ribulose 5P   Phosphogluconate dehydrogenase

1–3. G6P+2NADP+H_2O $\longrightarrow$ Ribulose 5P+CO_2+2$NADPH_2$

4. Ribulose 5P $\longrightarrow$ Ribose 5P   Phosphoribose isomerase

   Ribulose 5P $\longrightarrow$ Xylulose 5P   Phosphoribulose epimerase

5. Ribose 5P+xylulose 5P
   $\longrightarrow$ Triose P+sedoheptulose 7P   Transketolase

6. Triose P+sedoheptulose 7P $\longrightarrow$ F6P+erythrose 4P   Transaldolase

7. Xylulose 5P+Erythrose 4P $\longrightarrow$ Triose P+F6P	Transketolase
4–7. 6-Ribulose 5P $\longrightarrow$ 2-Triose P+4F6P	
8. 2-Triose P $\longrightarrow$ F1 : 6diP $\longrightarrow$ + H_2O $\longrightarrow$ F6P+P_i	See EMP
9. F6P $\longrightarrow$ G6P	Phospho-glucoisomerase
1–9. 6G6P+12NADP+7H_2O $\longrightarrow$ 6CO_2+12NADPH$_2$+P_i+5G6P	

Pentose Phosphate Cycle Diagram

of respiration; Krebs considered that they were concerned in the oxidation of pyruvate to carbon dioxide. He postulated a closed cyclic reaction sequence in which these acids were intermediates (Table 4.3b) and which resulted in the reformation of the initial reactant oxaloacetic acid. The operation of the cycle can be demonstrated by the use of specific inhibitors. For example, treatment with malonate inhibits the oxidation of succinate, and if other acids of the cycle, e.g. fumarate, are fed to malonate-inhibited tissue, succinate accumulates in equivalent amount.[90] The poisoning effect of high pressures of oxygen on plants has been shown to be due to an inhibition of the cycle resulting in an accumulation of citric acid.[6]

The mode of entry of pyruvic acid into the cycle was not understood for some time. It was known that pyruvic acid lost carbon dioxide and co-carboxylase was required as a cofactor. It is now known that the acetate remaining, condensed with lipoic acid, reacts with a fourth coenzyme, coenzyme A (CoA), to form acetyl CoA. It is this substance which condenses with the oxaloacetic acid in the presence of a condensing enzyme to form citrate, the first intermediate in the cycle (Table 4.3a). Coenzyme A is a derivative of

TABLE 4.3a

Entry of pyruvate into Krebs cycle

1. Pyruvic acid + lipoic acid $\longrightarrow$ CO_2 + acetyl hydrolipoate   Pyruvate dehydrogenase + pyrophosphothiamine

$$CH_3CO.COOH \qquad \begin{array}{c} S-CH_2 \\ | \\ CH_2 \\ | \\ S-CH \\ | \\ (CH_2)_4 \\ | \\ COOH \end{array} \qquad CH_2-CO-O-S-CH \qquad \begin{array}{c} HS-CH_2 \\ | \\ CH_2 \\ | \\ \\ | \\ (CH_2)_4 \\ | \\ COOH \end{array}$$

2. Acetyl hydrolipoate + CoA $\longrightarrow$
   Acetyl CoA + reduced lipoate   Thioltransacetylase

3. Reduced lipoate + NAD (CoI) $\longrightarrow$
   Lipoic acid + $NADH_2(CoIH_2)$ Lipoate dehydrogenase

pantothenic acid, which can act as an acetate or acetyl donor to other substances beside oxaloacetic acid.

When a tissue is placed under anaerobic conditions lactic acid or alcohol will accumulate according to the type of fermentation. If the tissue is subsequently placed in air the accumulated fermentation products may under certain conditions be oxidized via the Krebs cycle.

The oxidative capacity of a tissue homogenate with respect to Krebs cycle activity has been shown to reside in a particular fraction – the mitochondria. Mitochondria have now been successfully isolated from a wide range of plant material and their biochemical activities studied.[43] The operation of the whole sequence of Krebs cycle reactions depends on their particulate structure. Particulate preparations

TABLE 4.3b

Krebs (citric acid) cycle

4. Acetyl CoA + oxaloacetic $\longrightarrow$ Citric acid + CoA — Citric condensing enzyme

5. Citric acid $\longrightarrow$ Isocitric acid — Aconitase

6. Isocitric acid + NAD $\longrightarrow$
   (or NADP)
   $\quad\quad$ α-ketoglutaric acid + CO_2 + $NADH_2$ — Isocitric
   $\quad\quad$ (or $NADPH_2$)* — dehydrogenase

7. α-Ketoglutaric acid + lipoic acid $\longrightarrow$ Succinylhydrolipoate + CO_2 — Ketoglutarate dehydrogenase pyrophospho-thiamine

8. Succinylhydrolipoate + CoA $\longrightarrow$
   $\quad\quad$ Succinyl CoA + reduced lipoic acid — Thioltrans-acetylase
   Reduced lipoic acid + NAD $\longrightarrow$ Lipoic acid + $NADH_2$

9. Succinyl CoA + H_2O $\longrightarrow$ Succinic acid + CoA + ATP + ADP + P_i

10. Succinic acid $\longrightarrow$ Fumaric acid + 2H† — Succinic dehydrogenase

11. Fumaric acid + H_2O $\longrightarrow$ Malic acid — Fumarase

12. Malic acid + NAD $\longrightarrow$ Oxaloacetic acid + $NADH_2$ — Malic dehydrogenase

4–12. Acetyl CoA + 3NAD + $2H_2O$ $\longrightarrow$ $2CO_2$ + CoA + $3NADH_2$ + 2H

* Two isocitric dehydrogenase enzymes are known; one specific to coenzyme I, the other to coenzyme II. Probably the coenzyme I linked enzyme operates in plant mitochondria.

† As reduced dehydrogenase.

$$
\begin{array}{l}
CH_3 \\
| \\
C=O \quad \text{pyruvate} \\
| \\
COOH
\end{array}
$$

$$\searrow CO_2$$
$$\searrow 2H$$

$$
\begin{array}{l}
COOH \\
| \\
C=O \\
| \\
CH_2 \\
| \\
COOH
\end{array}
\quad + \quad
CH_3 \cdot CO.CoA \longrightarrow
\begin{array}{l}
COOH \\
| \\
HO-C-CH_2COOH \\
| \\
CH_2 \\
| \\
COOH
\end{array}
$$

oxaloacetate   acetyl coA   citrate

$$\uparrow 2H$$

$$
\begin{array}{l}
COOH \\
| \\
CH_2 \\
| \\
HCOH \\
| \\
COOH
\end{array}
\qquad
\begin{array}{l}
[COO]H \\
| \\
HC-CH_2.COOH \\
| \\
HCOH \\
| \\
COOH
\end{array}
$$

malate   isocitrate

$$\searrow 2H$$
$$\searrow CO_2$$

$$
\begin{array}{l}
COOH \\
| \\
CH \\
|| \\
CH \\
| \\
COOH
\end{array}
\xleftarrow{2H}
\begin{array}{l}
COOH \\
| \\
CH_2 \\
| \\
CH_2 \\
| \\
COOH
\end{array}
\xleftarrow{CO_2 \, 2H}
\begin{array}{l}
COOH \\
| \\
CH_2 \\
| \\
CH_2 \\
| \\
C=O \\
| \\
COOH
\end{array}
$$

Fumarate   succinate   α-ketoglutarate

Diagram of Krebs cycle

isolated from many plant tissues, e.g. mung bean seedlings, have been shown to oxidize all the acids of the Krebs cycle. The oxidation of pyruvate is dependent on the concomitant presence of one of the acids of the cycle and of inorganic phosphate and magnesium.

OXIDOREDUCTION REACTIONS
OF RESPIRATION

The oxidation of carbohydrates to carbon dioxide is accompanied by a concomitant removal of hydrogen which ultimately reacts with oxygen to form water.

Earlier theories regarded the essential feature of this process as an activation of oxygen to a state in which it was capable of reacting with the carbon intermediates. Early in this century Bach suggested that organic peroxides might be formed directly from oxygen. This led to the discovery of two enzymes, peroxidase and catalase. Peroxidase catalyses the oxidation of phenols by hydrogen peroxide; and catalase the oxidation of hydrogen peroxide itself. However, these proved not to be directly concerned in the oxidation of carbohydrates.

An alternative view of oxidation has been taken from 1920 onwards, chiefly due to Wieland and Thunberg. Wieland regarded oxidation reactions as not necessarily involving oxygen but rather the removal of hydrogen. He considered that the substrate must be activated by enzymes to make the hydrogen labile. Thunberg showed that there were enzymes in plant tissues, which he called *dehydrogenases*, which could activate substrates in this way and catalyse the transfer of hydrogen to such substances as methylene blue under anaerobic conditions, or to oxygen under aerobic conditions.

A third approach developed by Warburg was to consider the physiological features of respiration and show that they had some similarity to catalysis by inorganic metal compounds. If an enzyme contains a metal which can exist in two valency states it could both donate electrons (act as a reducing agent) and accept electrons (act as an oxidizing agent). Keilin subsequently showed the existence of haematin compounds containing iron in plants and animals, the cytochromes, which changed their oxidation reduction state from ferric to ferrous accordingly as the organism was subjected alternatively to aerobic and to anaerobic conditions.

Oxidation-reduction reactions can be considered as a transfer of electrons, for example in metal containing enzymes, or as the activation of oxygen to react and form water, or as the removal of hydrogen atoms from substrates. It is now realized that all three types of reaction play a part in the respiratory mechanism.

Dehydrogenases

Dehydrogenases catalyse the removal of hydrogen from substrates. The enzyme is specific to the substrate which is to undergo oxidation and to the substance to which the hydrogen is transferred, the hydrogen acceptor. The latter is generally a coenzyme and the dehydrogenase is specific to either coenzyme I (NAD) or coenzyme II (NADP). Dehydrogenases which respectively catalyse the oxidation of alcohol, lactic acid, malic acid, triose phosphate, and isocitric acid transfer hydrogen from these substrates to coenzyme I. Dehydrogenases

50

which transfer hydrogen to coenzyme II include those specific for the oxidation of glucose phosphate, phosphogluconic acid, and isocitric acid. Other dehydrogenases transfer electrons direct to cytochrome. Examples are succinic dehydrogenase, widespread in all tissues, and aldehyde dehydrogenase, found in potato and a number of other plant tissues. Another important dehydrogenase is that which catalyses the transfer of hydrogen from reduced coenzyme to cytochrome or alternatively to a dyestuff. It is called cytochrome reductase.

The substances coenzyme I and coenzyme II form an essential link

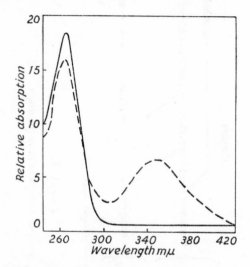

Fig. 4.3. The absorption curve for oxidised (————) and reduced (– – – – –) nicotinamide adenine dinucleotide

in the transfer of hydrogen from the carbon substrate to oxygen. They act as intermediates or carriers, themselves first becoming reduced and then, by transferring their hydrogen to other intermediates such as the cytochromes, becoming reoxidized (see Table 4.4). Oxidation and reduction of NAD and NADP is accompanied by characteristic changes in absorption spectrum in the ultra-violet (Fig. 4.3). This fact has been widely used to study their participation in reactions *in vitro*. *In vivo* the absorption of other plant constituents (e.g. proteins) in this region limits the usefulness of this technique.

The flavoproteins

An enzyme was mentioned previously which was concerned in the oxidation of reduced coenzymes I and II ($NADH_2$, $NADPH_2$). This

51

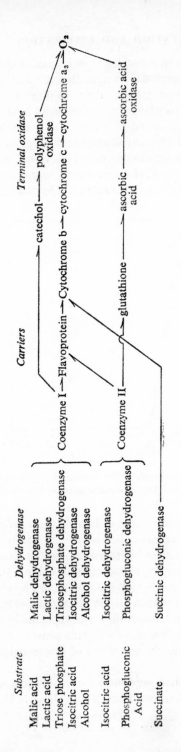

TABLE 4.4

Electron transport in respiration

is a member of a class of enzymes which contain flavin either as flavin mononucleotide (FMN) or flavin adenine dinucleotide (FAD) in their prosthetic group. There are a number of flavoprotein enzymes which catalyse hydrogen transfer. An important member of this group is NADP-cytochrome c reductase which is found in yeast and mammalian tissue. It catalyses the transfer of electrons between $NADPH_2$ and cytochrome b. This was first found by Haas. Warburg and Christian found another member of this class, referred to as yellow enzyme, which would react with $NADPH_2$, and a second

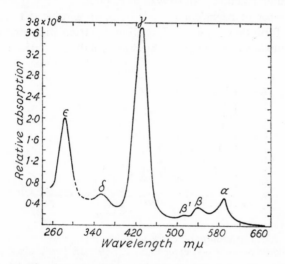

Fig. 4.4. *The absorption spectrum of the carbon monoxide complex with the oxygen transporting enzyme in yeast, i.e. of cytochrome oxidase. (After O. Warburg and E. Negelein*[151])

$NADH_2$-cyctochrome reductase is also known. Most reduced flavoprotein enzymes are slowly oxidized by oxygen without the presence of another enzyme. It has been suggested that they may play such a role in respiration, but it is more generally believed that their most important role is to catalyse electron transfer between the reduced coenzymes and the cytochromes.

Oxidases

A chain of carriers operates until a terminal substance is reached which reacts with oxygen directly (Table 4.4). Since the terminal reaction concerns oxygen itself, the enzyme catalysing the final step is referred to as an oxidase.

Oxidase activity was first characterized through the inhibition of respiratory activity by carbon monoxide. This inhibition was reversed by illumination and the extent of the reversal varied with the particular wavelength of light used. O. Warburg[151] measured the degree of reversal for equal amounts of light energy at different wavelengths. The 'action' spectrum obtained (Fig. 4.4.) was similar to that for photodissociation of inorganic catalysts containing iron, and Warburg postulated the existence of an iron haematin enzyme which by a change in valency from ferric to ferrous, and vice versa, catalysed the terminal reaction with oxygen in respiration.

A number of haem compounds occur in aerobic tissues. In the reduced form they show an absorption spectrum with three characteristic maxima at the approximate wavelengths 550–605 mμ, 520–30

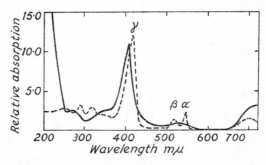

Fig. 4.5. The absorption curve of oxidised (————) and reduced (---------) cytochrome c. (After H. Lundegårdh[99])

mμ, and 415–50 mμ, which are referred to as the α, β, and γ peaks respectively. On oxidation the α and β peaks disappear and absorption in this region becomes diffuse (Fig. 4.5). Keilin[79] observed the spectrum of reduced cytochromes in a wide range of plant and animal tissues, under anaerobic conditions, and was the first to realize the significance of these compounds in oxido-reduction reactions in respiration. The characteristic absorption bands had been seen earlier by McMunn, but at that time they were not understood.

The cytochromes which occur in plants can be classified into groups according to the position of their α-absorption band. They form three groups; the c group containing cytochrome c, c_1, and f, the b group containing b, b_3, b_6, and b_7, and a third group containing a and a_3. Cytochromes f and b_6 are confined to the chloroplasts and their role in photosynthesis will be discussed in a later chapter.

The remaining cytochromes are concerned in electron transfer from a coenzyme linked dehydrogenase system to oxygen. This transfer takes place from cytochrome b to cytochrome c_1 and then to cytochrome c, a and finally to cytochrome a_3, which is now regarded as the oxidase. One of the most powerful methods of studying the cytochromes *in vivo* is by measuring changes in the absorption spectrum (Fig. 4.6), although this is made more difficult in plants

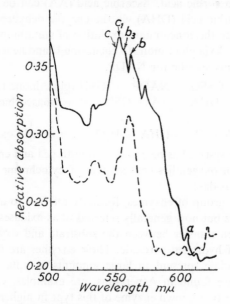

Fig. 4.6. Absorption curves for three-day-old barley roots under aerobic (------) and anaerobic (————) conditions. Under anaerobic conditions the bands of the reduced form of cytochrome a, b, b_3, c_1 and c become apparent. (After W. O. James and H. Lundegårdh[76])

than animals by the presence of other pigments and because of their relatively low concentration.[99]

An alternative terminal oxidase system to that mediated through cytochromes involves the oxidation of polyphenols. The enzyme polyphenol oxidase will catalyse the reaction between oxygen and polyphenols to form the corresponding quinone. The quinone can then oxidise reduced coenzyme and thus link back to the respiratory substrate via a dehydrogenase. This enzyme contains copper which is alternately oxidized and reduced just as is the iron in cytochromes.

The activity of polyphenol oxidase in the formation of quinones results in the browning of tissue, and can be seen when apples or potatoes are cut. The enzyme is generally believed to function mainly in damaged tissue and not to mediate any considerable part of the respiratory chain under normal conditions. It has a relatively low affinity for oxygen.

A third terminal oxidase is an enzyme containing copper which reacts with ascorbic acid. Ascorbic acid (AA) can be formed from dehydroascorbic acid (DHA) via the enzyme dehydroascorbic acid reductase with the concomitant oxidation of glutathione. This forms a complete link via glutathione to coenzyme II and hence to dehydrogenase systems specific for NADP.

$$NADPH_2 + GSSG \rightarrow NADP + 2GSH \text{ (glutathione reductase)}$$
$$2GSH + DHA \rightarrow AA + GSSG \text{ (dehydroascorbic acid}$$
$$\text{reductase)}$$
$$AA + O_2 \rightarrow DHA + H_2O \text{ (ascorbic acid oxidase)}$$

This enzyme system has been found in both pea and cress seedlings. Its affinity for oxygen lies between that of cytochrome oxidase and polyphenol oxidase.

There is a group of enzymes, formerly referred to as aerobic dehydrogenases but now generally referred to as oxidases, which catalyse hydrogen transfer between the substrate and oxygen with the formation of hydrogen peroxide. These enzymes are flavoproteins: xanthine oxidase, present in large amounts in milk, and glucose dehydrogenase found in Aspergillus, are examples. Glycollic acid oxidase is the best known enzyme of this type in higher plants. Such enzymes require the presence of catalase in a tissue or hydrogen peroxide may accumulate and poison the tissue.

Catalase is widespread in most aerobic tissue. It is a haematin derivative which catalyses the breakdown of hydrogen peroxide to give oxygen and water.

$$2H_2O \rightarrow 2H_2O + O_2 \text{ (catalase)}$$

Iron porphyrins which have catalase activity also oxidize other substances such as primary alcohols or phenols. This second type of reaction is characteristic of the enzyme *peroxidase*. The two types of catalysis are shared in common, but an individual enzyme will catalyse one reaction more than the other.

Inhibitors of oxidases

The demonstration of the activity of one oxidase rather than another in a particular tissue has generally been deduced from the effect of certain specific inhibitors.[74] Most oxidases contain metal complexes and their catalytic function depends on the ability of the metal to exist in two valency states. Hence they are inhibited by metal 'poisons' like cyanide, azide or, more specifically, for copper, dieca (diethyldi-thiocarbamate). Ascorbic acid oxidase and polyphenol oxidase both contain copper. Their functions can be differentiated from enzymes containing iron using inhibition by carbon monoxide which for copper – as distinct from iron – compounds cannot be reversed by illumination.

The interpretation of the evidence obtained by the use of inhibitors is not always unequivocal. In many tissues there is an oxygen uptake which is not inhibited by cyanide, referred to as cyanide-resistant respiration. The spadix of *Arum* is the best known example of an active oxidative metabolism which is not affected by carbon monoxide and cyanide.[75] This led to the view that this tissue could not function through a metal-containing oxidase system and that a flavoprotein must catalyse the reaction with oxygen. Subsequent work showed that this was not true but that this tissue contained a particular cytochrome component (cytochrome b_7) which is not affected by cyanide.[8] The present view is that the major part of oxidative metabolism under normal conditions *in vivo* takes place by a cytochrome mediated system.

PHOSPHORYLATIVE REACTIONS

The oxidation of triose phosphate to phosphoglyceric acid, a reaction common to fermentation and respiration, requires the presence of inorganic phosphate. During this oxidation the triose phosphate is first phosphorylated to diphosphoglyceric acid and then subsequently one phosphate group transferred to ADP. Phosphoenolpyruvic acid is formed from phosphoglyceric acid by the removal of the elements of water and another mole of ADP is phosphorylated in the formation of pyruvic acid from phosphoenolpyruvic acid. It should be noted that phosphoglyceric acid itself is incapable of transferring phosphate to ADP. In the Krebs cycle, in the formation of succinate, α-ketoglutarate is oxidized by NAD in the presence of coenzyme A to form succinyl coenzyme A, carbon dioxide, and $NADH_2$. Succinyl coenzyme A then reacts with ADP and phosphate to form free succinic acid, coenzyme A, and ATP. Thus there are three reactions in which the intermediates of the carbon path donate phosphate to ADP. All these processes involve phosphorylation at the *substrate* level.

Phosphorylation also takes place during the sequential transfer of hydrogen from $NADH_2$ and $NADPH_2$ to oxygen. This is referred to as *electron-transport phosphorylation*. It has been shown with isolated mitochrondia that the oxidation of reduced coenzyme ($NADH_2$) by oxygen can result in the formation of three molecules of ATP for each oxygen atom consumed.[106] In these experiments fluoride is used to inhibit the enzyme ATPase which would otherwise catalyse the breakdown of the ATP formed.

During the breakdown of a hexose sugar the balance sheet for phosphorylation (Table 4.5) shows under anaerobic conditions a net gain of two moles of inorganic phosphate (involving the uptake of two molecules of inorganic phosphate) per mole of hexose.

TABLE 4.5

Reactions involving phosphorylation

1. Fructose$+2$ATP $\longrightarrow$ F1 : 6diP$+2$ADP

2. 2PGA$+2$NAD(CoI)$+2$ADP$+2$P $\longrightarrow$
$\qquad$ 2TP$+2$ATP$+2NADH_2$(CoIH$_2$) $\left.\begin{array}{c} \\ \\ \\ \end{array}\right\}$ Substrate phosphorylation

3. 2PEP$+2$ADP $\longrightarrow$ 2Pyr$+2$ATP

Fermentation
$\quad$ 1–3. $\qquad$ F$+2$ADP$+2P_i+2$NAD $\longrightarrow$ 2Pyr$+2$ATP$+2NADH_2+2H_2O$

2*a*. $2NADH_2+O_2+6P_i+6$ADP $\longrightarrow$ $2H_2O+2$NAD$+6$ATP

4. 2Pyr$+6$NAD$+2H_2O+2$NADP*$+$
$\quad$ 2-succinic dehydrogenase $\longrightarrow$ $\qquad\qquad$ See Table 4.3b
$\qquad$ $6CO_2+6NADH_2+2NADPH_2+2$S.deh.H$_2$

5. $6NADH_2+3O_2+18$ADP$+18P_i \longrightarrow$
$\qquad\qquad$ 6NAD$+6H_2O+18$ATP$\left.\begin{array}{c} \\ \\ \\ \\ \end{array}\right\}$ Electron-
$\quad$ 2NADPH*$_2+O_2+6$ADP$+6P_i \longrightarrow$ $\qquad$ transport
$\qquad\qquad$ 2NADP$+2H_2O+6$ATP phosphorylations
$\quad$ 2S.deh.H$_2+O_2+4$ADP$+4P_i \longrightarrow$ 2S.deh.$+2H_2O+4$ATP

6. 2α-ketoglutarate$+2$ADP$+2P_i \longrightarrow$ 2-succinate$+2$ATP $\qquad$ Substrate phosphorylation

4–6 Oxidation of pyruvate
$\qquad$ 2-Pyr $+ 5O_2 + 30$ADP $+ 30P_i \longrightarrow 6CO_2 + 4H_2O + 30$ATP

1–6 Oxidation of hexose
$\qquad$ Hexose $+ 6O_2 + 38$ADP $+ 38P_i \longrightarrow 6CO_2 + 6H_2O + 38$ATP

* The table is written for the isocitric dehydrogenase which is specific to coenzyme II.

Under aerobic conditions the same phosphorylative reactions occur, but in addition, in the Krebs cycle, there will be five pairs of hydrogen atoms per molecule of pyruvate oxidized, transferred from the reduced coenzyme ultimately to oxygen. Four of these (from $NADH_2$) result in the uptake of three molecules of phosphate per oxygen atom consumed whilst the 2H atoms from succinic dehydrogenase require two further phosphate molecules. Thus 14 moles of phosphate are consumed in the hydrogen transfer reactions consequent upon the oxidation of one mole of pyruvate. In addition, a further molecule of phosphate will be taken up in the conversion of ketoglutarate to succinate. In all there will be 38 moles of ATP formed in respiration compared with two formed during fermentation per mole of hexose broken down (Table 4.5). If oxidation of carbohydrate takes place by the pentose shunt and not by the EMP, a maximum of 36 molecules of ATP may result per molecule of hexose from the oxidation of the $NADPH_2$ produced (probably taking place by prior conversion of $NADPH_2$ to $NADH_2$ catalysed by the enzyme pyridine nucleotide transhydrogenase). The consequence of this important difference between the number of moles of phosphate taken up per mole of hexose broken down under anaerobic and aerobic conditions will be discussed later in Chapter 5. The formation of ATP from ADP requires a supply of energy. It is not a reaction which will take place spontaneously. Hence the energy of oxidation of hexose is in part stored in the ATP which is formed during respiration.

Phosphorylation is a necessary concomitant to the oxidation of triose phosphate but certain agents will act as inhibitors and 'uncouple' phosphorylation from the oxidation, i.e. they will permit the oxidation to continue whilst suppressing the phosphorylation. When arsenate is fed to the tissue in place of phosphate the phosphorylation of the substrate is replaced by combination with arsenate and the arsenate derivatives (unlike the corresponding phosphates) spontaneously hydrolyse to give arsenate and free derivatives. Hence no transfer takes place to an acceptor molecule. Dinitrophenol acts as an inhibitor of electron-transport phosphorylation, and in many tissues, when phosphorylation is inhibited by this substance, the rate of oxygen uptake is increased. The mechanism has not yet been elucidated.

THE METABOLISM OF FAT AND PROTEIN

In the complete oxidation of carbohydrate to carbon dioxide one molecule of oxygen is consumed for each molecule of carbon dioxide produced. The ratio of the carbon dioxide produced to the oxygen consumed, called the *respiratory quotient* (RQ), equals 1·0. During the germination of seeds which are rich in fat reserves, values of the RQ considerably less than 1 have been observed. This led to the suggestion that fat may be utilized as a respiratory substrate, since a fat contains fewer oxygen atoms per carbon than a sugar and it requires more oxygen to complete its conversion to carbon dioxide. In other tissues, e.g. detached leaves, protein may be used as a respiratory substrate and the RQ will be greater than 1·0. One importance of the Krebs cycle is that it provides a common reaction mechanism for the oxidation of carbohydrates, fats, and proteins.

Fats

The first step in the oxidation of a fatty acid is the condensation of the fatty acid with CoA in the presence of ATP to form a CoA fatty acid complex. The complex is twice dehydrogenated, flavoprotein and NAD acting as the hydrogen acceptors, and then reacts with a further molecule of CoA. Two carbon atoms are removed from the chain with the formation of acetyl CoA, leaving a complex of the residual fatty acid now of shorter chain length. The new CoA-fatty acid complex can now undergo the same process again so that the fatty acid can be progressively reduced by two carbon atoms at a time.[141] The acetyl CoA formed can be oxidized in the Krebs cycle in the same manner as if it had been formed from carbohydrate via pyruvic acid. The aerobic reoxidation of the reduced flavoprotein and coenzyme produced during the formation of acetyl CoA can result in a net gain of 3 moles of ATP per mole of acetyl CoA formed. The reaction between fatty acids and acetyl CoA can be reversed to form fatty acids although the reaction mechanism is known to differ in the two directions. The formation of fats from carbohydrates can therefore take place through the E.M.P. pathway and the condensation of acetyl CoA units.

On the other hand, the formation of sugars from fats would require the reversal of the EMP. Two reactions in this sequence, namely the conversion of phosphoenolpyruvic acid to pyruvic acid, and second the decarboxylation of pyruvic acid to form acetyl CoA, are not readily reversible. Nevertheless, an extensive transformation of fat into carbohydrate has been observed during the germination of seedlings containing fat. The alternative route which avoids the loss of the carbon in acetyl CoA as carbon dioxide in the Krebs cycle was discovered by Krebs and Kornberg[81] and is called the glyoxylate bypass (Table 4.6). Acetyl CoA condenses with oxaloacetic acid to

TABLE 4.6

The glyoxylate shunt and fat-carbohydrate interconversion

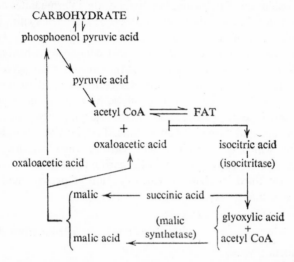

give isocitric acid as in the beginning of the Krebs cycle, but the isocitric acid is then split by the enzyme isocitritase to form succinic and glyoxylic acids. The glyoxylic acid reacts with a second molecule of acetyl CoA catalysed by the enzyme malic synthetase to form malic acid. Both the malic acid and the succinic acid are converted to oxaloacetic acid. This is in part decarboxylated in the presence of ATP to give phosphoenolpyruvic acid and in part forms oxalo-acetic acid to continue the cycle. The PEP is then converted to carbohydrate by reversal of the EMP pathway (Table 4.1a). The enzyme malic synthetase has been found widely distributed in plants which store fat as a reserve food substance. It has been demonstrated that during the germination of seeds rich in fat up to 75 per cent of the fat is converted to carbohydrate by the reactions discussed.[19]

Proteins

The keto acids of the Krebs cycle can be formed by deamination of the corresponding amino acids. Thus the amino acid glutamic acid can give rise to α-ketoglutaric acid, aspartic to oxaloacetic acid, and alanine to pyruvic acid. Hence during protein breakdown the carbon skeletons of these three particular amino acids can enter the Krebs cycle and be converted to carbon dioxide. A further discussion of these reactions is given in Chapter 7 on nitrogen metabolism.

THE KREBS CYCLE AND SYNTHESIS

The Krebs cycle has been considered so far as a catalytic mechanism for the oxidation of pyruvate, but many of the intermediates can also take part in other metabolic reactions. The keto acids can give rise to amino acids and hence take part in protein synthesis, acetyl CoA can give rise to fats, and succinate can condense with glycine to form δ-aminolaevulinic acid which is the precursor for pyrrole synthesis. But removal of acids from the cycle for synthesis can take place only at the expense of its catalytic functioning in respiration unless there is some other mechanism for replacing these acids. Three reactions are known which can do this. Two involve phosphoenolpyruvate, which can combine with carbon dioxide either in the presence of PEP carboxylase or PEP carboxykinase to form oxalo-acetate; the third involves the carboxylation of pyruvic acid in the presence of malic enzyme to form malate:

$$\text{Phosphenolpyruvate} + CO_2 \rightarrow$$
$$\text{Oxaloacetate} + P_i \text{ (PEP carboxylase)}$$

$$\text{Phosphoenolpyruvate} + CO_2 + ADP \rightleftharpoons$$
$$\text{Oxaloacetate} + ATP \text{ (PEP carboxykinase)}$$

$$\text{Pyruvate} + NADPH_2 + CO_2 \rightleftharpoons \text{Malate} + NADP \text{ (malic enzyme)}$$

Using radioactive carbon dioxide some dark fixation in heterotrophic plant tissues has been observed; there is still some doubt as to its significance. In addition, the enzymes isocitritase and malate syn-thetase catalyse the condensation of acetyl groups to form malate and oxaloacetate by the glyoxylate bypass. These latter enzymes are however largely confined to plants with fat reserves.

The Krebs cycle, together with the glyoxylate bypass, involves intermediates common to fat, carbohydrate, and protein metabolism. Hence through this central metabolic system carbohydrates, fats, and proteins can be interconverted.

GENERAL REFERENCES

H. BEEVERS (1961) *Respiratory Metabolism in Plants*. Row-Peterson
W. O. JAMES (1953) *Plant Respiration*. O.U.P.

CHAPTER FIVE

Energetics of Respiration and Biological Syntheses

In this chapter some of the factors which determine the position of equilibrium of a reaction system, i.e. the ratio of the products to reactants, will be considered. These factors are important in determining the influence upon each other of two reaction systems which have a common reagent and hence in analysing the metabolism of the cell as a whole. They also determine whether a reaction is likely to result in synthesis by proceeding in a forward direction or breakdown by proceeding in the reverse direction.

FREE ENERGY OF A REACTION

The equilibrium state of the reaction $A + B \rightleftharpoons C + D$ is defined by the following expression: $K = \dfrac{[C'] \, [D']}{[A'] \, [B']}$, where $[A']$, $[B']$, $[C']$, $[D']$ are the respective molar concentrations at equilibrium and K is the equilibrium constant. If K is large there will be a predominance of products relative to reactants at equilibrium; if K is small the ratio of products to reactants will be small.

An alternative way of expressing the equilibrium state is in terms of the free energy change of the reaction. That is defined by the expression $\Delta F = -RT \log_e K + RT \log_e \dfrac{[C] \, [D]}{[A] \, [B]}$, where ΔF is the free energy change expressed in cals/mole, R the gas constant ($2 \text{ cal}/^\circ\text{C/mole}$), T the absolute temperature, and $[A]$, $[B]$, $[C]$, $[D]$ the concentrations of the reagents present. The free energy of a reaction is the maximum work that can be obtained from a chemical reaction operating infinitely slowly (i.e. in a manner referred to in thermodynamics as perfectly reversible). It is important to note that it differs from the heat of the reaction.

The free energy change of a reaction depends on the concentration of all reagents. The standard free energy change (ΔF_0) is the energy change for the conversion of one mole of reactants to products under standard conditions, i.e. when the concentrations of A, B, C, and D are all unity. If ΔF_0 is negative, i.e. if K is large, the reaction will tend to take place spontaneously with the formation of C and D from A and B. When $\Delta F_0 = 0$ the system is in equilibrium. If K is very small, ΔF_0 will be positive and the spontaneous reaction will be for A and B to be formed from C and D. By the removal of products so that their concentration is maintained low or by increasing the concentration of the reactants the free energy change will be altered so as to favour the formation of products. For each ten-fold increase in concentration of reactant the free energy of the reaction will change by 1·36 kcal at 25°C. Thus a reaction whose standard free energy is +2·7 kcal, which would convert products to reactants spontaneously under standard conditions, will take place in the reverse direction only if the ratio of the concentration of reactants to products is maintained greater than 100 to 1. In the plant there are a limited number of reactions whose standard free energy is positive but which can be made to proceed in the forward direction by an increase in concentration of reactants relative to products. The formation of the peptide bond involves a relatively small increase in free energy of between 0·5 and 4·0 kcal. This is sufficiently small so that a change in ratio of the concentration of reactants to products can result in detectable synthesis, and a reversal of the hydrolysis reaction catalysed by endopeptidases has been observed.

The free energy change of a reaction determines whether a reaction may or may not take place spontaneously. It does not follow that if a reaction is thermodynamically possible it will in fact take place at a measurable rate. Certain reactions which involve a large decrease in free energy take place only very slowly: they require the presence of a suitable catalyst to lower the activation energy of reaction (as discussed in Chapter 3).

THE LIBERATION OF ENERGY IN RESPIRATION

In respiration the transfer of hydrogen or electrons from the substrate to oxygen takes place by a number of reaction steps. Thus the energy liberated in the oxidation of carbohydrate is not liberated as a whole but in a number of reactions each of smaller free energy change. This can be seen by comparing the energy liberated in the oxidation of each of the intermediate carriers by oxygen. This is greatest for the carbon substrates and coenzymes, less for the flavoproteins, and smallest for the cytochromes. The free energy of oxidation is often expressed in terms of the oxidation-reduction potential, and Table 5.1 shows the relationship between the free energy of oxidation of a compound, its oxidation-reduction potential and its place in the respiratory sequence of hydrogen transfer. Within reasonable ratios of concentration of the oxidized and reduced forms the sequence of operation of carriers in hydrogen transfer must be in the direction of an increasing oxidation-reduction potential referred to hydrogen, i.e. of a decreasing free energy change (Fig. 5.1).

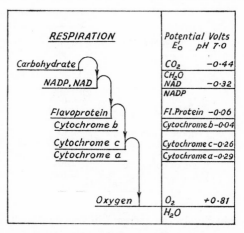

Fig. 5.1. The hydrogen or electron transport chain in respiration showing the oxidation reduction potentials

From Table 5.1 it will be seen that 24·6 kcal are liberated per two electrons transferred in the reaction between cytochrome c and oxygen; 14·0 kcal are liberated per two electrons transferred between cytochrome b and cytochrome c; and 12·2 kcal are liberated per two electrons transferred between flavin and coenzyme.

COUPLED REACTIONS

Reactions involving a positive free energy change take place only when they are accompanied by a second reaction in which there is a greater negative free energy change and with which they have a common reagent. The two reactions are then said to be 'coupled'.

Part of the energy derived from the successive oxidation steps in respiration is used to convert ADP to ATP, a reaction which in

TABLE 5.1

Standard oxidation reduction potentials

The following table lists the standard oxidation reduction potential E'_0 at pH 7·0 and at 25° C referred to the standard hydrogen electrode. It also gives the standard free energy ((ΔF_0) for the reaction $A + H_2 \longrightarrow AH_2$ per hydrogen atom or electron transferred and the standard free energy ($\Delta F'_0$) for the reaction $AH_2 + \frac{1}{2} O_2 \longrightarrow A + H_2O$. The relation between ΔF_0 and E'_0 is

$$\Delta F_0 = -23,068n \; (E'_0 + 0.06 \; pH)$$

in which n, the number of electrons transferred, has been taken as unity.

A	Reduced product	Standard		
		Potential E_0' volts	Free energy ΔF_0 kcals	Free energy $\Delta F_0'$ kcals
$\frac{1}{4}O_2$	H_2O	0·81	−28·4	0
Cytochrome c	Reduced cytochrome c	0·28	−16·1	−12·3
Succinate	Fumarate	0·02	−10·1	−18·0
Cytochrome b	Reduced cytochrome b	−0·04	− 9·1	−19·3
Flavin phosphate	Reduced flavin phosphate	−0·06	− 8·4	−20·0
Malate	Oxaloacetate	−0·16	− 6·0	−22·4
Coenzyme	Reduced coenzyme	−0·32	− 2·3	−26·1
H^+	$\frac{1}{2}H_2$	−0·42	0	−28·4

isolation would involve an increase in free energy. The energy required to convert one mole of ADP to ATP has been calculated on the assumption that the energy content of a molecule can be arithmetically summed from the energy content of the individual bonds. This gives a calculated value for the free energy of the reaction of about +12,000 cal/mole.[96] Measurements of the equilibrium constant of reaction between ATP and various other phosphate compounds suggest a rather lower value of the free energy of phosphorylation.[29] However, it is clear that the value is unlikely to be less than +8,000 cal/mole.

From the preceding section it is clear that if the electron flow from the reduced coenzyme to oxygen is coupled to phosphorylation it would be thermodynamically possible for one ATP molecule to be formed per 2 electrons transferred in the oxidation of coenzyme by flavin, for two ATP molecules to be formed in the oxidation of cytochrome b by cytochrome c, and three ATP molecules to be formed in the oxidation of cytochrome c by oxygen. Experimentally, the formation of a maximum of three molecules ATP has been demonstrated in the oxidation of one molecule of reduced coenzyme by isolated plant mitochondria, and it is probable that one is formed at each of these steps. In a similar way, in photosynthesis, phosphorylation accompanies electron flow through the cytochromes in association with the plastid pigments (see Chapter 6).

Acetyl phosphate, ATP, ADP, and creatine phosphate all liberate approximately the same energy on hydrolysis of the phosphate. A second class of phosphates including glucose-6-phosphate, GIP, F6P, AMP, and phosphoglyceric acid liberate considerably less energy on hydrolysis of the phosphate. The second group have therefore been referred to as low energy phosphates in contrast to the first group called the high energy phosphate esters which are able to phosphorylate compounds the low energy ones cannot. Further, the formation of a low energy phosphate ester from a high energy one liberates free energy which can be utilized in a concomitant synthesis which takes place as a 'coupled' reaction.

In many biological syntheses the formation of a condensed product is coupled to the hydrolysis of ATP to ADP and phosphate. The formation of glucose-6-phosphate from glucose and phosphate has a standard free energy change at pH 7·0 of $+3·0$ kcal approximately. Therefore it cannot take place spontaneously unless the concentration of glucose and phosphate relative to that of glucose phosphate is maintained high. But if glucose and ATP react to give glucose-6-phosphate and ADP and P the overall free energy change is -5 kcal (assuming the energy of formation of ATP from ADP and P to be approximately 8,000 cal). Hence the formation of glucose phosphate from glucose can take place spontaneously in the presence of ATP. From glucose-1-phosphate (which may be formed from glucose-6-phosphate) the synthesis of starch can take place spontaneously with an overall negative free energy change catalysed by the enzyme starch phosphorylase. Thus the synthesis of starch from glucose can take place only if it is coupled to the formation of ADP from ATP. By contrast, the hydrolysis of starch to glucose (catalysed by the enzymes amylase and maltase) is a spontaneous reaction with a negative free energy change. Again, hydrolysis of sucrose to glucose and fructose takes place spontaneously with a considerable loss in free energy, but the formation of sucrose must take place via phosphorylated derivatives of glucose and fructose so that the free energy change of the hydrolysis of ATP may be utilized in the synthesis.

A similar situation occurs in the formation and breakdown of amides. The hydrolysis of an amide to the corresponding amino acid has a free energy change of -6 kcal. The synthesis of an amide must therefore be dependent on the presence of a coupled reaction and the utilization of ATP is essential to make the overall reaction spontaneous. The synthesis of protein in the plant is again dependent on coupled reactions in which ATP is consumed.

Respiration results in the formation of a considerable number of phosphate bonds in contrast with the formation of relatively few by fermentation. Since the potential rate of production of ATP is related to the respiratory activity, synthesis of polymeric compounds in the plant is dependent in non-photosynthetic tissues or in the dark on oxidative respiration.

FACTORS AFFECTING POLYMER FORMATION

Several investigators have studied the factors which determine what proportion of the assimilatory products remain in the leaf and accumulate as sugar and what proportion is converted into the polymer starch. The proportion varies widely between different plants; the monocotyledons form relatively little starch, whereas many dicotyledons form starch as their main reserve. The formation of starch from sugar can take place in the dark, as may be shown by feeding detached leaves with sugar solution. For each plant a characteristic minimum concentration of sugar is required before visible starch formation takes place. This concentration may be taken as a measure of the position of balance characteristic of the tissue. Within the same plant the balance may vary between different tissues since there is a greater tendency for starch formation in storage organs like seeds and a lesser tendency in foliage.

These observations indicate that a balanced state or 'dynamic equilibrium' is established between the polymer and monomer and must result from the operation of at least two independent enzymic pathways. The position of balance will be determined by the relative activity of the two systems and changed by any factor which affects the two systems differentially. Lowering the temperature can be shown to move the balance in the direction of monomer rather than polymer. Again, removal of oxygen from the tissue moves the balance in favour of the monomer form. These effects suggest that metabolic activity is required for the formation of starch, and this is confirmed by the use of inhibitors, such as cyanide and iodoacetamide, which inhibit respiration and also inhibit starch formation.

The activity of the enzymes which catalyse the conversion of starch to glucose is probably independent of respiratory activity and hence the synthetic path must be dependent on respiratory activity.

The synthesis of starch *in vivo* takes place via the formation of a phosphorylated sugar intermediate. This could be glucose-1-phosphate, which condenses to form amylose in a reaction catalysed by starch phosphorylase.[61] More recently a second enzyme, amylose synthetase, has been found which catalyses formation of amylose from uridine diphosphoglucoside (UDPG).[91] UTP (uridine triphosphate) is first formed from UDP by reaction with ATP: UTP then condenses with glucose-1-phosphate to form UDPG and pyrophosphate as follows:

$$UDP + ATP \rightarrow UTP + ADP \quad \text{(nucleotide transferase)}$$
$$UTP + G1P \rightarrow UDPG + PP \quad \text{(UDPG pyrophosphorylase)}$$

In vivo phosphorylase is now considered to be possibly concerned in the degradation of amylose and synthesis is thought to take place primarily from UDPG. Thus the synthesis of amylose from sugar requires a supply of ATP both for the formation of glucose-1-phosphate from glucose and also for the formation of UTP from UDP. Since ATP is produced in respiration, an indirect relationship is established between starch synthesis and respiratory activity. The function of the amylases *in vivo* is not certain.

Similar considerations apply to the balance between protein and amino acids (see Chapter 7) and between sucrose and hexose in the plant. The enzyme invertase catalyses the hydrolysis of sucrose and the equilibrium is largely towards the formation of hexose. The enzyme, sucrose phosphorylase, obtained from the bacterium *Pseudomonas saccharophila*, catalyses the condensation of glucose-1-phosphate and fructose to form sucrose. This is essentially the same type of reaction as that catalysed by starch phosphorylase, but this enzyme is absent from higher plants. A different enzyme found in wheat germ catalyses the condensation of uridine diphosphate glucoside (UDPG) with fructose-6-phosphate to form sucrose phosphate (sucrose phosphate synthetase). Another enzyme, sucrose synthetase, also catalyses the condensation of UDPG and fructose to form sucrose, but this reaction is believed *in vivo* to operate in the direction of degradation rather than synthesis. Thus the balance between sucrose and hexose is determined by two reaction systems, the one dependent on the production and supply of ATP from respiration, the other, the hydrolytic, not dependent on respiration.

Factors which inhibit aerobic respiration will tend to shift the balance between sucrose and hexose in the direction of hexose. The difference in balance between hexose and sucrose observed between plants of different families may be attributed to differences in the relative activity of the hydrolytic and the synthetic enzyme systems.

In general, the dependence of synthesis on respiratory activity follows because the formation of the condensed compound is an energy-requiring process and cannot take place spontaneously. Hydrolysis is generally an energy-yielding process and can take place spontaneously. The simultaneous operation of both reaction systems results in a balanced state or dynamic equilibrium, the position of balance depending on the supply of ATP from respiration.

SELF REGULATION OF METABOLISM

Pasteur noted in certain tissues that the rate of breakdown of hexose under aerobic conditions was considerably less than under anaerobic conditions. This effect, known as the *Pasteur effect*, has been described as a sparing effect of oxygen on carbohydrate breakdown. It is more marked in dormant than in actively growing tissues. No single mechanism has been suggested which fully explains this effect.

In the actively growing tissue, whilst the respiratory activity may be high and consequently the rate of production of ATP high, synthesis may take place at a considerable rate and there may be no *net* accumulation of ATP. However, in a dormant tissue the production of ATP in respiration may result in an increase in the steady state concentration of ATP relative to that under anaerobic conditions. Hence in tissues whose synthetic activity is at a minimum, ATP tends to accumulate under aerobic conditions with a corresponding depletion of inorganic phosphate and adenosine diphosphate. Since phosphorylation is necessarily coupled to the oxidation of phosphoglyceraldehyde, the absence of phosphate and phosphate acceptor will slow down this reaction step. Under fermentative conditions the production of ATP will be smaller per mole of hexose broken down and the relative concentrations of phosphate and ADP correspondingly higher. Hence one explanation of the Pasteur effect is in terms of a change in the relative concentration of ATP and ADP and P_i under aerobic and anaerobic conditions. The fact that uncoupling agents like DNP (which prevents the formation of ATP) also generally result in an increased rate of oxidation is consistent with this viewpoint. The type of mechanism by which a process produces conditions which are unfavourable for its continuation is sometimes referred to as a *feedback* mechanism by analogy with certain electronic systems.

A number of synthetic reactions, including nitrate and sulphate reduction (Chapter 7), the amination of ketoglutarate to glutamate (Chapter 7), and fat synthesis from acetyl groups (Chapter 4), utilize reduced coenzymes ($NADH_2$, $NADPH_2$). Under conditions favouring synthesis (aerobic rather than anaerobic conditions) the ratio of reduced to oxidized coenzymes may be lowered. In dormant tissue the contrary will tend to be true.

Both the accumulation of ATP and the accumulation of reduced, relative to oxidized, coenzyme will tend to slow down the oxidation of triose phosphate to phosphoglyceric acid in the same way.

$$TP + NAD + ADP + P_i \rightleftharpoons PGA + NADH_2 + ATP$$

For, since $\dfrac{[PGA]\,[NADH_2]\,[ATP]}{[TP]\,[NAD]\,[ADP]\,[P_i]}$ must remain constant at or near equilibrium, the higher the ratio $[ATP]/[ADP]\,[P_i]$ and the higher $[NADH_2]/[NAD]$, the higher will be $[TP]/[PGA]$. Thus the latter ratio will be dependent on the whole range of synthetic activity taking place. The oxidation of triose phosphate may then be the 'pace maker' for the EMP pathway.

The utilization of $NADPH_2$ in synthetic reactions with a consequent relative increase in $[NADP]/[NADPH_2]$ may also lead to an increase in the rate of oxidation of glucose 6 P to gluconate 6 P. This reaction is considered as probably the 'pace maker' for the pentose phosphate pathway.

The different types of metabolic activity in the plant cell, such as carbohydrate, fat, and nitrogen metabolism utilize a large number of reagents in common. A change in rate of one of these processes may result in a change in rate of all the others. Furthermore, the rate of biosynthetic reactions will generally be related to the rate of respiration which in the green plant may itself be related to photosynthetic activity. The complexity of the physiological responses of the plant becomes apparent from a detailed study of the biochemistry of individual aspects of metabolism. In considering the changes which take place in physiological processes during development, for example in the ripening of the apple fruit (Fig. 5.2), it is still not possible to evaluate the relative importance of biochemical and biophysical factors. Nevertheless, many of the matters discussed in this chapter must play an important part.

71

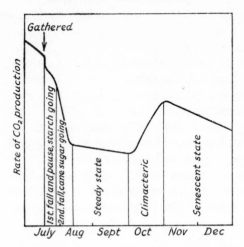

Fig. 5.2. The change in respiration rate of apple fruits during development showing the rise during ripening (which is associated with the production of ethylene). (After F. L. Kidd and C. West[80])

GENERAL REFERENCES

D. D. DAVIES (1961) *Intermediary Metabolism in plants.* C.U.P.

M. FLORKIN and H. S. MASON (eds) (1960) *Comparative Biochemistry* vol. I *Sources of Free Energy*, vol. II *Free Energy and Biological Function*, Academic Press.

F. F. LIPMANN (1941) 'Metabolic generation and utilization of phosphate bond energy'. *Adv. Enzymology* **1**, 99.

CHAPTER SIX

Photosynthesis

The reactions in plants which take place spontaneously must all take place with a loss of free energy. For life to continue there must be a compensating process whereby energy is received by the plant. This is the process of photosynthesis in which light energy is absorbed and used to convert inorganic carbon dioxide to organic compounds. The subsequent oxidation of these organic products in respiration results in the liberation of energy which may be used in biosynthesis (see Chapter 5).

The free energy required to convert a molecule of carbon dioxide to carbohydrate (with liberation of a molecule of oxygen from water) is very considerable, being of the order of 110 to 120 kcals/mole. The precise value will vary within this range according to the partial pressure of carbon dioxide and the concentration of other substances involved. But differences due to variations in concentration are comparatively small and the energy required for the reaction is, under all conditions, very large.

The necessary energy is obtained through the absorption of light energy by the plant pigments. Chlorophyll preferentially absorbs light both in the blue and the red part of the spectrum. In the bacteria, bacteriochlorophyll replaces chlorophyll, and this pigment absorbs light in the infra-red beyond the visible part of the spectrum. Absorption of light donates to the absorbing molecule energy in indivisible discrete units called '*quanta*', raising the molecule to an excited energy state. Some of the energy absorbed by chlorophyll can be re-emitted as fluorescence, although the amount of light re-emitted in this way *in vivo* is very small. Regardless of whether blue or red light has been absorbed, the fluorescence emitted is of the same wavelength, indicating that the same excited state of chlorophyll results from absorption of either red or blue light. Therefore the energy content of excited chlorophyll must be less than that of the smallest quantum of red light absorbed, i.e. 40 kcal/mole quantum. This is much less than that required for the conversion of one molecule of carbon dioxide to carbohydrate. Hence photosynthesis must

73

be a complex process involving a number of steps obtaining energy from an absolute minimum of three quanta for each molecule of carbon dioxide reduced.

Measurements of the amount of O_2 produced by the plant show that six or more quanta are absorbed by chlorophyll per molecule of oxygen.[52] This represents a high efficiency of energy utilization – approximating to 50 per cent. There is some uncertainty in this measurement because respiration and photosynthesis take place simultaneously and the rate of respiration cannot easily be measured for the green plant in light. Some respiratory intermediates, e.g. ATP, are involved also in photosynthesis, and it would appear probable *a priori* that photosynthesis and respiration might interfere with each other. On the other hand, the interaction may be minimized by the spatial isolation of the mitochondria and chloroplasts. By using higher light intensities when photosynthesis takes place at a rate many times faster than respiration the complications due to respiration are minimized, and the number of quanta required is observed to be six or more.

The rate of oxygen production in light measures the apparent rate of photosynthesis: when the oxygen consumed in respiration (usually measured in the dark) is added to this the real rate of photosynthesis is obtained. This procedure is valid provided that the rate of respiration observed in the dark continues unchanged in light. A. Brown[26] has devised a technique to distinguish oxygen uptake due to respiration in the light from oxygen production in photosynthesis. The oxygen produced during photosynthesis has been shown to be largely derived from the water molecules present, whereas the oxygen consumed in respiration is taken from the gas phase. Hence if photosynthesis takes place in ordinary water containing O^{16}, the gas produced is O^{16}. This can be distinguished from the consumption of oxygen if O^{18} is added to the gas phase. The experiments show that, in general, the rate of oxygen consumption, measured by the rate of uptake of O^{18}, is the same in the light as in the dark.

The Early Physiological Experiments

LIMITING FACTORS

In 1905 F. F. Blackman investigated the effect of varying light intensity on the rate of photosynthesis at different concentrations of carbon dioxide. He showed that the rate of photosynthesis increased with an increase in carbon dioxide concentration up to a certain value and then became relatively independent of any further increase. He referred to the region of the curve where the rate was independent of carbon dioxide concentration as light-limited and considered that the maximal rate was determined solely by the number of light quanta absorbed. The concentration at which dependence changed to independence corresponded to a higher rate and a higher concentration at a higher light intensity (Fig. 6.1). He deduced from this interaction of factors that photosynthesis must consist of at least two sequential reactions, a light reaction, and a dark reaction involving carbon dioxide.[14] Either may limit the rate of the whole process according

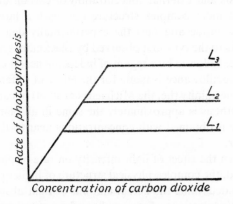

Fig. 6.1. The relationship between rate of photosynthesis and carbon dioxide concentration at different light intensities according to F. F. Blackman's theory of limiting factors

to conditions. Furthermore, the effect of a change in any one factor on the rate will be maximal when the other factors are at such a level that increase in them will not cause an appreciable change in rate.

EXTERNAL FACTORS[70]

The maximum effect of varying the carbon dioxide concentration will occur when the light intensity is so high that increasing it causes no appreciable increase in rate. Under these conditions the relationship between rate of photosynthesis and concentration of carbon dioxide was found to differ in different plants. At first this caused confusion, until it was realized that the relationship measured was that between the rate of photosynthesis and the concentration of carbon dioxide external to the plant. But the carbon dioxide available for photosynthesis is that which has reached the chloroplasts within the plant, and the concentration there will differ more from that outside the plant the larger the diffusion path between the chloroplast and the outside. Thus the measured relationship confuses the effect of diffusion of carbon dioxide from outside the plant with the effect of internal concentration on rate. With an organism such as *Chlorella*, a small unicellular alga, the diffusion path is very short and the concentration of carbon dioxide available to the photosynthetic centres is very nearly the same as that in the external medium. In this case a relatively simple hyperbolic relationship, of the type characteristic of a simple enzymic reaction, was observed between the rate of photosynthesis and external concentration of carbon dioxide. With organisms of more complex structure (i.e. with a larger diffusion path between inside and out) the experimentally determined relationship tends to the type first observed by Blackman, giving a region of dependence followed by a region of independence. It can be shown that when due allowance is made for the effect of differences in diffusion path the affinity (i.e. the Michaelis constant) of carbon dioxide for photosynthesis is approximately the same in all plants. Half the maximal rate is obtained with concentrations near to that normally present in air.

Again, when the effect of light intensity on rate of photosynthesis is investigated, the complex physical structure of higher plants makes it difficult to determine the actual amount of light absorbed by the photosynthetic pigments. Even with such a simple organism as *Chlorella*, which forms a relatively homogeneous suspension in an aqueous medium, the problems of light scattering are appreciable. With *Chlorella* the relationship between the rate of photosynthesis and light intensity, for a concentration of carbon dioxide so high that further increase has little effect on the rate, approaches a hyperbolic form characteristic of simple reaction kinetics.

It may be concluded that the rate of photosynthesis can be determined *either* by a dark enzymic process involving the uptake of carbon dioxide, which is limiting at low concentrations of carbon dioxide, *or* by a photochemical reaction which limits the rate at very low light intensities.

Further confirmation that two reaction steps occur in photosynthesis was obtained when the effect of temperature on the process was observed. The temperature coefficient was observed to vary appreciably according to the conditions of the experiment. With a high light intensity and a high concentration of carbon dioxide the rate increased some $2\frac{1}{2}$ times for each 10°C rise of temperature; with a high light intensity but a low concentration of carbon dioxide the rate of the reaction increased fourfold for every 10° rise in temperature. On the other hand, with a sufficiently low light intensity and a high concentration of carbon dioxide the rate increased very little with increase in temperature. In the last case, the rate of the process might be expected to be determined solely by the photochemical reaction, and it is hardly surprising that the rate is independent of temperature since increasing temperature cannot increase the number of quanta absorbed. On the other hand, the high temperature coefficient at low concentrations of carbon dioxide must be a characteristic of the dark enzymic process.

Again the effect of various inhibitors was shown to differ according to the conditions under which they were investigated. Thus inhibition by cyanide was found to be greater the higher the concentration of carbon dioxide. This would imply that cyanide mainly inhibited the dark process with little effect on the photochemical reaction. Hydroxylamine inhibits photosynthesis equally at all light intensities and for this reason cannot simply effect the photochemical reaction. Here a complex explanation is required, and it has been suggested that hydroxylamine inhibits an enzyme whose effective concentration is a function of the light intensity.

INTERNAL FACTORS

In 1918 various workers tried to find a quantitative relationship between the rate of photosynthesis and the chlorophyll content of a plant. Willstatter and Stoll[158] measured the photosynthetic activity of a number of green plants which had yellow varieties, such as the elm and privet. They found that in general the yellow varieties had a higher rate of photosynthesis per unit of chlorophyll (i.e. assimilation number) than did the green (also Fig. 6.2). They suggested that there must be some component in the plant other than chlorophyll which determined the rate of photosynthesis and which was present in the yellow varieties to a greater extent than in the green. In later work Briggs[22] showed with *Phaseolus vulgaris* that the chlorophyll first formed in the seedling leaves was relatively ineffective in photosynthesis compared with that formed later in development. However, if the seedling was allowed to mature by placing it in the dark (when no chlorophyll was formed) and then the chlorophyll allowed to form subsequently in the light, even the first formed chlorophyll had full activity. Thus Briggs argued that some factor essential for photosynthetic activity had been formed by the plant during its development in the dark. This was referred to as an internal factor and it is clear that it is something other than chlorophyll.

By the use of intermittent illumination Emerson and Arnold[45] were able to measure the concentration (relative to that of chlorophyll) of an internal factor which might limit the efficiency of chlorophyll. They used extremely brief but very intense flashes. The duration of the flash was so brief that little reaction could take place during the flash except the photochemical process. If each molecule of chlorophyll absorbed energy during the flash and could effectively

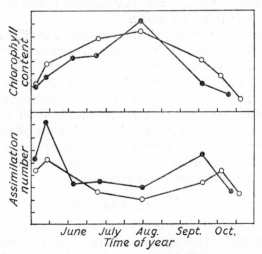

Fig. 6.2. The variation throughout a season of chlorophyll content and assimilation number in Tilia cordata (●) *and* Acer pseudoplatanus (○). (*After R. Willstatter and A. Stoll*[158])

use it in photosynthesis, the maximal yield of oxygen from a single flash might have been expected to be equivalent to the total chlorophyll content. In fact, the maximum yield which was obtained with *Chlorella* was 1 mole of oxygen for each 2,000 moles of chlorophyll. Therefore they postulated that the yield was limited by some internal factor to which chlorophyll must transfer its energy. Since there is not time for a chlorophyll molecule to become activated twice during a single flash, clearly the maximum yield is a measure of the internal factor and it is present to the extent of 6/2000 or 1/333 of the chlorophyll on a molar basis, assuming each chlorophyll molecule absorbs one quantum and that six quanta are required per molecule of oxygen. When successive flashes were spaced too closely together the yield per flash decreased. The minimum time which must elapse between individual flashes for each to have a maximal effect must be the time necessary for the internal factor to complete its reactions. Thus in addition to measuring the concentration of internal factor it was possible to determine its working time; at 25°C it was found to be 0·01 second.

The earlier physiological experiments led to the view that there were two separate and distinct possible rate-determining processes in photosynthesis: (i) the combination of carbon dioxide in some enzymic system which could be poisoned by cyanide and which had a high temperature coefficient; and (ii) a photochemical reaction in which light was absorbed by chlorophyll and transferred through some internal factor present in an amount small compared with that of chlorophyll. This broad distinction between a dark carboxylation process and a photochemical stage has been substantiated in recent biochemical investigations of photosynthesis.

Biochemical Investigations

DARK REACTIONS: THE USE OF RADIOACTIVE CARBON

Immediately prior to the Second World War and in the years following, the use of radioactive carbon isotopes became widespread in biology. The pre-war experiments were made with the relatively short-lived isotope carbon 11 and few real conclusions could be reached with an isotope whose half-life is only 20 minutes. After the war the long-lived isotope carbon 14 became available and this was exploited by Calvin and his colleagues. In their first experiments they determined the compounds into which radioactive carbon was incorporated during its assimilation by the plant. Within a few seconds of exposure to a high concentration of carbon dioxide containing some radioactive carbon dioxide, radioactivity appeared in *Chlorella* in five compounds, namely, phosphoglyceric acid, malic acid, ribose and sedoheptulose phosphates, and alanine. Within five minutes appreciable radioactivity was detected in sucrose, fats, and proteins. It was necessary to develop a technique for determining the sequence of formation of these intermediates. It was realized that if the percentage activity in any one compound, as a fraction of the total activity incorporated, was determined for each intermediate this quantity would decrease with time for the first intermediate alone. Using this criterion, it was found that phosphoglyceric acid was formed first, and in more recent experiments using extremely short times it has been shown that almost all the radioactive carbon incorporated in the first second of illumination appears in phosphoglyceric acid. For intermediates formed from a second reaction step the percentage radioactivity will show an increase with time followed by a subsequent decrease; ribose and sedoheptulose phosphates were

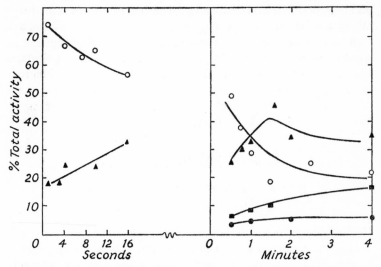

Fig. 6.3. The percentage radioactivity incorporated in different compounds as a function of time of photosynthesis in $C^{14}O_2$ in Scenedesmus. $\circ$ = phosphoglyceric acid. $\blacksquare$ = malic and aspartic acid. $\blacktriangle$ = sugar phosphates. $\bullet$ = alanine. (After J. A. Bassham, A. A. Benson, L. D. Kay, A. Z. Harris, A. T. Wilson and M. Calvin[7])

found to behave in this way. Final products, e.g. sucrose, showed a continuous increase in percentage activity with time of exposure (Fig. 6.3).

In later experiments the time sequence of labelling of individual atoms in a compound which became radioactive was determined. For short periods of exposure phosphoglyceric acid was found to have its radioactivity almost entirely in the carboxyl group. This suggested that phosphoglyceric acid was formed by carboxylation of a non-radioactive precursor probably containing two carbon atoms.

Later, radioactivity appeared in the other two carbon atoms in PGA suggesting that the precursor was formed, in part, from the products of the reaction. Again the glucose formed initially was labelled only in the middle two carbon atoms (C3 and C4); with longer periods of exposure the other atoms of the molecule also become labelled. By a reversal of the reactions discussed in Chapter 4 (EMP pathway), and in the presence of a supply of reduced coenzyme and ATP, phosphoglyceric acid can be reduced to triose and the triose can then form hexose. The fact that radioactivity in hexose is confined at first to C3 and C4 is consistent with its formation from C3 labelled PGA in this way. Because radioactivity later spreads throughout the PGA and hexose molecules, some products of the reaction must react to reform the acceptor for carbon dioxide. The process by which they do this is called the photosynthetic or Calvin cycle. At first a 2C

Table 6.1

Calvin photosynthetic cycle

1. 6 Ribulose diP + $6CO_2$ + $6H_2O \rightarrow$ 12PGA	Carboxydismutase (diphosphoribulose carboxylase)
2. 12PGA + 12ATP + $12NADPH_2$ ($CoIIH_2$) $\rightarrow$ 12 Triose P + 12 ADP + $12P_i$ + 12NADP(CoII)	See reaction 4 of Table 4.1*
3. 6TP $\rightarrow$ 3F1:6diP + $2H_2O \rightarrow$ 2F6P + $2P_i$ + F1:6diP	See reaction 2 of Table 4.1
4 2F6P + 2TP $\rightarrow$ 2 Erythrose P + 2 ribose P (RMP)	Transketolase
5. 2 Erythrose P + 2TP $\rightarrow$ 2 Sedoheptulose diP	Aldolase
6. 2 Sedoheptulose diP + $2H_2O \rightarrow$ 2 Sedoheptulose P + $2P_i$	Phosphatase
7. 2 Sedoheptulose P + 2TP $\rightarrow$ 4RMP	Transketolase
2–7. 12PGA + 12ATP + $12NADPH_2$ + $4H_2O \rightarrow$ 12NADP + 12ADP + $16P_i$ + 6RMP + F1:6diP.	
8. 6RMP $\rightarrow$ 6 ribulose P; 6 ribulose P + 6ATP $\rightarrow$ 6 ribulose diP + 6ADP	See reaction 4 of Table 4.3
1–8. $6CO_2$ + $10H_2O$ + $12NADPH_2$ + 18ATP $\rightarrow$ F1:6diP + 12NADP + 18ADP + $16P_i$	

* The triose phosphate dehydrogenase of the chloroplast is specific to NADP.

acceptor compound was sought, but the acceptor proved to be a 5C compound which was carboxylated to give two molecules of PGA.[7] The triose produced from reduction of PGA combines with a molecule of hexose to form sedoheptulose and then ultimately ribose monophosphate. (The reactions are shown in detail in Table 6.1 and Figs. 6.4 and 6.5.) The ribose phosphate is then phosphorylated to ribulose diphosphate, which can react with carbon dioxide to form two molecules of phosphoglyceric acid in a reaction catalysed by the

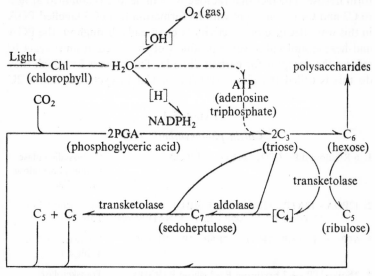

Fig. 6.4. Outline of the photosynthetic cycle

enzyme carboxydismutase. This enzyme has since been found in non-photosynthetic as well as photosynthetic tissues.

More recently Kandler and Gibbs[78] in similar experiments to those of Calvin found that initially the 4C atom in hexose was more active than the 3, and later there was more activity in the 1 and 2 than the 5 and 6. Benson has pointed out that this could result from the presence of a large pool of 3C compounds, which equilibrated with the labelled dihydroxyacetone formed. This would reduce the radioactivity of the 3C atom compared with the 4C in hexose. Maruo and Benson reported large concentrations in algae and higher plants of α-glycerophosphate and $\alpha\alpha'$-diglycerophosphate and of the phosphatidyl glycerol. Saturation of the glycerol 'pool' with C14 was observed to take many hours. The relative greater activity of C1 and 2 compared with 5 and 6 of hexose is attributed to a relative protection of these groups from equilibration with starch due to their utilization in transketolase reactions.

In a third type of experiment the change in concentration of various radioactive intermediates of photosynthesis was investigated when the external conditions were suddenly changed. When the concentration of carbon dioxide was rapidly diminished the concentration of

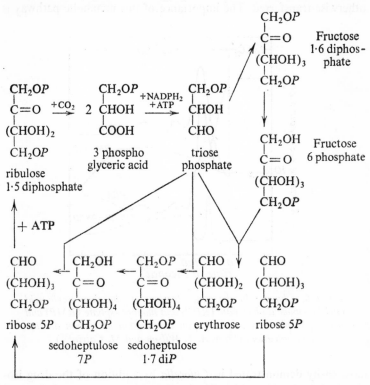

Fig. 6.5. The photosynthetic carbon cycle (after Calvin)

ribulose diphosphate showed a marked increase and of phosphoglyceric acid a corresponding decrease[159] (Fig. 6.6). This was in agreement with the proposed mechanism. Similarly on darkening there was a large increase in phosphoglyceric acid and a corresponding decrease in ribulose diphosphate. This result is also consistent with the mechanism formulated.

Most of the investigations of photosynthesis made by Calvin and his colleagues were in the presence of concentrations of carbon dioxide far higher than that in normal air. Several workers (including Tolbert in America, Warburg in Germany and Whittingham in the United Kingdom) have shown that during photosynthesis at lower concentrations of carbon dioxide a large fraction of the carbon dioxide fixed may be converted to glycollic acid and other compounds derived from it. The glycollic acid is believed to be derived from the Calvin cycle as the result of the removal of 2C fragments which are otherwise transferred. The importance of this metabolic pathway is

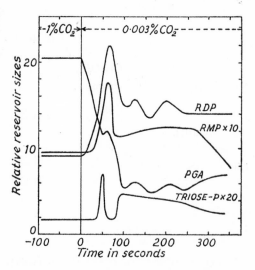

Fig. 6.6. Changes in the concentrations of phosphoglyceric acid (PGA), ribose diphosphate (RDP) and monophosphate (RMP) and triose phosphate consequent upon a reduction of carbon dioxide concentration. (From A. T. Wilson and M. Calvin[159])

most easily demonstrated in *Chlorella* by addition of the drug iso-nicotinyl hydrazide which blocks the subsequent metabolism of glycine causing glycollate and glycine to accumulate. Under certain conditions nearly one half of the carbon incorporated during photosynthesis may be metabolised through 2C compounds.[125]

Racker,[126] using a homogenate prepared from ground-up spinach leaves, showed that, when reduced coenzyme (NADPH$_2$), adenosine-triphosphate, and ribulose-diphosphate were supplied together with radioactive carbon dioxide, carbon dioxide could be incorporated into sugars even in the dark. Hence the essential products of the photochemical reaction in photosynthesis must be NADPH$_2$ and

ATP. Provided that both of these substances are available, the Calvin cycle will operate in the direction of incorporation of carbon dioxide.

PHOTOCHEMICAL REACTIONS

The study of the photochemical process received a great impetus when R. Hill[67] showed that it was possible to demonstrate photochemical activity of chloroplasts removed from the living plant. He isolated chloroplasts from higher plants and showed that if ferric salts were added and the system illuminated, the ferric salts were reduced to ferrous and oxygen was evolved. This suggested that the essential photochemical step was a 'splitting' or photolysis of water molecules. The oxidizing radical produced from water [OH]* gave rise to the evolution of oxygen and the reducing radical [H]* reacted with the ferric salt.

The view that water-splitting resulted from the photochemical reaction of photosynthesis had been suggested by Van Niel[148] on the basis of his studies of the photosynthetic bacteria. Van Niel distinguished two large groups, the *Thiorhodaceae*, which require not only light energy and carbon dioxide to grow but in addition a reduced sulphur compound such as hydrogen sulphide, and the *Athiorhodaceae*, which require in place of the sulphur compound an organic carbon substrate. In no case in the photosynthetic bacteria was oxygen produced. Van Niel suggested that in these organisms the oxidizing radical [OH] produced from the splitting of water did not give rise to oxygen as in the green plant but was disposed of necessarily by reaction with the additional substrate which thus became oxidized (Fig. 6.7). This was in agreement with the observation that in *Thiorhodaceae* sulphur was a product of photosynthesis, and in *Athiorhodaceae* an oxidation product of the organic substrate.

A number of hydrogen acceptors have been shown to be capable of stimulating oxygen production by illuminated chloroplasts. These include quinones which are reduced to hydroquinones and dyestuffs such as dichlorphenolindophenol. At first it was not realized that during the preparation and isolation of the chloroplasts certain soluble factors were lost from the chloroplasts. If these were added back in the form of a concentrated water extract it was found that chloroplasts could reduce NADP in light with the simultaneous production of oxygen.[42, 132, 144]

* Square brackets indicate the radicals are probably in a combined form.

Arnon and his colleagues[3] also showed that if adenosine diphosphate were supplied, together with inorganic phosphate and magnesium ions, chloroplasts produced ATP in the light. For this phosphorylative activity light is essential and oxygen is not; so that the process was called photophosphorylation to distinguish it from the analogous reactions of mitochondria which require oxygen (oxidative phosphorylation). Arnon showed that when hydrogen acceptor and phosphorylative reagents were added at the same time, both the rate of phosphorylation and that of oxygen evolution increased.

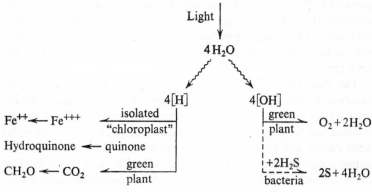

General equation: $4H_2O + 2A \xrightarrow{hv} 2H_2O + O_2 + 2AH_2$

Fig. 6.7. The diagram shows how van Niel's hypothesis that water is split in the photochemical reaction integrates the reactions of chloroplasts and photosynthesis in green plants and bacteria

Under certain conditions the amount of reduced product $NADPH_2$ was stoichiometrically equivalent to the amount of ATP produced. This suggested a 'coupling' between the phosphorylative and the oxidoreductive reactions.

$$2NADP + 2ADP + 2P_i + 2H_2O$$
$$\xrightarrow{hv} 2NADPH_2 + 2ATP + O_2$$

In addition an enhanced phosphorylative activity of isolated chloroplasts was found when such substances as vitamin K_3 or FMN were added to the chloroplasts without any externally added hydrogen acceptor. Under these conditions an alternative sequence of reactions resulted in the production of ATP as the sole product, without any accumulation of reduced product. This was called cyclic photophosphorylation. It has been suggested that, when a plant is placed under conditions where carbon dioxide is absent, it might use this alternative path to utilize light energy to accumulate ATP which could then be used in a variety of synthetic reactions (see Chapter 5).

If the essential feature of the photochemical reaction in photosynthesis is the photolysis of water, then during the transfer of hydrogen to an intermediate hydrogen acceptor phosphorylation must take place. The hydrogen acceptor normally reacts ultimately through NADP with carbon dioxide in the green plant or in isolated chloroplasts with added substances such as ferric ions. However, in the presence of vitamin K it must be reoxidized by the [OH] radical reforming the water molecule and thus reversing the initial photolysis. There would then be no net oxidation-reduction reaction, and if the reoxidation were coupled to phosphorylation ATP would result as the sole product.

Later Arnon compared the photochemical activity of chloroplasts isolated from higher plants with that of chromatophores isolated from bacteria.[2] Not all the photochemical activities exhibited by chloroplasts were shown by isolated bacterial chromatophores. For example, addition of NADP was found to have little effect on the photophosphorylative activity of chromatophores. One reaction shown to be common to both types of organelle was the formation of ATP in the presence of vitamin K but absence of an external hydrogen acceptor, i.e. cyclic photophosphorylation. Arnon was then led to suggest that it is not necessary to regard the photochemical process as involving water splitting. He suggested that during excitation by light, chlorophyll (or bacteriochlorophyll) loses an electron which is expelled with a high energy. This electron may be returned to the chlorophyll molecule by a series of carriers of which vitamin K is one, and during this sequence of reactions a phosphate bond is formed. In the green plant the electron expelled from chlorophyll is used to reduce carbon dioxide, the final carrier being $NADPH_2$. In this case an electron must be restored to the chlorophyll molecule from some other substance, e.g. a water molecule. In bacteria the electrons used in the reduction of NADP can come from the externally added hydrogen donor (such as H_2S) in the dark and there is no need to postulate any reaction involving water. The essential feature of photosynthesis common to green plants and photosynthetic bacteria is the release of an electron from chlorophyll (Fig. 6.8) which can be used either for reduction or returned by a cyclic reaction path.

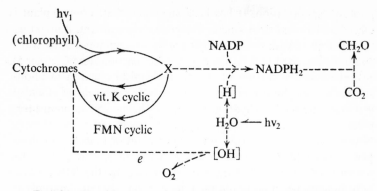

Fig. 6.8. Possible paths of electron flow in photosynthesis. The electron ejected from chlorophyll by light (hv₁) may return by a cyclic route (via vitamin K in bacteria and via FMN in higher plants) or may be transferred to NADP. In the latter case an electron must be returned to the system from water probably involving a second photochemical reaction (hv₂)

Role of cytochromes

It is probable that cytochromes are concerned in the return of the electron to chlorophyll both in green plants and photosynthetic bacteria. Arnon has suggested that the bacteria have a single cyclic pathway (using vitamin K as the carrier) in which only one cytochrome is concerned; in higher plants there are two possible return paths for the electron (either via vitamin K or FMN) and two cytochromes may be concerned. There is good evidence for the occurrence of cytochromes peculiar to photosynthetic organisms, both in green plants and in bacteria.[69] Moreover, since the photosynthetic bacteria include obligate anaerobes, the cytochromes in these organisms cannot be concerned in aerobic metabolism. Two cytochromes have been observed which are confined to the chloroplasts of higher plants, one of the c type, cytochrome f, and one of the b type, cytochrome b_6 . Neither can be oxidized by cytochrome oxidase. In *Rhodospirillum*, a facultative aerobic photosynthetic bacterium, two cytochromes, one a c type and one a b type, have been observed. Both cytochrome f and the *Rhodospirillum* c type have potentials nearer to the oxygen electrode than cytochrome c. In *Chromatium*, an obligate anaerobic photosynthetic bacterium, four separate absorption peaks have been observed, suggesting the presence of four cytochrome components, two of which have been extracted by Newton and Kamen. Again, components of both c and b type were found.

The main experimental evidence that cytochromes are concerned in photosynthesis is that in the plant they change their oxidation state when exposed to light. Duysens[44] showed a change in absorption spectrum consistent with the oxidation of a cytochrome upon illumination, first in the bacterium *Rhodospirillum* and later in *Porphyridium cruentum*, a red alga. In *Rhodospirillum rubrum* Chance and Smith[34] showed that the light-induced absorption changes were similar to those which resulted from addition of oxygen to cells in darkness. However, whereas the light-induced changes were not sensitive to addition of cyanide or carbon monoxide, the oxygen-induced changes were. Thus in aerobic organisms the effects of a photo-oxidase are superimposed on those of a dark oxidase. This complication was avoided by Olsen and Chance, [117] who investigated an obligate anaerobic bacterium, *Chromatium*, and showed that in light there was a change in both the f and the b type cytochromes. Whereas cytochrome f became relatively more oxidized in light, cytochrome b became relatively more reduced.

According to the cyclic mechanism proposed by Arnon, an electron expelled from chlorophyll is transferred either to NADP or to FMN and thence via cytochromes back to the chlorophyll. Hill has suggested that in the chloroplast, cytochromes b_6 and f play a similar part to that of b_3 and c in the mitochondria. Electron flow in mitochondria and also in chloroplasts is related to a concomitant phosphorylation. In mitochondria, electrons originate from the oxidation of a carbon substrate and finally react with oxygen via the oxidase cytochrome a_3: in chloroplasts, electrons originate from chlorophyll after absorption of light quanta and return to chlorophyll via cytochromes without any requirement for oxygen or an oxidase. The two cytochromes of green plants may be specifically concerned in two separate electron transport steps, and this will be discussed further later in this chapter.[68]

THE ROLE OF THE PIGMENTS

Structure of the pigments

Chlorophylls

In the leaves of higher plants four pigments are present: the green chlorophylls a and b, the yellow xanthophyll, and orange carotene. Chlorophyll a is universal in all green plants. Chlorophyll b is absent from the brown and red algae, but in its place chlorophyll c occurs in the brown and chlorophyll d in the red algae. The amount of chlorophyll a relative to that of chlorophyll b varies, but there is generally two or three times as much *a* as *b*. Leaves of natural yellow varieties are relatively abundant in chlorophyll *a*, although the total chlorophyll content is very considerably reduced. The chlorophyll content of normal green leaves varies between 0·05 and 0·2 of the fresh weight; in algae it may be several times higher than this. The chlorophylls are readily extracted from fresh green leaves with acetone or from powdered dry leaves with acetone or alcohol. They are

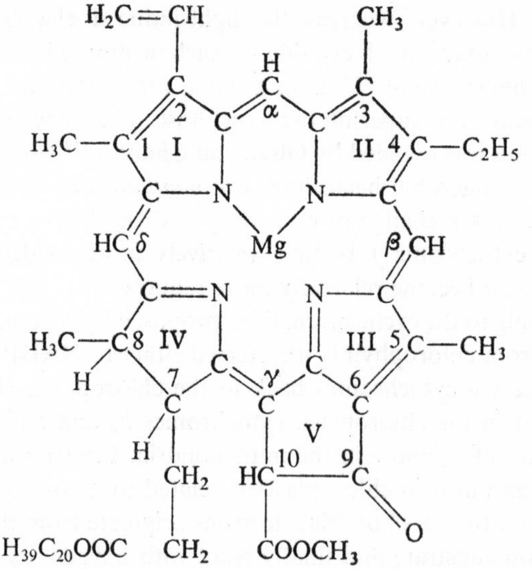

Fig. 6.9. The structural formula of chlorophyll a. *Chlorophyll* b *has a formyl group replacing the methyl group attached at carbon atom 3. Protochlorophyll does not have the two hydrogens at C atoms 7 and 8 and bacteriochlorophyll has two additional hydrogen atoms at carbon atoms 3 and 4 and the group at carbon atom 2 is oxidised to* —CO—CH₃

insoluble in water and may be separated from acetone either by fractionation with organic solvents or by chromatography.

The basic structure of the chlorophyll molecule consists of a tetra-pyrrolic ring forming a porphyrin to which is attached a long chain alcohol phytol. Magnesium is conjugated in the centre of the porphyrin ring (Fig. 6.9). Chlorophyll *a* and *b* differ chemically by one substituent group; the methyl group in chlorophyll *a* being replaced by a formyl group in chlorophyll *b*. Chlorophyll absorbs light with characteristic absorption bands in the red and the blue (Fig. 6.10) and its concentration is most easily determined from the amount of light absorbed. In certain photosynthetic bacteria the pigment present is bacteriochlorophyll, which differs from chlorophyll *a* in possessing two additional hydrogen atoms and a different substituent group in one pyrrole ring.

In most angiosperms no chlorophyll is formed in the dark and etiolated seedlings are a very pale green due to the pigment protochlorophyll. On illumination, protochlorophyll is reduced to chlorophyll. By contrast, gymnosperms and certain of the lower plants are able to produce chlorophyll even in darkness.

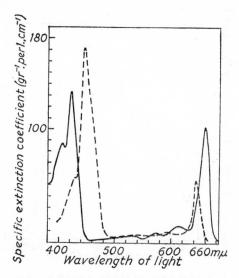

Fig. 6.10. Absorption curves of chlorophyll a (——————) and chlorophyll b (– – – – – –) in ethyl ether. (After F. P. Zscheile and C. L. Comar[165])

Carotenoids

The carotenoids are yellow, orange, or red pigments and are divided into the carotenes which contain only carbon and hydrogen and the xanthophylls which possess hydroxyl or ketonic groups. The carotenoids are insoluble in water but soluble in organic solvents such as acetone. They all contain a characteristic central unsaturated carbon chain but differ in their terminal groups. The existence of the double bond structure accounts for the existence of a large number of isomers. *In vitro* the unsaturated nature of the molecule makes it easily oxidizable by molecular oxygen. In green leaves the commonest pigments are carotene amongst the carotenes and luteol and zeaxanthol amongst the xanthophylls. A variety of carotenoids occur in the photosynthetic bacteria. The carotenoids absorb light mainly in the yellow and blue part of the spectrum (Fig. 6.11).

The phycobilins; phycoerythrin and phycocyanin.

These red and blue pigments occur together in the red and blue-green algae. They differ from the chlorophylls and carotenes in being soluble in dilute aqueous salt solutions. Like the chlorophylls, they are tetrapyrrolic derivatives, but the pyrrole rings are in a linear chain. No metal has yet been shown to be associated in them. In the cell

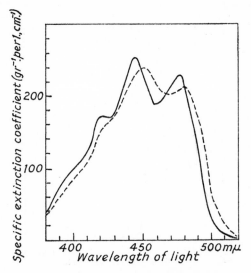

Fig. 6.11. Absorption curves of the carotenoids luteol (————)
and zeaxanthol (— — — — —) in ethanol

taey are present as protein complexes, the protein being of the globulin class which is easily denatured. For example, when marine red algae are placed in fresh water, the algae change from a brown to a bright pink colour. After denaturation it is not possible to extract the pigments in aqueous salt solution. Phycoerythrin absorbs in the yellow region of the spectrum with three absorption peaks, and phycocyanins absorb in the red (Fig. 6.12).

Properties of photosynthetic pigments *in vitro*

Since chlorophyll *a* (or bacteriochlorophyll) is the pigment common to all photosynthetic plants, chemists have sought to interpret the role of chlorophyll in photosynthesis in terms of some special chemical property of this molecule.[97, 150]

Chlorophyll has two absorption bands in the visible spectrum in the blue and the red. The quantum of blue light has a higher energy (since the energy of a quantum is inversely proportional to its wavelength), but within 10^{-11} second part of the blue excitation energy is lost as heat and the same state results as if absorption had taken place of red light. This excited state common to both red and blue absorption has 41 kcals energy in excess of the ground state. Its lifetime is of the order of 10^{-9} second, and energy is released either as heat, or by the emission of fluorescent light, or by taking part in a chemical reaction. Alternatively, it may lose part of its energy

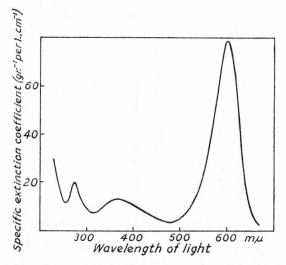

Fig. 6.12. Absorption curve of phycocyanin from Aphanizomenon flos aquae. (*After T. Svedberg and T. Katsurai*[143])

(probably some 10 kcals) and change into another excited but longer-lived state, sometimes called the *triplet state*. This has a relatively long lifetime compared with that of the other excited states, probably of the order of 10^{-2} second. This relatively long life increases the probability of this state taking part in chemical reaction before its energy is dissipated as heat or is lost by the emission of phosphorescent light (Fig. 6.13). It thus seems probable *a priori* that the triplet state should be the excited state which initiates photosynthesis. *In vitro* the triplet state can be shown to have an absorption spectrum which is markedly different from that of the ground state.

In addition to the different states of excited molecule, there are chemically different forms in the ground state which may also play a part in photosynthesis. Chlorophyll in organic solution is reversibly bleached when illuminated in the complete absence of oxygen. Krasnovski and colleagues[86] have studied the oxidation-reduction reaction sensitized in the absence of oxygen by chlorophyll dissolved in organic solvents between electron donors such as ascorbic acid

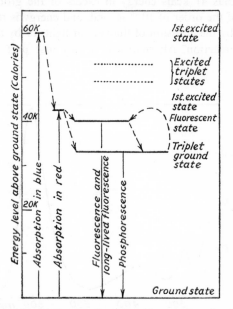

Fig. 6.13. Energy levels of the chlorophyll molecule

and electron acceptors such as coenzymes. They suggest that during the reaction the chlorophyll is reduced. Chlorophyll *a* in toluene is photoreduced in presence of phenylhydrazine and then shows characteristic absorption bands at 518 and 585 mμ.

By the use of very sensitive methods of measurement of absorption, changes in absorption spectrum of photosynthetic organisms during photosynthesis have been observed. In part these may be attributed to changes in cytochrome components. Other changes, which have not yet been fully explained, may be due to changes in pigment molecules. In *Chlorella*, Witt[160] studied the kinetics of an increased absorption in light at 518 mμ which accompanied a corresponding decrease at 475 mμ, an effect also observed by Duysens (Fig. 6.14). Chance and Strehler showed that these absorption changes were more pronounced for cells illuminated under anaerobic conditions. Oxygenation of cells in darkness gave similar effects but of only half the magnitude. In a carotenoid-deficient mutant of *Chlamydomonas* no change in absorption at 518 mμ was observed, and the effect was likewise absent in a carotenoid-free purple bacteria mutant. Hence it is probable that a carotenoid is associated with the change at 518 mμ. With higher light intensities additional absorption changes have been observed in the red region of the spectrum consistent with

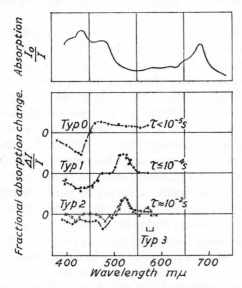

Fig. 6.14. Upper: Absorption curve for spinach chloroplasts. Lower: The change in absorption spectrum following flash illumination (10⁻⁴ sec.) in a Chlorella *mutant (type 0) and in spinach chloroplasts (type 1) and following a longer flash (10⁻² sec.) in* Scenedesmus *(type 2 ×———×) and spinach chloroplasts (type 2 ●———●). (After H. T. Witt[160])*

the formation of an oxidized pigment form referred to as P 700 with an oxidation-reduction potential near that of cytochrome *f*.

THE PIGMENTS *IN VIVO*

The chloroplasts

An alternative and more popular view is that an understanding of the role of the pigments in photosynthesis is not to be found solely from a study of the properties of the individual molecules *in vitro* but rather of their properties when they are located in the chloroplast. All the pigments concerned in photosynthesis are localized in the chloroplast; the red and yellow anthocyanins which are present in the cell sap play no part in photosynthesis. In higher plants the chloroplasts are ellipsoidal bodies, but in algae there is a great diversity of shape. Nevertheless, the basic structure in algae and higher plants is probably analogous. In the blue-green algae and purple bacteria which have no chloroplasts the pigments are concentrated in particles.

There has been some speculation as to how the different pigments are organized together with proteins and fats in the chloroplast. Whilst the chemical organization is still not clear, studies with the electron microscope have elucidated the physical structure of the chloroplast. Earlier studies with the light and fluorescence microscopes had shown that chloroplasts were not optically homogeneous but separated into regions in which the pigments are relatively concentrated, the *grana*, amongst the less pigmented *stroma* regions. Studies with the electron microscope have shown that both the grana and the stroma have a laminated structure (Plate 4). There is some evidence that this structure is related to photosynthetic activity. One type of experiment has been to compare photosynthetic activity and chloroplast structure during the greening of an etiolated plant. As the plant develops chlorophyll there is a progressive development in the chloroplast from a granular to a laminated structure; furthermore, as the structure develops so does the photosynthetic activity.

Wolken[161] has suggested that the chlorophyll molecules form a monomolecular film separating lipid from protein layers (Fig. 6.15). The chemical structure of chlorophyll makes it well suited to occupy an interface between fat and protein, whereas the carotenoids might be expected to occur in the fatty layer and the phycobilins in the protein layer. If one calculates the average number of chlorophyll molecules present in the plastid, and the lamellar surface area, the surface area of interface is of the right order to accommodate all the chlorophyll molecules in a monolayer.

One consequence of such an orderly arrangement is that the effective concentration of pigment within the granum is very high, perhaps of the order of 0·1 M. This close packing has important consequences. It increases the probability that energy from light can be transferred from an absorbing molecule within the very short time available before it is degraded into heat. Tentative calculations indicate that excitation energy may move from the actual molecule which absorbed the light through perhaps as many as several hundred or even one thousand molecules before it is dissipated. This transfer of energy can take place not only from chlorophyll molecule to chlorophyll molecule, but also from many of the accessory pigments.

The existence of energy transfer can be demonstrated experimentally. If allowance is made for a shift in the wavelength for maximum

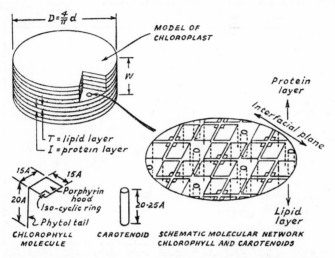

Fig. 6.15. The arrangement of chlorophyll and carotenoid pigments in monolayers in the granum, according to the suggestion of Wolken. (After J. J. Wolken and F. A. Schwertz[161])

absorption together with some broadening of absorption bands *in vivo*, the absorption spectrum of a green cell can be related to the corresponding spectrum for the isolated pigments with a reasonable degree of certainty. However, when the cell is illuminated with monochromatic light absorbed mainly by a single pigment it is often found that the fluorescence emitted is characteristic of a second pigment present. For example, in a suspension of diatoms illuminated with light which is predominantly absorbed by the carotenoid fucoxanthol, the fluorescence is similar in quality and intensity to that emitted when the exciting light is absorbed only by chlorophyll. Hence in a cell, the energy must have been transferred from the fucoxanthol which absorbed the light to chlorophyll. Similarly, transfer of energy has been demonstrated from chlorophyll *b* to chlorophyll *a* in green algae, from the carotenoid fucoxanthol to chlorophyll *b* in diatoms, and from the phycobilins to chlorophyll in the red and blue-green algae (Fig. 6.16).

Hence the presence of the other pigments extends the range of wavelengths of light which may be utilized by the plant, allowing some specialization of the plant to particular environments, as for example the well-known zonation of seaweeds with the green *Chlorophyceae* in shallow waters, the red algae in deep waters, where the light is blue-greenish and the brown algae in between.

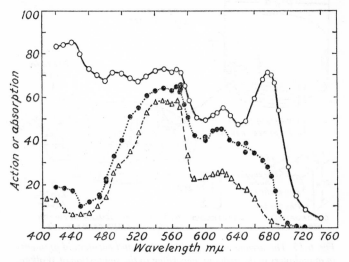

Fig. 6.16. *The absorption spectrum* ○———○ *and action spectrum* △------△ *for the red alga* Porphyra naiadum, *together with the absorption curve for the pigments extracted in aqueous medium* ●·········●. *The absorption near to 680 mμ due to chlorophyll is ineffective in contrast with that near 540 and 600 mμ due to phycobilins which is effective.* (*After F. T. Haxo and L. R. Blinks*[62])

Prior to studies of sensitization of fluorescence of one pigment due to absorption by another, it has been shown that the photosynthetic efficiency of light absorbed by carotenoids in the green algae *Chlorella* was about half that of light absorbed by chlorophyll; that of light absorbed by fucoxanthol in diatoms was about as efficient as that absorbed by chlorophyll; and that of light absorbed by phycobilins in blue-green algae about as efficient as that absorbed by chlorophyll.[46] These measurements indicate that transfer of energy must occur within the plant with high efficiency. In the photosynthetic bacteria energy transfer from carotenoids to bacteriochlorophyll has been demonstrated in a similar manner. In the red algae it was found that the photosynthetic efficiency of light absorbed by phycoerythrin was greater than that for light absorbed by chlorophyll;[62] and later this was found to be the case for the excitation of fluorescence also. This was attributed to the existence in these plants of a form of chlorophyll which is inactive both with respect to fluorescence and to photosynthesis, and it was suggested that phycocyanin and phycoerythrin transfer excitation energy preferentially to the active form of chlorophyll.

The mechanism of energy transfer is assumed to take place by a process called inductive resonance. The excited molecule is associated with an electric field with vibration frequencies determined by that of the light it emits; if a nearby molecule has ability to absorb energy of these frequencies, it may itself become excited. With the concentrations of chlorophyll b and a in *Chlorella*, theoretical considerations predict almost complete transfer of excitation energy from b to a, resulting in the absence of any fluorescence characteristic of chlorophyll b; this has been confirmed experimentally. Similarly, it can be shown that the findings of almost complete transfer of energy from phycoerythrin and phycocyanin to chlorophyll are not inconsistent with theory.

A detailed study by Brown and French[51] of the absorption band of green plants in the red region of the spectrum indicated the presence of several chlorophyll components. These workers developed an instrument to determine the first derivative of the optical extinction as a function of wavelength, a method which is more sensitive than measuring the extinction itself. The observed derivative spectrum can be analysed as the summation of a number of normal probability curves each representing one constituent with a single absorption maximum (Fig. 6.17). With this technique it was shown that the absorption in the red region of the spectrum for a leaf of a higher plant could be analysed in terms of the presence of at least four distinct constituents. One of these with an absorption maximum at 650 mμ was attributed to chlorophyll b, the other three to different forms of chlorophyll a having absorption maxima at 673, 683, and 695. It has been suggested that these different forms may represent combinations of the pigment with different proteins. The proportion of the different forms varies from organism to organism, and in the case of micro-organisms may be modified according to the conditions of culture.

The existence of these different forms of chlorophyll clarified the earlier observations of Emerson and Lewis[46] that the quantum efficiency of photosynthesis in the green algae *Chlorella*, decreased very rapidly in the region between 680 and 700 mμ where there was still appreciable absorption. The effect in a red alga where the quantum yield declined beyond 650, although there was appreciable absorption up to 680 is illustrated in Fig. 6.16. It now appears that the

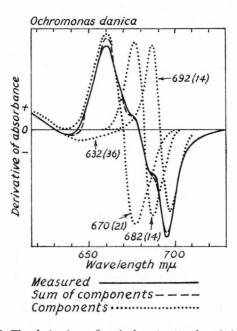

Fig. 6.17. The derivatives of optical extinction for whole cells of Ochromonas danica (————). This curve can be analysed in terms of three components which have symmetrical absorption curves (··············). The addition of the derivative absorption spectra for the three components (------) is seen to correspond closely to the measured spectrum. (After C. S. French[51])

forms of chlorophyll which absorb in the far red at 683 and 695 cannot by themselves result in photosynthesis.

Emerson and co-workers subsequently showed that absorption in the far red could be made effective if it was supplemented by simultaneous absorption at a shorter wavelength. The action spectrum for the increased rate of photosynthesis resulting from a second wavelength superimposed on monochromatic light of 697 mμ showed two characteristic peaks, one at 650 mμ and one at 670 mμ. The peak at 650 mμ is characteristic for absorption by chlorophyll b, and Emerson concluded that the simultaneous excitation of chlorophyll b must improve the photosynthetic efficiency of the light absorbed in the far red by chlorophyll a. An increased photosynthetic activity (enhancement effect) due to simultaneous illumination by two different wavelengths has now been found in a large number of organisms.

The general conclusion is that it may be necessary to have simultaneous excitation of two pigment systems for efficient photosynthesis. In studies with monochromatic light, the relative inefficiency of absorption by chlorophyll a alone appears only at the far red end of the spectrum because this is the only region in the visible where chlorophyll a is the sole absorbing pigment.

The two photochemical reactions required for efficient photosynthesis have been called the long wave chlorophyll reaction and the accessory pigment reaction. French and Fork have suggested that both chlorophyll a 683 and chlorophyll a 695 are capable of a single photochemical step referred to as the long wavelength chlorophyll reaction. The accessory pigment reaction can be affected by absorption by chlorophyll a 673 and chlorophyll b in *Chlorella*, by chlorophyll b in the higher green plant, by chlorophyll c in fucoxanthin in the brown algae, and by phycoerythrin and phycocyanin in the red algae.

Duysens showed that the action spectrum for the oxidation of the cytochrome (probably cytochrome f) in *Porphyridium cruentum* showed a maximum at 680 mμ, whereas the action spectrum for oxygen production in photosynthesis was known to have a maximum at 560 mμ where phycoerythrin absorbs. He proposed that two pigment systems were present – system (i) containing the phycobilins in association with that part of chlorophyll a to which energy transfer can readily take place from the phycobilins, and system (ii) containing the remainder of the chlorophyll a which is not in association with phycobilins. It is probable that system (ii) is capable of effecting only the return of an electron to chlorophyll from cytochrome; system (i) may be concerned in a photochemical process which transfers electrons from chlorophyll[154] (Fig. 6.8) to cytochrome. Hence system (ii) can result only in the oxidation of cytochrome; by itself it cannot result in photosynthesis. System (i) must also be excited for efficient photosynthesis and sensitizes the reduction of the cytochrome which has become oxidized as a result of reaction with water in system (ii). Hill and Bendall[68] have proposed that cytochromes b_6 and f might act as carriers between systems (i) snd (ii).

Since light energy can be transferred from pigment to pigment molecule in the chloroplast, a limited number of centres at which excitation energy can be converted to chemical energy will suffice. Energy conversion centres may be present in an amount of the order of only 1/300th of the chlorophyll, if we assume that the maximum yield which can be obtained from photosynthesis in intense brief flash illumination (discussed earlier) is determined by the number of centres. An energy conversion centre might require the presence of a special enzyme (e.g. a cytochrome or coenzyme) or of a particular physical structure. Electrons expelled from a chlorophyll molecule after absorption of a quantum could migrate within the chloroplast to a conversion centre localized on one surface of the lamella. There they could react with some acceptor which ultimately reduces carbon dioxide. The residual positive charge would migrate to the other surface where ultimately it could react with an electron produced from water by a second photochemical process in which oxygen was produced. In the bacteria and under certain conditions in the higher plant the positive charges and electrons may recombine with the liberation of energy resulting in the formation of ATP in a closed cyclic process as proposed in Arnon's scheme.

Evidence which may be interpreted as indicating that chloroplasts can separate charges upon illumination comes from three types of experiment.[1] The formation of free radicals in illuminated chloroplasts has been demonstrated by measurements of electron spin-resonance. These measurements suggest that light energy reacts in a single electron transfer from a molecule, thus giving rise to a magnetic field. Even when the chloroplast is illuminated at $-111\,^{\circ}\text{C}$ free radicals are formed, suggesting that enzymic reactions are unlikely to be responsible but rather that the radicals result directly from photochemical reaction. Second, algal cells and chloroplasts show an emission of light for a brief period immediately following illumination. This chemiluminescence or bioluminescence is thought to result from the recombination of charges which persist in the dark with a relatively long life. Third, dried chloroplast films have been shown by Arnold to be photoconductive. When carefully prepared layers of chlorophyll and carotenoid were made, it was found that illumination resulted in the development of a potential across the junction. These three types of evidence are consistent with the view that the chloroplast can physically separate charges resulting from light-absorption by chlorophyll. If this view is established, then the most formidable problems remaining in photosynthesis are biophysical rather than biochemical.

GENERAL REFERENCES

J. A. BASSHAM and M. CALVIN (1957) *The Path of Carbon Photosynthesis*. Prentice Hall Inc.

R. HILL and C. P. WHITTINGHAM (1957) *Photosynthesis*. (2nd ed.) Methuen

E. I. RABINOWITCH (1945–56) *Photosynthesis*. (3 vols.) Academic Press

CHAPTER SEVEN

Nitrogen Metabolism

The Nitrogen Compounds of the Plant

In common with both carbon and sulphur most nitrogen compounds
in the plant are relatively more reduced than those in the plant's
environment. Both carbon and nitrogen compounds can be reduced
directly by light energy in photosynthetic organisms, but in general
the elements other than carbon are reduced in the dark indirectly
with a concomitant oxidation of photosynthetic product. Again, as
with the carbon compounds, the nitrogen compounds of the plant
exist in two forms; as polymeric, or large, condensed molecules, and
as monomers, the smaller building units. Thus the chemistry of the
nitrogen compounds of the plant is concerned first with the intermediate forms in reduction to the amino level and the formation of
amino acids, and second with the distribution between the long chain
polymer, the proteins, and the smaller molecules, the amino acids
and their derivatives.

The Formation of Amino Groups

Nitrogen gas

A few plants can utilize nitrogen gas directly. Reduction of nitrogen
in light has been observed in some blue-green algae and in photosynthetic bacteria. In this case the reducing power is derived directly
from light energy. Some free-living bacteria, e.g. *Azotobacter* and
Clostridium, can fix nitrogen in the dark, but higher plants utilize
nitrogen in the dark only if they have root nodules. It is generally
known that leguminous plants, e.g. peas and lupins, increase the
nitrogen content of the soil in which they are grown. Nodules occur
not only in the *Leguminosae* but also in *Betulaceae*, *Rubiaceae*,
Rhamnaceae, and other families.[17] The formation of nodules on the
roots has been shown to be due to the presence of the bacterium
Rhizobium.

Virtanen has suggested that nitrogen is reduced by the formation
of hydroxylamine and demonstrated that under conditions un-

favourable for growth of higher plants derivatives of hydroxylamine are excreted from the plant roots into the soil. Hydroxylamine is toxic to plants when fed at only moderate concentrations, and it has been questioned whether it can be an intermediate in normal metabolism. Burris and Wilson have suggested that ammonia rather than hydroxylamine is the first reduced intermediate formed from nitrogen gas. They showed that when nitrogen containing the heavy isotope N^{15} was fed either to leguminous plants or nitrogen-fixing bacteria the immediate intermediates formed were ammonia or near derivatives of ammonia and relatively little activity was found in hydroxylamine.[163]

Enzymes concerned in the process of nitrogen reduction have not yet been isolated from higher plants. This has been in large part due to the fact that it has not been possible to obtain nitrogen fixation by the bacterium *Rhizobium* outside the living host plant. Fixation by homogenates has recently been reported and should lead to a rapid development in a study of the enzymes concerned. The presence in the nodules of leghaemoglobin, a form of haemoglobin, has been known for some time, but the role of this substance in nitrogen fixation is still not clear.

Nitrate

Nitrate is taken up in solution from the soil (see Chapter 8) and occurs as such in the mature plant to a small extent in the leaves and often to a considerable extent in the roots.[16] Nitrate reduction does not require light and can take place at the expense of stored carbohydrate. Reduction can take place both in the leaf and the root and there is evidence that the relative activity of root and leaf differs in different plant species. The actual level of nitrate in a plant tissue will depend on the relative rate of nitrate uptake and nitrate reduction. Nitrate will be high when conditions are such as to favour uptake and lower reducing activity.

Reduction of nitrate

$$\text{Nitrate} + \text{NADPH}_2 \xrightarrow[\text{reductase}]{\text{nitrate}} \text{Nitrite} + \text{NADP} + \text{H}_2\text{O}$$
$$\text{HNO}_3 \qquad\qquad\qquad\qquad\qquad \text{HNO}_2$$

$$\text{Nitrite} + 2\text{NADPH}_2 \xrightarrow[\text{reductase}]{\text{nitrite}} \text{Hydroxylamine} + 2\text{NADP} + \text{H}_2\text{O}$$
$$\text{HNO}_2 \qquad\qquad\qquad\qquad\qquad \text{NH}_2\text{OH}$$

$$\text{Hydroxylamine} + \text{NADPH}_2 \xrightarrow[\text{dehydrogenase}]{\text{ammonia}} \text{NH}_4\text{OH} + \text{NADP}$$
$$\text{NH}_2\text{OH}$$

Nitrate reductase, a flavoprotein enzyme containing molybdenum, catalyses the reduction of nitrate to nitrite.[115] It has been found in many plants both in roots and leaves. The reduction requires reduced pyridine nucleotide. A second enzyme nitrite reductase has also been demonstrated in many plants and catalyses the formation of hyponitrous acid from nitrite.[114] It has been postulated that the next stage of the reduction is via hydroxylamine to ammonia, but the enzymes concerned with this have not been isolated from higher plants. One complete sequence proposed is

$$\text{nitrate (NO}_3') \rightharpoonup \text{nitrite (NO}_2') \rightharpoonup \text{hyponitrite (H}_2\text{N}_2\text{O}_2) \rightharpoonup$$
$$\text{hydroxylamine (NH}_2\text{OH)} \rightharpoonup \text{ammonia (NH}_3)$$

In most higher plants ammonia can act as a nitrogen source but some plants, including barley, oats, rye, and sugar beet, preferentially take up nitrate. If the embryo is isolated from a pea it is found that the isolated embryo can utilize ammonia, but can only use nitrate if reducing power in the form of glucose is provided. The alga *Chlorella*, if fed ammonia and nitrate together, will utilize the ammonia preferentially, only using the nitrate after all the ammonia has been exhausted. Other micro-organisms, e.g. *Euglena* among algae, and yeasts among the fungi, are unable to use nitrate and must be fed ammonia. Most higher plants and many algae can in addition utilize reduced organic nitrogen compounds which already contain amino groups.

The Formation of Amino Compounds*

The most important utilization of ammonia in plant metabolism is in the formation of α-amino acids, that is acids with an amino group substituted on the carbon atom adjacent to the carboxyl group. A wide range of amino acids are known in living organisms both with aliphatic and aromatic groupings. The probable reaction mechanism by which amino acids are formed is the reaction between ammonia and an α-keto acid giving rise to the corresponding amino acid. In this reaction the keto group is reduced so that a reducing substance $NADH_2$ and the corresponding dehydrogenase are required. The most important reaction is the reductive amination of α-ketoglutaric acid to form glutamic acid, catalysed by the enzyme glutamic dehydrogenase.

* See the Appendix for a brief description of the chemistry of some amino compounds.

An alternative enzyme system catalyses the condensation of ammonia with an unsaturated acid such as fumarate to give aspartate.

Formation of Amino acids

$$\alpha\text{-Ketoglutarate} + NH_3 + NADH_2 \xrightarrow[\text{dehydrogenase}]{\text{Glutamic}} \begin{array}{l} \text{glutamate} + NAD \\ + H_2O \end{array}$$

$$\text{Fumarate} + NH_3 \underset{}{\overset{\text{Aspartase}}{\rightleftharpoons}} \text{aspartate}$$

$$\text{L-Glutamate} + H_2O \underset{\text{decarboxylase}}{\overset{\text{Glutamic}}{\rightleftharpoons}} \text{aminobutyrate} + H_2CO_3$$

The importance of this reaction in living organisms is still not clear, although it certainly plays a less important role than reductive amination. A third reaction is the carboxylation of amino derivatives, e.g. the carboxylation of γ-amino butyric acid to form glutamate, catalysed by the enzyme glutamic decarboxylase. This is not believed to be an important route of amino acid synthesis in the plant. Thus the most significant pathway of synthesis is reductive amination, producing amino acids corresponding to the keto acids available in the plant. Three keto acids play a particularly important role in respiratory activity, namely pyruvate, α-ketoglutarate and oxaloacetate. Reductive amination of α-ketoglutarate to form glutamate is well established, is probable for pyruvate which forms alanine, and may occur with oxaloacetate to form aspartate.

If amino acids are to be formed corresponding to keto acids other than ketoglutarate they are probably formed by transamination. Transaminases are enzymes widely distributed in all plant tissues, particularly in roots. They catalyse reactions between a keto acid and an amino acid; exchange of the keto group for the amino group resulting in the formation of a new amino acid and the keto acid corresponding to the old amino acid. Pyridoxal phosphate is a necessary co-factor.

Transaminase reactions

L-Glutamate + oxaloacetate $\rightleftharpoons$ Ketoglutarate + L-aspartate

L-Glutamate + pyruvate $\rightleftharpoons$ Ketoglutarate + L-alanine

L-Glutamate + glyoxylate $\rightleftharpoons$ Ketoglutarate + glycine

Animals are incapable of making all the amino acids necessary for their nutrition and they must be provided with certain essential amino acids in their diet. This is not the case with plants, which can synthesize the whole range.

Peptide compounds

Two amino acids can condense together between the carboxyl group of one and the amino acid group of the other, resulting in the formation of the peptide linkage. When two amino acids condense a dipeptide is formed, and when a large number condense together to form a long chain molecule ultimately a protein is formed. A simpler condensation of this type is between free ammonia and an amino acid forming the peptide linkage in an amide.

Enzymes which catalyse the hydrolysis of the peptide link, the peptidases, are widely distributed in plants. In general they are of two types, the exo- and the endo-peptidases. The former include the amino-peptidases, which attack a terminal peptide linkage only in the vicinity of a free amino group, and the carboxy-peptidases which attack a terminal peptide link only in the vicinity of a carboxyl group. The endo-peptidases do not attack the end of a chain but specifically attack peptide links in the middle of a chain. The two commonest endo-peptidases (formerly called proteases) are papain, obtained from papaya, and bromelin, obtained from pineapple juice. These enzymes after extraction are only active in the reduced form, so that a reducing agent such as cysteine is added.

The Balance between the Synthesis and Breakdown of Compounds containing Polypeptide Bonds

AMIDE FORMATION AND BREAKDOWN

Under conditions of protein breakdown amino groups may be liberated. These may be evolved as ammonia or they may react with amino acids to form amides. When seeds germinate normally, protein is broken down in the seed, translocated to the growing point and then re-formed as protein. If the seedling is kept in the dark the amino groups after translocation to the growing tip accumulate as the amides glutamine and asparagine (Fig. 7.1). In light there is little accumulation of amide except during a very brief initial period; but in the dark a progressive accumulation of amide may take place over many days. If the embryo is removed from the endosperm of a seed (depriving it of a source of carbohydrate) the breakdown of protein results in the accumulation of ammonia; but if the embryo is treated with glucose, amide is formed. If lupin seeds are fragmented and treated with toluene as a poison, ammonia is liberated and little amide is formed. The accumulation of amide under normal growth conditions can be stimulated by treatment with excess ammonia. For example, if rye grass is excessively fertilized with ammonia sulphate, glutamine crystals appear on the leaves. Amide formation takes place only when carbohydrate is supplied and respiration is active. Otherwise free ammonia is liberated and the death of the plant tissue follows. In some plants glutamine alone is formed, in some asparagine, and in others both.

Amide formation is also an important feature of the metabolism of excised leaves. When leaves are removed from the plant, protein

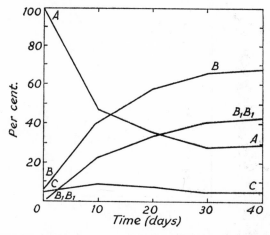

Fig. 7.1. The change in protein nitrogen AA, amino acids and amides BB, organic nitrogenous bases CC, and asparagine B_1B_1 in seedlings of vetch. (D. Prianischnikov. Nitrogen in the Life of Plants, publ. Kramer Inc. Madison (1951))

breakdown occurs, and at first amides accumulate. Feeding with sugar does not appreciably prevent the breakdown of protein in the detached leaf, nor does exposure to light. If the leaf is old and the respiratory activity is low, ammonia begins to be formed at a relatively early stage, after only a brief period of amide accumulation (Fig. 7.2). In an attempt to investigate the compounds from which amides are formed various liquids have been infiltrated into the intercellular spaces of excised leaves. This is done by placing the leaf under a vacuum, to remove air from the intercellular spaces, and then allowing liquid to penetrate back into the space on release of the vacuum. Mothes[111] showed that a number of ammonium salts such as ammonium succinate, malate, or aspartate all stimulated amide formation. Chibnall subsequently showed that ammonium sulphate had a similar effect, demonstrating that under conditions of adequate carbohydrate supply the infiltrated salt is used primarily as an ammonium source.

The distribution of amino groups between amide and amino acid is determined by a 'balanced state' or *dynamic equilibrium*. The amidases are predominantly hydrolytic enzymes, for which the equilibrium is very much in the direction of free amino acid. Amide

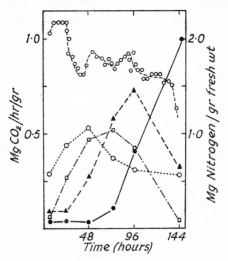

Fig. 7.2. The changes in the nitrogen compounds in detached barley leaves. $^-$O$^-$ CO_2. □⋯⋯⋯⋯□ *unstable amide* (× 2). O⋯⋯⋯⋯O *amine N.* ▲‒‒‒‒▲ *stable amide* ●————● *ammonia.*
(After E. W. Yemm[162])

synthesis takes place by a different enzyme system involving a phosphorylated derivative of the amino acid, and this requires a supply of ATP and Mg^{++} (see eqn. 1 below). The tripeptide glutathione can be formed in a similar manner by incubating together a bean seedling homogenate, ATP, magnesium ions, and the amino acids, glutamic acid, cysteine, and glycine (see eqn. 2 below). *In vivo*, synthesis of amide depends on a supply of ATP which will be available only during active aerobic respiration; the rate of hydrolysis on the other hand is largely independent of respiration. Thus the balance state between amide and amino acid will be moved to favour accumulation of amino acids rather than amides by all factors which inhibit respiration.

Peptide bond synthesis

1. Glutamate $+$ NH$_3$ $+$ ATP $\xrightarrow{\text{Mg}^{++}}$ Glutamine $+$ ADP $+$ P

(glutamine synthetase)

2. Glutamate $+$ cysteine $+$ ATP $\rightleftharpoons$ Glutamylcysteine $+$ ADP $+$ P

glutamylcysteine $+$ glycine ($+$ ATP) $\rightleftharpoons$ Glutathione (glutamyl cysteinyl glycine)

THE RELATIONSHIP BETWEEN PROTEIN AND AMINO ACID NITROGEN

As in the case of amide synthesis, the formation of protein is dependent on a supply of ATP, while the hydrolytic enzymes, the endo-peptidases, catalyse an equilibrium in favour of the amino acid form. If the balance between proteins and amino acid *in vivo* is determined by these two enzyme systems, the relative concentrations of protein and amino acid will be dependent on respiratory activity. The protein in the plant is in a 'dynamic state', as has been shown by feeding with $N^{15}H_4{}^+$, when, for example, the incorporation of protein into tobacco leaves during a given period was far greater than could be accounted for by synthesis of new protein.[149] Factors which stimulate respiratory activity will tend to favour a balance towards protein and those which suppress respiratory activity will favour a balance towards amino acids.

An excised leaf placed in the dark shows a marked loss of protein both from the chloroplast and the non-chloroplast protein; feeding a large excess of glucose can suppress protein hydrolysis but only to a limited extent. Wood has shown that in various grasses the amino acid/protein balance depends on the water content of the leaf. Under conditions of wilting the formation of protein was suppressed, a result opposite from that which would be expected if only a simple chemical equilibrium existed between amino acids and protein. The age of the tissue also affects the protein balance. Pearsall and Billimoria floated daffodil leaves on nitrate solutions and showed a gradation from the top to the bottom of the leaf in its ability to form protein; this was believed to be related to the gradation in age of the tissue (Fig. 7.3). The older portion at the tip showed no protein formation, but under the same conditions the younger portion showed active synthesis. Under conditions of mineral deficiency which affect respiratory activity a general correlation between aerobic respiratory activity and protein content can be seen. Furthermore, vacuum infiltration of leaves with protein hydrolysate can be shown to result in some incorporation of N^{15}, provided the tissue has an active aerobic metabolism. Thus there is general evidence that there is a correlation between respiratory activity and the synthesis of protein.

The sequence of amino acids along a protein chain is characteristic for a particular protein. Not only is chemical energy required for the formation of peptide links (which can be supplied from ATP), but also 'information' is required as to the sequence in which the individual residues are to be joined. For this reason, in addition to requiring

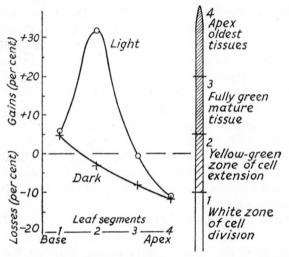

Fig. 7.3. *The percentage change in protein content of different portions of the daffodil leaf immersed in sterile solution of nitrate and glucose in light* (○) *and dark* (+). (*After W. H. Pearsall and M. C. Billimoria*[120])

ATP, nucleic acids, which are believed to programme the amino acid sequence, are also necessary.

The necessity of nucleotides for protein synthesis can be shown particularly clearly in the case of enzyme adaptation because during the formation of an adaptive enzyme, net protein synthesis must take place. Some mutants of *Escherichia coli* are unable to synthesize particular nucleotides and have been shown to be incapable of forming certain adaptative enzymes; when fed the nucleotide they can then form the enzyme.[119] Certain mutants which require thymine and without it cannot form DNA can form adaptive enzymes. This suggests that RNA and not DNA is the required nucleic acid.

Some success has been achieved with protein synthesis by isolated particulate cell fractions; for example, in the case of fragmented mammalian tumour or liver cells protein synthesis has been shown by feeding radioactive amino acids. At least two stages were involved. First, incorporation of amino acid into an activated form took place requiring ATP and a series of soluble enzymes – the amino acid activating enzymes.[53] Second, for the further condensation into protein a microsomal fraction* was required. In this reaction another phosphorylative compound, guanosine triphosphate (GTP), was required. Similarly, protein synthesis was demonstrated with sonically disrupted *Staphylococcus* cells. Removal of RNA by treatment with ribonuclease prevented the incorporation of amino acids.[88] When only a limited amount of nucleic acid was removed the ability to form enzyme was restored by addition of RNA but not of DNA; if depletion had gone further, then DNA restored the activity to a greater extent than RNA.

The sequence of amino acids in protein could result from the sequential action of a large number of enzymes, each one specific for one amino acid. Alternatively, a single large molecule could act as an organizer or template which orientates the activated amino acids into suitable positions and then binds them together by a 'zipper'-like action. The latter is now thought to be the case and nucleic acid to provide the template. The general characteristics of the organism are determined by the DNA of the nucleus, but protein synthesis takes place in the ribosomes which contain RNA. The problem remains as to how the DNA in the nucleus determines the type of protein manufactured by the ribosomes. When amino acids containing C^{14} are fed into animal tissues, radioactivity appears first in the soluble RNA of the cytoplasm, later in the RNA of the ribosome, then in the protein of the ribosome, and finally in the soluble protein of the cell. It is thought that the activated amino acids attach themselves to the soluble (or 'transfer') RNA and that this process requires ATP. The soluble RNA, after combination with the amino acid, fits on to the ribosome. The microsomal RNA is not itself the template, but will synthesize a particular protein according to the sequence of bases (the 'code') in a fraction of the cytoplasm[20] called 'messenger' RNA. The type of messenger RNA produced in the

---

* A particulate cell fraction obtained by centrifugation at 100,000 g and containing endoplasmic reticulum. Treatment with sodium desoxycholate removes much of the protein and phospholipid, resulting in a particulate preparation – the ribosomes.

cytoplasm is determined by the DNA of the nucleus. This mechanism, deduced largely from work with animal tissue, probably applies also to micro-organisms and, it is presumed, also to higher plants. The process of detaching a leaf leads to protein hydrolysis which can be only partially stopped by feeding amino compounds or sugars. It may result from some interference with the nucleotide metabolism, and recent evidence shows that kinetin (6-furfuryladenine) fed to detached leaves prevents protein breakdown to some extent.[128] Chibnall had earlier suggested that some substance essential for protein synthesis must be supplied to the leaves from the roots. Removal of the leaf from the plant removed the supply of this substance and this resulted in protein hydrolysis. Chibnall proposed a hormonal control of the protein balance of the leaf, and this is still the probable explanation.

In conclusion, it will be noted that there are still a number of problems remaining in the study of nitrogen metabolism. The biochemistry of nitrogen fixation is still not fully elucidated, and in spite of the recent advances in our knowledge of the mechanism of protein synthesis in micro-organisms, a full understanding of the factors controlling protein balance in the higher plant has yet to be attained.

GENERAL REFERENCES

A. C. CHIBNALL (1939) *Protein Metabolism in the Plant.* Yale U.P.
G. C. WEBSTER (1959) *Nitrogen Metabolism in Plants.* Row Peterson.

PART TWO

Plant Processes

It is the practice amongst biochemists to limit the word metabolism to the synthesis and degradation of organic material in living organisms. In the first part of this book it has been shown that metabolism may be regarded as an essential concomitant of all energy-requiring processes in the plant. This suggests that a process which consumes energy, such as the uptake and accumulation of salts by a plant cell, must be linked to metabolism. Ultimately it may be possible to relate all the processes taking place to sequences of defined chemical reaction steps. At the present time we are further from achieving this end with complex processes such as growth or water movement which involve multicellular structures than with respiration or photosynthesis which can be considered at the cellular level.

With processes such as growth the behaviour of the plant as a whole is measured and the part played by the individual cells must be deduced. To do this it is necessary to determine the role of the physical structure of the plant in its functioning. Only after this can the role of chemical reactions at the cellular level be assessed.

CHAPTER EIGHT

Osmotic Relations of the Individual Cell

Water is an important constituent of the higher plant. Eighty to ninety per cent of the fresh weight of a plant is water; the actual percentage varying from tissue to tissue, for example, being less in the xylem than in the phloem. The water can exist in three forms: as the solvent of a true solution in the vacuole, as the dispersal medium for the colloidal system in the cytoplasm, or as water held in the pores of the cell wall by capillary forces. The factors which affect the distribution of water between these three phases differ. In this chapter we shall be concerned primarily with the relationship between the water in the vacuole of the cell and its surroundings.

In so far as a solution contains molecules of a dissolved substance, the solute, the concentration of the solvent molecules, is less than in pure solvent. Therefore, when a sugar solution is placed in contact with pure water, sugar will diffuse from the solution into the water, but equally water will diffuse from the pure water into the solution (because the latter has a lower concentration of water). If two solutions are separated by a porous membrane which has pores of such a size that water molecules can pass freely through it but sucrose molecules cannot, water will pass from the weaker to the more concentrated solution without the complication of sucrose moving in the opposite direction. Such a membrane would be termed a semipermeable membrane (or better, a selectively permeable membrane). The movement of water is called *Osmosis*. The forces involved in the movement both of water and the solute are determined by the laws of diffusion. Solvent movement could be prevented by applying a pressure to the solution so that effectively the concentration (or activity) of water molecules was made equal to that in the solution. Then no movement would take place. The force required is defined as the *osmotic pressure* of the solution and is that force which must be applied to a solution to maintain it in equilibrium with pure solvent.

117

As well as movement by diffusion during osmosis a bulk mass flow of water may take place through the pores of the membrane. This will result when the rate of movement of solute through the pores of the membrane is potentially less rapid than that between the surface of the membrane and the external solutions. Under these conditions, a decrease in pressure will result just inside the pores of the membrane and a hydrostatic pressure develop along the pore. Mass flow will become more important as the pore radius increases relative to its length; Dainty and Hope have suggested 15Å as likely to be the critical diameter in natural membranes. Thus according to the structure of the membrane the flow of water may include both a diffusional and hydrostatic term.

METHODS OF MEASURING OSMOTIC PRESSURE

The osmotic pressure can be measured mechanically by determining the hydrostatic pressure required to maintain the solution in equilibrium with pure solvent. However, the relatively lower concentration of solvent molecules in a solution has its effect on other physical properties. The vapour pressure of a solution is less than that of pure solvent and the lowering of the vapour pressure can be readily determined experimentally. Also the freezing point of a solution is lower than that of pure solvent. From the depression of the freezing point or the lowering of the vapour pressure the osmotic pressure can be calculated.

Measurements of the osmotic pressure at different temperatures and concentrations have shown that the fundamental relationships of a weak solution are of the same form as those for an ideal gas. For a gas the pressure P, volume V and temperature T are related by $PV = RT$, where R is the gas constant; for a solution $OP = RTC$, where $OP = $ osmotic pressure in atmospheres, and $C = $ concentration in moles/1.

It follows that all molar solutions should have an equal osmotic pressure of 22·4 atmos. at 0°C. The osmotic properties of a solution are dependent on the number of dissolved particles and not on their chemical form. In the case of salt solutions which ionize, the number of particles is greater than the number of dissolved molecules. If a solution of sodium chloride were to ionize completely there would be twice as many particles as if no dissociation took place and consequently its osmotic pressure would be double the expected value. Equally, if the solute associates to form aggregates with itself or solvent molecules, there would be relatively fewer particles and the osmotic pressure would be less than expected. For this reason the equation is normally written $OP = iRTC$, where i is the isotonic coefficient. For sodium chloride i has a value near to 2 if that for sucrose is taken as 1.

OSMOTIC RELATIONS OF A PLANT CELL

The osmotic pressure of the vacuole of the cell is determined by the amount of dissolved substances. If a cell is placed in pure water one would expect an increase in the volume of the vacuole resulting from the diffusion of water from outside the cell into the salt solution of the vacuole. The cell wall basically composed of microfibrils with innumerable submicroscopic interstices is relatively permeable to water and most dissolved substances. The outer membrane of the protoplast, the plasmalemma, will in the first place be assumed to be relatively permeable to small molecules; then effectively an external solute may permeate up to the tonoplast. The tonoplast acts as a semi-permeable membrane and the changes of volume resulting when a cell is placed in a solution will, until the final stages, be confined to the vacuole. This is a limiting case, as we shall discuss later. Ultimately, the vacuole will increase so much in volume that the cytoplasm is pressed against the cell wall. The cell wall will stretch within the limits of its elasticity but cannot expand indefinitely. Thus the final volume of the cell will depend on two opposing forces – one resulting from the difference in osmotic pressure of the vacuole and the external solution, the other being the wall pressure which prevents unlimited expansion of the cell. The resulting net force which is the combined effect of the osmotic pressure of the cell sap and of the forces restraining the cell expansion is called the *suction pressure* (S.P.) or diffusion pressure deficit (DPD).* It follows that S.P. $= OP - WP$, where WP is the force exerted by the wall. For a cell in a tissue WP will consist of the forces exerted not only by the wall of the cell under consideration but all the forces on the wall due to the surrounding cells. If the cell is placed in a solution more concentrated than that in the vacuole the volume of the vacuole will diminish; eventually the cytoplasm will no longer press against the cell wall. At this point we refer to the cell as at the stage of *incipient plasmolysis*. If the vacuole continues to shrink the cytoplasm will eventually draw completely away from the cell wall and the cell will be plasmolysed. Under these conditions the wall of the cell and all

* The term DPD has been favoured by most American authors.

119

surrounding cells can no longer exert any effect upon the suction pressure, and then S.P. = *OP*. As the cytoplasm withdraws from the cell wall, external solution enters through the cell wall and fills the space between the cytoplasm and the wall. In the case of a cell exposed to dry air which is losing water by evaporation the vacuole will decrease in volume. As the vacuole shrinks the cytoplasm moves with it, and in this case the cell wall remains adherent to the cytoplasm. Now the tendency is for the wall to return to its original condition, and the force which it exerts is working in the same direction

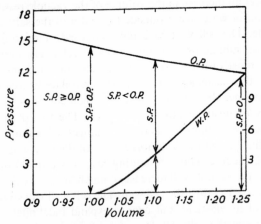

Fig. 8.1. The relationship between volume within the semipermeable membrane and turgor pressure, osmotic pressure, and suction pressure of the cell. The suction pressure is always less than the osmotic pressure in a turgid cell but equal to it at the point of incipient plasmolysis and in the plasmolysed cell. The curve for osmotic pressure is derived from the gas laws. If the cell wall stretched elastically according to Hooke's Law it would change linearly with volume. In fact it increases more than this as the volume decreases

as the osmotic force. Thus for a wilted cell S.P. = *OP* + *WP*. These relationships are illustrated in Fig. 8.1.

So far in this discussion the vacuole alone has been considered to change its shape because the tonoplast has been regarded as *the* semipermeable membrane of the cell. Recent work shows that according to the nature of the solute, penetration may take place to varying depths into the cell. Then the limiting layer into which penetration does not take place represents the semi-permeable membrane. The majority of investigators believe that no penetration of cytoplasm takes place and the plasmalemma is the effective membrane.[93] It is convenient to refer to the volume within the cell which changes with change in osmotic pressure as the *osmotic volume*. The space external to this limiting layer, which an external solution is regarded as freely penetrating, is called the *free space*. The osmotic volume of a plant tissue can be measured by using Archimedes' principle. If the weight of tissue (W_1 and W_2) is determined in two solutions of different strength but known densities (D_1, D_2) then, if W is the weight in air,

$$W_1 = W - VD_1 \text{, and } W_2 = W - VD_2 \text{. Therefore } V = \frac{W_2 - W_1}{D_1 - D_2},$$

where V is the volume not penetrated. In practice, a number of complicating factors must be considered, for which reference must be made to original papers. It is found experimentally that with discs cut from carrot root the osmotic volume is less for potassium nitrate than for sucrose, indicating that the smaller molecule can penetrate further into the cell.[25] The change in volume of a cell with time $\left(\dfrac{dV}{dt}\right)$ during plasmolysis can be expressed in terms of the osmotic pressure gradient, the area of the cell A, and a constant K_w, the permeability coefficient to water, as follows:

$$\frac{\Delta V}{\Delta t} = K_w \, A \, [OP_o - SP_i]$$

where OP_o is the osmotic pressure of the internal solution and SP_i the suction pressure of the cell. Measurements with isolated protoplasts give essentially the same value for K_w as with the whole cell, demonstrating that the wall offers little resistance to water movement. This is consistent with our knowledge of the porous structure of the wall. A slightly smaller value for K_w is obtained from observations of deplasmolysis than for plasmolysis. The permeability coefficient for a turgid cell can be determined from the rate of entry of isotopic water. The values obtained by the two methods are significantly different, suggesting either that the permeability of the cell is different in the plasmolysed and the turgid state or that the plant cell membrane is such that the flow of water during osmosis is not purely diffusional.

Measurement of the osmotic pressure of plant material

At the point of incipient plasmolysis the suction pressure is equal to the osmotic pressure of the cell sap. If a solution can be found in which a tissue is at the point of incipient plasmolysis and can maintain this state indefinitely, the osmotic pressure of the external solution is the same as the O.P. of the cell sap. In practice, sections of plant tissue are prepared and the percentage of cells plasmolysed in solutions of different strength determined. It may be assumed that the average cell is just about to be plasmolysed, i.e. is at the point of incipient plasmolysis, when 50 per cent of the cells of the tissue have plasmolysed and 50 per cent have not. The percentage of cells plasmolysed is determined for a number of different concentrations, using sections which are believed to be taken from homogeneous tissue. From a graph of the percentage of cells plasmolysed plotted against concentration of solution, the concentration which corresponds to

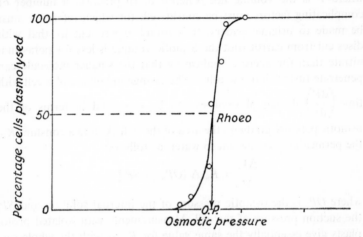

Fig. 8.2. The percentage of cells plasmolysed as a function of osmotic pressures of the external solution in which the tissue is bathed. The solution resulting in 50 per cent of the cells being plasmolysed has an osmotic pressure equal to that of the osmotic pressure of the average tissue

the point of average incipient plasmolysis can be deduced (Fig. 8.2). In this method a number of errors arise. First, the osmotic relationship of the cells will be disturbed because tissue tensions and hence wall pressures are altered as a result of cutting. Second, it is necessary to use a solute which is not accumulated by the cell. If a permeable substance is used the percentage of cells plasmolysed will change with time, rising to a maximum and then falling again as the solute permeates into the cell. It is also desirable, for reasons to be discussed later, to use a substance which does not affect the metabolism of the cell. For these reasons mannitol has frequently been chosen. The osmotic pressure determined (P_i) will be that corresponding to the osmotic volume at incipient plasmolysis (V_i); the corresponding value at any other volume V will be given by the equation $P = P_i \cdot \left(\dfrac{V_i}{V} \right)$.

If the volume of the protoplast is used in this expression it assumes that any free space in the cytoplasm does not change its volume during plasmolysis. This may not always be true; if potassium thiocyanate is used as plasmolyticum the cytoplasm swells whilst the vacuole shrinks. This is referred to as 'cap' plasmolysis. It is now believed to be true to a greater or less extent with other plasmolytic agents.

Attempts have been made to express the sap from plant tissues and directly determine the osmotic pressure by physical methods. This is a straightforward experimental technique, but the results are difficult to interpret since it is not clear that the liquid expressed is unchanged vacuolar sap. The solution collected may contain water and substances which were not originally in the vacuole, and also to some extent may have been diluted by the contents of the free space during the process of extraction. These difficulties lead to some uncertainty as to the value of this method.

Measurement of suction pressure (or diffusion pressure deficit)
The S.P. is the net force acting on the water in the plant cell and is dependent on the osmotic pressure of the contents, the extensibility of the cell wall, and any tissue tensions. These forces must remain unchanged during the measurement of S.P. Hence it is necessary to find the concentration of a solution which has no osmotic effect on the tissue; when this is done the net forces on the water in the tissue are balanced by the osmotic forces of the external solution. It follows that the osmotic pressure of a solution in which a tissue is unchanged is equal to the average suction pressure of the tissue cells. The absence of any effect on the tissue can be shown by measuring its weight, its volume (difficult in practice), or the length of a single dimension; alternatively, the external solution can be analysed for any change in concentration by measurement of the refractive index or density, or by chemical analysis. In practice, if sections are made from a root tissue such as carrot, it is convenient to determine the solution which results in no change of weight after immersion (Fig. 8.3). The thinner the sections the greater will be the error due to a change of tissue tensions consequent upon cutting. Alternatively, the thicker the sections the slower will water penetrate into the tissue and the longer will be the time for the experiment and the greater

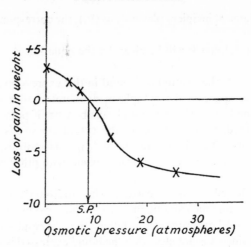

Fig. 8.3. The percentage change in weight of similar samples of tissue as a function of the osmotic pressure of the bathing solution. The osmotic pressure of the solution which results in no change in weight equals the suction pressure of the tissue

the error due to the uptake, if any, of the solute. Slices of 1–2 mm thickness are most often used. Measurement of a single linear dimension is frequently used with tissue cut from such material as the hollow dandelion peduncle. Here the cells on the interior are relatively more permeable than those of the epidermis; hence uptake or loss of water results in an easily detectable change in curvature of the tissue.

Active Water Uptake

When the osmotic pressure of plant cells has been determined by two different methods, such as the plasmolytic method and the determination of the lowering of the freezing point of the expressed sap, the value obtained from the expressed sap has usually been a few atmospheres less than that obtained from plasmolytic measurements.[10, 39] This result might be expected if the liquid obtained by applying pressure to a tissue is not only vacuolar sap but includes some more dilute solution expressed from the cytoplasm of the cell.[9] Indeed, observations show that the osmotic pressure of the expressed liquid does vary with the pressure that has been applied in expressing it. Nevertheless, the discrepancy between the two values led to the suggestion that in addition to an osmotic uptake of water by plant cells there might be some additional uptake resulting from vital forces peculiar to a living system. A second type of evidence used to support this view came from observations of the water uptake by a tissue in which the respiration was markedly inhibited. For example, using potato discs suspended in water aerated with a gas mixture containing either 20 per cent or 7 per cent of oxygen, it was found that reduction in the oxygen content reduced both the respiratory activity and the water uptake.[59] In addition, various inhibitors, e.g. azide, were found to inhibit both the respiratory oxygen uptake and the water uptake. More extensive observations showed that there was no simple quantitative relationship between the degree of inhibition of water uptake and the degree of inhibition of respiration. Dinitrophenol was shown to increase the oxygen uptake due to respiration but to decrease the water uptake. However, this was in accordance with the hypothesis, since, as discussed in Chapter 4, dinitrophenol essentially prevents the utilization of energy obtained from respiration without affecting oxygen uptake and might be expected to decrease an active process. Hence there is a broad correlation between the effect of certain inhibitors on respiration and on water uptake. In a third type of observation the volume of the cell was determined in isotonic salt and sugar solutions and found to differ. Also, changes in volume consequent upon the transfer of tissue from one solution to the other were observed. These observations were made before the concept of free space had been formulated; it can be explained if the osmotic volume of the cell differs for the two solutes. Hence it need not indicate the operation of non-physical forces. Measurements have been made to investigate the relationship between the volume of protoplasts isolated from cells and the osmotic pressure of the medium surrounding them. These observations show that the pressure volume relationships were those to be expected for a non-living system, i.e. $p(v - b) =$ constant, when b represents a volume related to the free space.

Other factors affect water uptake which at first sight would not appear to affect the physical process of osmosis. For example, treatment of tissue with indoleacetic acid (IAA) will often facilitate the uptake of water.[18] There is, however, reason to believe that IAA may alter the plastic properties of the cell wall and thus affect water movement by affecting the extensibility of the cell wall and cytoplasm. Some of the effect of a change in the concentration of oxygen or of treatment with various poisons may be due to an action which these factors have on the cell wall or protoplasmic structure, and consequently on the permeability of the cell to water. At present it must be concluded that there is no convincing evidence that water movement into the cell has any component necessarily related to the metabolism of the cell.[84]

Uptake of Solutes

DIFFUSION

The uptake of substances by plant tissue can take place by physical diffusion. For a non-electrolyte the concentration inside the cell cannot exceed the concentration outside and diffusion will take place until the concentrations inside and outside are equal (i.e. the chemical potential gradient is zero). The amount of substance ds entering in time dt is given by

$$\frac{ds}{dt} = P(C_o - C_i).A$$

where A is the area of the cell, C_o and C_i the concentrations outside and inside the cell, and P is the permeability coefficient. The equality of concentration will refer only to the form in which the substance is transported. If, after entry into the cell, the penetrating substance forms some chemical complex, or is absorbed at a surface, then the concentration of free substance inside the cell may be maintained lower than that outside, and transport into the cell by diffusion will continue, although the total concentration inside may exceed that outside. In the case of electrolytes, involving the movement of changed ions, the existence of electrical potential differences must also be taken into account. In the presence of a potential difference there will be an unequal concentration of ions on the two sides of the membrane, such that at equilibrium the electrochemical potential gradient is zero.

The study of the diffusion of un-ionized substances into the cell has shown that the rate of penetration is far less than that of water and is dependent on certain molecular properties. First, penetration is more rapid the greater the fat-solubility of the penetrating substance. This is consistent with the view that the membranes of the plant protoplast contain lipids. Second, penetration is more rapid the smaller the relative size of the molecule, provided that when a molecule or ion is associated with a number of water molecules these are also taken into account (see Fig. 8.4). The correlation with molecular size indicates the existence of a porous membrane, and this is consistent with the high rate of water movement relative to that of larger molecules. Both of these properties together suggest that the

126

OSMOTIC RELATIONS OF THE INDIVIDUAL CELL

resistance to free penetration into the living protoplast resides in a structure consisting of a double layer in part fat and in part protein.[36] The protein is assumed to form the outer layers since measurements indicate a low surface tension between the plant cell surface and

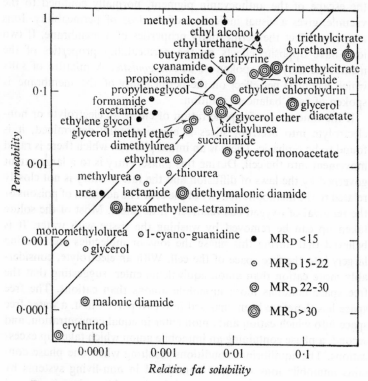

Fig. 8.4. *The permeability of cells of* Chara ceratophylla *to various organic non-electrolytes showing that the permeability increases with the fat solubility (as measured by partition between olive oil and water) and decreases with molecule size (the size of the point indicating the size of the molecule). (After R. Collander and H. Bärlund*[37])

water. Ionization of the protein results in a surface charge which will be a function of the pH.

The selective permeability of plant membranes is only maintained under physiological conditions. Heating above 50°C, treatment with various salts, or extreme alkalinity or acidity, results in a loss of selective permeability. These effects presumably arise from denaturation of the protein component of the membrane. Similarly, treatment with chloroform, which will extract lipid components from the membrane, also results in a loss of selective permeability. After such treatments, substances can freely diffuse in and out of the cell. This can be most easily demonstrated using beetroot discs from which the escape of the anthocyanin pigment, normally confined to the vacuole, gives a visual indication of the loss of permeability. Ions may also affect the permeability properties of a membrane. If two ions have opposite effects on the permeability properties of the membrane they are spoken of as *antagonistic*. A mixture of salts which has little net effect on the permeability of the membrane is spoken of as a 'balanced' solution.

If the time course for penetration of either an electrolyte or non-electrolyte into beetroot slices is experimentally determined, it is found to be biphasic. There is an initial phase in which there is rapid movement into the cell. During this phase, entry is to a large extent governed by the laws of diffusion and the rate of entry is not closely related to the metabolic activity of the cell. The addition of poisons or the removal of oxygen has relatively little effect. Most of the solute taken up can be removed by washing the tissue with water. It is believed that during this phase the ions or molecules are entering largely into the free space of the cell. With an electrolyte, considerably more cation than anion equivalents enter, suggesting that the free space contains more immobile anions than cations. The free space has therefore been analysed into two parts – first, a water-free space into which cation and anion enter in equal concentration, and second, a phase containing an immobile anion which takes up excess cations. The equilibrium conditions resulting when one phase contains immobile ions was first considered in non-living systems by Donnan; hence the free space containing immobile anions is referred to as the Donnan free space. Much, if not all, of it is likely to be associated with the cell wall.

If the quantity, Q, taken up of a non-electrolyte (which can be shown neither to be accumulated nor metabolized by the cell) is measured, the volume of the water-free space can be calculated as Q/C, when C is the concentration in the external solution.

ACTIVE UPTAKE

Ionic substances

The second phase in the time relationship of salt uptake represents a continuous incorporation, often at a slower rate than the initial uptake, which is clearly different in type from the initial uptake.

All conditions that affect the metabolic activity of the cell affect this phase of salt uptake. Moreover, during this phase salt is accumulated to a concentration inside the cell which is greater than that in the surrounding medium. This process is referred to as *salt accumulation* and is an active process.[142] It continues throughout the first and second phase. It is believed to represent the accumulation of salts in the vacuole and requires the expenditure of work in transporting ions through part of the cytoplasm and the tonoplast. Both ions, cation and anion, are accumulated during this phase, often to different extents.

Experiments which show the dependence of salt accumulation on respiratory activity include those in which the effect of the removal of oxygen, the addition of cyanide, changing of temperature, or the addition of various inhibitory substances or activators such as methylene blue has been determined. All these factors show that when respiratory activity is decreased, salt accumulation is also decreased.[131] In addition to this general relationship between salt accumulation and metabolic activity, the addition of salt to a plant tissue results in a marked increase in the rate of respiration. The enhanced respiratory activity associated with salt accumulation is called *salt respiration.* When salt accumulation is inhibited by the addition of cyanide, so also is the salt respiration. This close correlation between respiratory activity and salt accumulation has led to the belief that part of the respiratory system is directly connected with the accumulation of salt.

Lundegårdh[98] has proposed that anions form a complex with cytochrome. In barley roots the oxidation-reduction state of the cytochrome can be observed by absorption spectrophotometry and it can be shown that it changes on addition of salt. Lundegårdh postulated a mechanism whereby the iron of the cytochrome complexes with an external anion, transports it through the cytoplasm and liberates it at the site of reduction; cations enter by a process of exchange with the hydrogen ions which are produced during respiration (Fig. 8.5).

According to this hypothesis the maximum number of anions accumulated should be equal to the number of electrons transported by the cytochrome, which can be determined from the rate of oxygen uptake. Attempts to demonstrate a general relationship between salt and oxygen uptake have succeeded, but claims have been made that more anions may be taken up than the equivalent of the oxygen uptake.[130] Moreover, there is the biophysical problem that salt accumulation takes place in the vacuole, whilst the cytochromes concerned in respiration are thought to be largely confined to the mitochondria. There have therefore been a number of suggestions that other stages in respiration, probably involving phosphorylated derivatives, may be concerned in salt uptake. The observation that treatment of tissue with dinitrophenol results in a reduction in salt uptake (but not of oxygen consumption) gives support to this view.

According to Lundegårdh's mechanism, it would not be possible

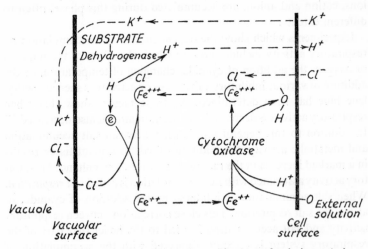

Fig. 8.5. Diagram to indicate the mechanism of salt (or anion) absorption proposed by Lundegårdh. The iron of cytochrome is oxidised at the cell surface from ferrous to ferric: it takes up an additional chloride ion (or other anion) to balance the extra charge. It moves to the tonoplast where the chloride is liberated into the vacuole and simultaneously the iron is reduced to the ferrous state. The cytochrome returns to the outside surface and continues the cyclic process. Cations enter by exchange with the hydrogen ions produced

to accumulate more cations than anions, but some plant tissues accumulate excess cations and others excess anions, dependent on the chemical nature and valency of the ions in the external solutions. When differential uptake of ions takes place, other changes must occur in the tissue to maintain electrical neutrality. For example, when excess cations are taken up in the vacuole the tissue may preserve neutrality by accumulating organic acids which are produced in the cytoplasm during metabolism. This effect has been observed in a number of roots when they are supplied with a salt containing a relatively mobile cation and a less mobile anion (e.g. potassium sulphate).[147]

Generalized carrier mechanisms

The Lundegårdh hypothesis is one particular form of a general carrier mechanism. In order to accumulate a substance within a permeability barrier, one possible mechanism is to transport the substance through the membrane, not in a free form but in the form of a complex. If on the outside of the membrane conditions are such as to favour the formation of the complex and on the inside such as to favour the dissociation of the complex, this would provide a mechanism for accumulation across the membrane (Fig. 8.6). The kinetics

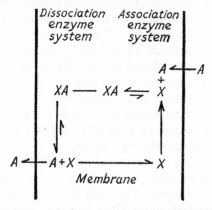

Fig. 8.6. A diagram to illustrate a generalized carrier mechanism for accumulation of substances by plant cells

of potassium accumulation by a number of root tissues has been shown to be similar in form to a simple enzyme catalysed reaction.[47] This is consistent with the suggestion, but does not establish that a complex might be formed between the ion and some carrier. Furthermore the addition of rubidium ions has been shown to inhibit competitively the uptake of potassium ions, although further detailed study showed that an explanation in terms of competition by ions for a single carrier in a membrane is inadequate.

The nature of the carrier will determine the nature of the substance accumulated. Glucose is accumulated by plant tissues to a considerable extent under conditions of active respiratory metabolism. It has been suggested that glucose could be converted to glucose phosphate in the cytoplasm, transported across the tonoplast, and then at the vacuole hydrolysed into glucose and phosphate. This would mean that glucose was transported in the form of glucose phosphate. Adenosine triphosphate (ATP) and hexokinase would be required to phosphorylate the glucose, and the regeneration of ATP would be dependent on active respiration. At the tonoplast, phosphatase could catalyse the hydrolysis of glucose phosphate to glucose and free phosphate. Such a carrier mechanism would be related to respiratory activity and capable of continuous recycling. Continuous accumulation would require a spatial separation of the condensing and hydrolytic enzymes, suggesting a predominance of condensing enzyme in the outer part of the cell or membrane and a dominance of hydrolysing enzyme near the vacuole or on the inner side of the membrane. At present there is no convincing experimental evidence that the particular enzyme localization suggested above for glucose, exists, but this example serves to illustrate the principle.

An amphoteric molecule, e.g. lecithin, could serve as a carrier for the simultaneous accumulation of both cations and anions. Alternatively, two carriers, one concerned with anions and the other with cations, may be present. If one carrier only is concerned, it must change its state in time so that at one time it is acting as an anion and at another as a cation carrier. ATP may be consumed either in the formation or functioning of a carrier.

The use of isotopes has permitted for the first time the measurement of the rate of influx and efflux and not merely the net flux (which is given by chemical analysis alone) of ion into the cell. Detailed measurements of ion fluxes into plant cells compared with the measured electrical potential difference between the cell and the surrounding medium has established the existence of ion 'pumps' which actively move ions against an electrochemical potential gradient. Dainty and MacRobbie have shown for *Nitellopsis obtusa* an inwardly directed (accumulation) pump for chloride ions and an outwardly directed (excretory) sodium ion pump. By analysis of the average concentrations in the vacuole and cytoplasm and measurements of the potentials at these sites in the cell, it has been suggested that the chloride pump is located at the tonoplast and the sodium pump at the plasmalemma, but owing to the complex heterogeneity of the cytoplasm it is not possible to interpret measurements concerning localized concentrations or potentials unequivocally.

A completely different view has been proposed primarily with respect to animal cells. Ions or other molecules are believed to be bound to the surface of membranes in the cytoplasm; by movements of the membranes the absorbed substance may become enclosed in

132

an invagination and ultimately isolated as a vesicle. Subsequent decomposition of the vesicle may result in the release of ions in a free state. So far, there is little evidence that this mechanism, which depends on active metabolism to provide continuous changes in membrane structure, operates in the plant cell.

Briggs, Hope, and Robertson have summarized the features of salt accumulation as including the active transport of at least one ion, a sufficiently great resistance to its passive efflux so that a large difference in concentration between inside and outside is maintained, and the passive movement of the ion of opposite sign along the electrochemical potential gradient created.

The movement of water molecules *per se* in and out of a plant cell has probably little to do with plant metabolism, but there is good evidence that the movement of salts is related to metabolic activity. But precisely how salt uptake is linked to the energy yielding process of plant metabolism has still to be discovered.

GENERAL REFERENCES

T. A. BENNET-CLARK (1959) 'Water relation of cells'. In *Plant Physiology*. Vol. 11. ed. F. C. Steward. Academic Press.

G. E. BRIGGS, A. B. HOPE, and R. N. ROBERTSON (1961) *Electrolytes and Plant Cells*. Blackwell.

J. DAINTY (1962) 'Ion transport and electrical potentials in plant cells'. *Ann. Rev. Pl. Physiol.* **13**, 379.

R. O. SLAYTER (1962) 'Internal water relations in higher plants'. *Ann. Rev. Pl. Physiol.* **13**, 351.

CHAPTER NINE

Water Relations of the Whole Plant

The supply of water to the whole plant involves not only uptake by individual root cells but its subsequent movement to all the tissues of the plant. The mechanism by which water rises to the top of a tall tree has intrigued plant physiologists for many years. It is considered here as a biophysical problem and placed in perspective with other plant processes. Only after the biophysical features have been discussed is it possible to consider how far water movement through the plant is dependent upon cellular metabolism.

Water movement through the whole plant involves the uptake of water through the root hairs, the transport of water through the plant and its subsequent loss from the leaves, petiole, and stem surface into the atmosphere. This movement of water and subsequent loss by transpiration involves by far the greatest water traffic in the plant, the amount of water concerned in metabolic processes being negligible by comparison.

Water Uptake by the Root

OSMOTIC RELATIONSHIPS

The osmotic relationships of a single cell have been discussed in Chapter 8. Water will enter the root hairs from the soil when the S.P. of the root hair exceeds the S.P. of the soil water. The latter depends both on the surface forces which bind water to the soil particles, measured as the soil moisture tension, and on the osmotic contents of the soil solution. The soil moisture tension increases greatly as the soil moisture content falls, ultimately rising to such a value that the plant can no longer take water from the soil. The value at this stage (called the permanent wilting percentage) will depend very much on the physical properties of the soil, being higher in clay soils than in sand. It corresponds to a S.P. of the order of 15 atmospheres.

Ursprung and Blum have attempted to determine whether the

movement of water through the root from the root hairs to the xylem could be explained solely by osmosis, the water passing from vacuole to vacuole of adjoining cells. If this were the case, one would expect there to be a gradient in suction pressure from the outermost to the innermost tissues. Ursprung and Blum tried to show this experimentally by taking thin sections from different parts of the root and observing their change in volume when placed in solutions of different osmotic pressure. Their observations showed that there was indeed a progressive increase in suction pressure from the root hair across the root tissues into the xylem. The one marked discrepancy existed at the endodermis, the cells immediately inside the endodermis having a lower suction pressure than those outside. The cells of the endodermis have a Casperian strip around the radial and transverse walls which reduces their permeability to water, and whilst the passage cells probably permit considerable flux it is doubtful if they account for all the movement into the stele of the root. In order to prepare sections of the root the stem must be cut down; when this is done the tension which normally exists in the xylem (see later) is released, causing water to flood back into the xylem of the root. Owing to difficulty of permeation through the endodermis wall, water will tend to accumulate on the inside, lowering the S.P. of these cells. Thus it is argued that this single discrepancy is an experimental artefact and does not vitiate the view that there is a suction pressure gradient through the root in the direction from inside to outside. Water movement may alternatively take place largely through the cell wall and free space of the cortical cells without entering the cell vacuoles. Mees and Weatherley showed that the water flux per unit pressure difference through detached tomato roots was twice as great for a hydrostatic pressure as for an equal osmotic pressure gradient. This suggests that mass flow as well as diffusional flow may be important in root tissue.

The movement of bromide ions through barley roots was investigated by Broyer, who found that radioactive potassium ions were taken up from potassium bromide in about the same quantity, regardless as to whether the root had previously accumulated potassium bromide or not. Moreover, the bromide taken up appeared in the xylem exudate equally in both cases and at a concentration higher than that in the cell vacuoles. He suggested that salts pass mainly through the free space and not through cell vacuoles. The ions must be taken up by the surface cells but then move into the xylem passively.

Simultaneous measurements of the rate of water uptake and salt uptake have failed to establish any simple relationship between them. As yet there is no evidence for movement of salt against a concentration gradient through a tissue, so that the process of salt accumulation is probably confined to the cell vacuole.

ROOT PRESSURE

From the time of Stephen Hales plant physiologists have been intrigued by the fact that when stems are cut from certain plants, e.g. vine or marrow, liquid is forced out from the cut surface. If a manometer is placed on the cut surface, pressures of three to five atmospheres can be measured. This ability of a plant to force out liquid under pressure has been called root pressure. The root pressure can also be measured by placing the roots in an external solution and then, after decapitation, adjusting the osmotic pressure of the external solution so that no liquid escapes from the cut surface. Then the root pressure is balanced by the osmotic pressure of the external solution, and this gives the most reliable method of measurement of root pressure. Root pressure shows both a diurnal and a seasonal rhythm, in general, the pressure being greater at midday and in spring.

Various factors affect root pressure. Roots placed in an atmosphere deficient in oxygen have a considerably lower root pressure. If roots are treated with potassium cyanide, which suppresses respiration, root pressure is again considerably reduced. Indoleacetic acid stimulates the root pressure of tomato roots at low concentrations but is inhibitory at high concentrations. It is clear that root pressure is related to the metabolic activity of the root.

The magnitude of root pressure seems to have little relationship to the rate of loss of water from the top of the plant. When a plant is placed under conditions where the air is saturated with water vapour so that the transpiration loss is reduced to zero, root pressure may continue to operate and force water out of the vein endings in the leaves. This phenomenon is called *guttation*.

The volume of the exudate from the cut stem is small, probably some 5 per cent of the total amount of water which is being transported through the plant. Root pressure is not therefore believed to be the primary mechanism by which water is moved through the root. It is a subsidiary force, of negligible magnitude at certain times of the year, producing only a small fraction of the total water movement required for maximal transpiration.[85] It is absent from conifers. The primary movement upon which the plant depends for its water supply must be related to osmotic forces; root pressure is an additional force dependent on the metabolic activity of the plant. The mechanism by which metabolism gives rise to root pressure is still unknown.

MEASUREMENT OF NET WATER UPTAKE BY THE ROOT

The water uptake of a plant or cut shoot is generally determined with a potometer (Fig. 9.1). This measures the volume (or in other designs the weight) of water which is being taken in by the root of a plant or

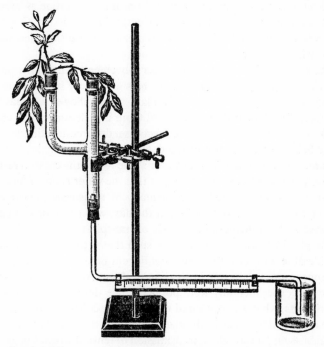

Fig. 9.1. The potometer in which the rate of uptake of water by a cut shoot is measured by the movement of water along the horizontal capillary (indicated by momentarily moving the beaker and introducing an air bubble into the end)

cut end of a stem. Errors may arise owing to temperature changes of the apparatus, and to minimize these it is important that the volume of water should be small in relation to the size of the plant. If a cut shoot is used, care must be taken to see that no air enters the cut surfaces.

Movement of Water through the Wood

The water, which has moved from the root hair to the xylem, must now pass up the stem. Measurements have been made of the resistance of wood to the movement of water through it,[49] by measuring the amount of water which can be forced through a piece of wood when water is supplied at one end subject to pressure. Forces of only a few atmospheres produce an appreciable flow. It is found that there is no polarity in resistance to movement. Furthermore, there is little change in the rate of movement through a piece of wood after it has been killed by steaming or by poisons until such time as various products accumulate and block the paths in the tissue. Conifers, which have only tracheids, offer a greater resistance than deciduous trees, which have vessels in their wood.

The xylem is the main path of water movement through the plant. If a ring of xylem is removed from the stem a very marked loss of turgidity of the upper part of the plant soon follows, whereas, by contrast, if a phloem ring is removed there is little immediate effect on the state of turgidity. The xylem acts as a dead connecting system water being lost at the top of the column and being regained at the bottom. The continuous loss of water at the top of the column results in a pull on the water in the xylem, so that the water is under tension. This can be demonstrated experimentally by measuring the external diameter of a tree trunk throughout the day, which can be shown to decrease with an increase in the rate of transpiration.

The physical structure of water is such that it can be subjected to considerable tension without any contingent breakdown resulting in the appearance of vapour in the liquid phase. Attempts to demonstrate this experimentally were popular some time ago, but in these experiments, what was measured was often the coherence of water to some other surface (such as the glass containing the water) rather than of water itself. Nevertheless, transmission of tension stresses in excess of 100 atmospheres were observed in these experimental water columns, a force far greater than that required to pull water up the xylem to reach the top of the tallest tree. When the water has arrived at the top of the xylem it moves out from the xylem to the mesophyll along a suction pressure gradient.

Transpiration—Loss of Water from the Aerial Parts of the Plant

MEASUREMENT OF TRANSPIRATION RATE

The rate of loss of water by the plant in the process of transpiration can be measured by a number of methods. The water vapour given off by plants may be collected and condensed or determined in the vapour phase by physical or chemical methods. Alternatively, the change in total weight of a pot plant can be measured, provided that loss from the soil is prevented. A suitable balance is required, since the relative change in weight may be quite small, if a large volume of soil is present. The loss in weight of a detached plant organ can be determined more easily and accurately. If the plant is in the light there is in addition a gain in weight due to photosynthesis; if in the dark, a loss in weight, due to respiration. In most conditions the changes in weight resulting from these two processes are negligible compared with the decrease in weight due to the loss of water vapour.

THE NATURE OF TRANSPIRATION

Loss of water from a woody stem with a covering of bark takes place largely through the lenticels, with only a small loss through the bark tissue. Cuticular transpiration represents only 1/10th or 1/20th of the total loss from a leaf, as shown by comparing the loss of weight of an untreated detached leaf with that of a similar leaf in which the stomata have been blocked.[13] The loss of water from a leaf surface takes place mainly through the stomata, the water vapour originating from the wet surface of mesophyll cell walls which open on to the sub-stomatal cavity. If the air surrounding the leaf is not fully saturated, water will evaporate from the free water surface within the leaf, diffuse through the stomata or lenticels and out into the air.

Transpiration is a purely physical process and evaporation and transpiration can both be considered in terms of Fick's law of diffusion. An equation can be written relating the rate of transpiration, R, to the following principal factors: (i) the difference in water vapour content of the air within the leaf and that outside, (ii) the area available for evaporation, (iii) the distance through which diffusion must take place, and (iv) a constant, K, the coefficient of diffusion of water vapour in air. The rate of transpiration,

$$R = KA \frac{(C_i^{H_2O} - C_0^{H_2O})}{d}$$

139

when A represents the mean area of the diffusion path, d represents the mean length of the path, and C_iH_2O, C_0H_2O are the concentrations of water vapour at the mesophyll wall surface and in the air respectively. These quantities are not easily determined for the complex structure of a leaf.

From a consideration of this equation the factors which affect the rate of transpiration can be deduced. For example, factors which affect the difference in water vapour content are of two kinds, those which affect the humidity of the surrounding air, e.g. air temperature, and those which affect the humidity in the leaf, e.g. leaf temperature. Within the leaf, the free water surface from which evaporation takes place is in the wall of the cells lining the sub-stomatal cavity. The water within the cell is not pure water and therefore its vapour pressure is less than that of pure water. However, for the range of suction pressures occurring within the plant cell, this is a small correction, and a change in suction pressure of the mesophyll cells will not change the concentration gradient sufficiently to affect significantly the rate of transpiration. When the leaf is fully turgid the water contained in the mesophyll wall will fill the fine micro-spaces of the wall and will have a plane surface. When transpiration takes place to a considerable extent the superficial water layer may be lost and the water will retreat within the pores of the cell wall. The water surface will become curved rather than plane, and this will result in a lowering of the vapour pressure and hence of the rate of evaporation.

THE TRANSPIRATION PATH

The non-stomatal external diffusion path

The diffusion path for transpiration originates at the mesophyll cell wall, continues across the sub-stomatal cavity, through the stomatal pore, and then through a layer of still air beyond the leaf surface. This layer of still air, referred to as the *shearing layer*, is the air path through which the diffusing water molecule must pass before it can be regarded as free and part of the external air. Its thickness will vary with wind velocity and will be greater the larger the total area of the leaf. Its magnitude in still air can be calculated from the physical dimensions of the leaf; this gives a maximal value since the air is in fact never completely still.

The stomatal path

At the end of the nineteenth century many workers doubted whether the relatively small stomatal openings in the leaf could provide the major pathway for the gaseous exchange of plants. F. F. Blackman[13] showed that when the stomata on the lower epidermis of leaves of *Nerium oleander* were blocked the transpiration rate was reduced to 10 per cent of its previous value. This suggested that cuticular transpiration was only 10 per cent of the total. Brown and Escombe approached the same problem by means of physical models. They determined experimentally the rate of diffusion of gases through lead discs containing small holes. First, they placed a lead disc with a single hole over the top of a beaker containing sodium hydroxide. As carbon dioxide entered it reacted with the soda and from the change in strength of the soda it was possible to calculate the amount of carbon dioxide which had entered in a given time. Their observations showed that with a single hole the rate of diffusion was proportional to the perimeter rather than to the area of the disc. This fact could have been predicted from the physical laws of diffusion as a special case when the thickness of the disc is small compared with the diameter of the hole.* Second, Brown and Escombe[27] investigated the rate of diffusion through a disc with a number of holes. They compared the rate of diffusion with that of a similar disc with a single large hole whose area was the same as that of the total area of all the smaller holes. The rate of diffusion through the multiperforate disc was greater than that through the disc with the single hole, the difference being greatest when the holes were relatively far apart. It can be shown that their results are consistent with expectation from the physical laws of diffusion, and that the rates of diffusion observed by them are consistent with the established value for the diffusion constant of carbon dioxide in air. If the dimensions of stomata are known the maximum diffusion which can take place through them can be calculated; it is far in excess of the observed rate of transpiration.

Measurement of stomatal aperture

The simplest method of measuring stomatal aperture is by direct observation with a microscope preferably fitted with a vertical light source. The aperture can be measured at various depths by means of focusing so that both the aperture and effective length can be determined. Difficulties arise in the case of hairy leaves, leaves with sunken stomata, and leaves in which the cuticle overhangs the guard cells. An alternative method devised by Lloyd is to strip off the epidermis,

---

* Since the effective length of the hole is $l + 2\pi r/4$, where l is the thickness of the septum, and $2\pi r/4$ the end correction for the two ends, the ratio of the area of the pore to its effective length is $\pi r^2/l + 2\pi r/4$, which is proportional to r, if $l \ll r$.

plunge it rapidly into absolute alcohol, in an attempt to fix the stomata in the state in which they were on the leaf, and then examine it microscopically. Even so, there is a possibility of some change during the time taken for this procedure. A simple qualitative method to

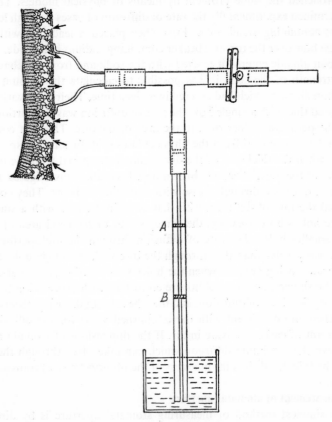

Fig. 9.2. *The simple porometer. The pressure is reduced in the poro-meter cup and liquid is drawn up the centre capillary tube. As air enters the cup through the stomata of the leaf the liquid falls and the time taken to fall from A to B is a measure of the diffusion resist-ance of the leaf*

determine the relative stomatal size is by the use of various liquids of different surface tension. A small drop is placed on the leaf surface and penetration or failure to penetrate is noted. Penetration into the sub-stomatal space is shown by a darkening of the leaf area surrounding the point of penetration owing to the air space becoming filled with liquid. Alcohol, benzene, and xylol form a progressive series, alcohol penetrating only widely open stomata but xylol entering those which are slightly open. An alternative method is to form an impression of the stomata using a silicone rubber liquid which hardens on the leaf and can then be stripped off.

The classical instrument for studies of *relative* stomatal aperture is the porometer (Fig. 9.2). In this method air is drawn bodily through the leaf and the rate of movement of air is determined under a fixed pressure gradient. A cup is sealed on to the leaf surface and the air pressure within it is lowered by suction. Air enters through the stomata in that part of the leaf outside the cup, moves through the intercellular spaces and enters the cup via the stomata within to restore normal atmospheric pressure in the cup. The time course of pressure within the cup is observed, using a manometer. An alternative method using the instrument called a diffusion porometer has been devised to avoid a mass flow of air through the leaf. In this apparatus the porometer cup is filled with a gas, such as hydrogen. When the cup is sealed, hydrogen will pass from the cup through the stomata and into the leaf more rapidly than air enters the cup from the leaf. The time course of the subsequent fall of pressure in the cup is recorded. Successive measurements with either type of apparatus result in a flushing of the leaf with air or hydrogen and some drying out of the leaf takes place. Also, changes in the carbon dioxide content of the gas in the porometer cup during the experiment (particularly probable if the plant is illuminated) may affect the stomatal aperture. The times measured in the porometer depend on the combined resistance to gas flow offered by the stomata and the intercellular spaces which connect the sub-stomatal cavity within the cup with those outside. It is generally believed that the limiting effect is that of the stomata within the cup, but this may not always be the case.

An estimate of the stomatal contribution to the total diffusion path is most easily determined from the measurement of pore size and depth; these can be best obtained by direct observation combined with Lloyd's method.

The non-stomatal internal diffusion path

The remaining part of the diffusion path is across the sub-stomatal cavity. Its relative magnitude will vary considerably according to the anatomy of the leaf, depending on both the total surface area of the cells abutting on to the sub-stomatal cavity and on the mean length of path across the sub-stomatal cavity. Attempts have been made to cut a series of sections and examine the three-dimensional structure of the sub-stomatal cavity. This is an arduous experimental task.

There is an alternative physical method by which the overall contribution of the sub-stomatal cavity and the stomata, taken together, can be determined. In order to do this an indicator of the rate of loss of water vapour, such as a piece of paper impregnated with cobalt chloride, is placed on the leaf surface.[107] This will change colour from blue to pink as it takes up water vapour. The cobalt chloride is placed in immediate contact with the leaf surface and the time for a given colour change to take place determined. Now the same piece of cobalt chloride paper is placed a known distance away from a free water surface. This is conveniently done by taking as a free water surface a piece of moistened blotting paper and placing the cobalt chloride impregnated paper a fixed distance above it, using a plastic spacer. If the time for the change of colour in the cobalt chloride paper is the same for the leaf as for the physical model, the leaf may be regarded as having an equivalent air diffusion path equal to the thickness of the plastic spacer. Hence it is possible to determine the total equivalent diffusion path in centimetres for the stomata and the sub-stomatal cavity combined. If the physical dimensions of the stomata are known the diffusion path equivalent to the stomata can be calculated and hence the relative contribution of the sub-stomatal cavity and stomata determined.

Relative magnitude of the parts of the diffusion path

Thus it is possible to estimate approximately the relative contributions of the three parts of the diffusion path. For a sunflower leaf with widely open stomata these values are approximately one unit for the stomata, one unit for the shearing layer (but dependent on wind conditions), and three for the substomatal cavity, i.e. the stomata represent only one-fifth of the total diffusion path. As the stomata close, their contribution to the total path will increase. It follows that since when fully open any change in the stomatal path is a change in only one-fifth of the total path, stomatal changes have little effect on the rate of transpiration. But when the stomata are nearly closed the stomata will exert a considerable degree of control over the rate of transpiration. Stålfelt experimentally demonstrated with leaves of *Betula pubescens* that the degree of control was less the more widely open the stomata (Fig. 9.3).

The same considerations determine the rate of diffusion of carbon dioxide into the leaf and hence the rate of photosynthesis. But the total diffusion path for carbon dioxide into the leaf must also include

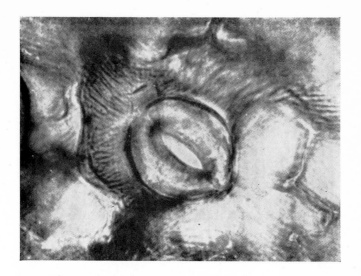

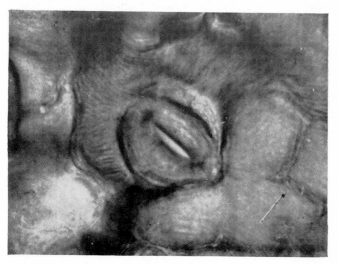

Plate 5. *The open stoma of* Cyclamen persicum (*above*) *and the same after puncture of the upper guard cell* (*below*). *The inner wall of the punctured guard cell has straightened suggesting that stomatal movement cannot be due to wall structure but is dependent on the osmotic properties of the guard cells.* (*After O. V. S. Heath*[63])

diffusion through the cell wall and entry into the chloroplast. Thus in addition to the three parts of the diffusion path which were concerned in transpiration, namely stomata, shearing layer, and substomatal cavity, there are two additional terms, the cell wall and the internal cell path, to be taken into account. By comparing observed rates of photosynthesis for a sunflower leaf with the calculated maximum rate of diffusion through the stomata alone, it appears that the total equivalent diffusion path for carbon dioxide is of the order of nine times that due to the stomatal path alone. Hence with fully open stomata, changes in the stomata are changes affecting only one-

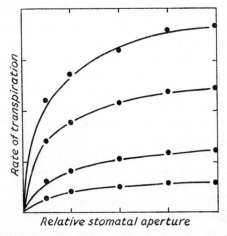

Fig. 9.3. The effect of stomatal aperture on the rate of transpiration from the leaf of Betula pubescens. The four curves are at differing light intensities. (After M. G. Stalfelt[140])

tenth of the total diffusion path for photosynthesis and can have only a small effect on the rate. But as the stomata close they begin to have a greater effect; furthermore, closure will affect the rate of transpiration more than the rate of photosynthesis and will preferentially decrease transpiration relative to photosynthesis.

In the above discussion the important effect of the anatomy of the leaf on gas exchange has been emphasized. Classically the effect of external morphology was emphasized. Plants with sunken stomata and/or hairy surfaces were regarded as potentially likely to have lower rates of transpiration and thus to be adapted to live in drier places. But measurements by Maximov showed that all such plants did not have significantly lower transpiration rates than plants without such characteristics when measured under the same conditions of adequate water supply. It is therefore important to distinguish between *xeromorphic* leaves which have specialized morphological characteristics that have sometimes been thought to limit water loss and leaves of those plants called *xerophytes* which actually grow under dry (xerophytic) conditions.

FACTORS WHICH INFLUENCE STOMATAL APERTURE

The opening and closing of stomata depends on changes in the suction pressure of the guard cells relative to that of the surrounding epidermal cells (see Plate 5). The wall of the guard cells is thickened in such a way that changes in volume result in movement of the guard cells relative to one another; when they swell they open the aperture between them and when they shrink they close it. Early measurements of the osmotic pressure of the guard cells showed that the osmotic pressure was greater when the stomata were open than when closed.

Numerous factors influence the opening and closing of the stomata. It has long been realized that, in general, stomata open in the light and close in the dark. This was assumed to be the cause of the diurnal changes in stomatal aperture. Lloyd and Loftfield both attempted to show that the starch content of the guard cells showed a diurnal change, in a manner correlated with the change in aperture of the stomata. This has been most conclusively demonstrated recently by Williams,[156] who devised an approximately quantitative method for measuring starch content. Another major factor which influences the opening and closing of stomata is the concentration of carbon dioxide. Darwin found that a high concentration of carbon dioxide caused the stomata to close. Linsbauer[95] showed that regardless of whether the leaf was in the light or dark, provided the concentration of carbon dioxide was sufficiently high, the stomata would close. This has been confirmed in recent work by Heath and his collaborators,[64] who have shown an interaction between light intensity and carbon dioxide concentration. Thus in darkness, 0·017 per cent carbon dioxide was required to cause closure of the stomata; with an illumination of ninety foot-candles 0·049 per cent was required, and with eight hundred foot-candles 0·084 per cent was required. In a systematic investigation of the effect of varying light intensity and carbon dioxide concentration Heath and Milthorpe showed that the effects of light and of carbon dioxide were partially dependent and partially independent (Fig. 9.4).

146

The classical explanation of the way in which changes in light intensity or carbon dioxide concentration affect stomatal aperture was to assume that these factors influenced the pH of the cells surrounding the sub-stomatal cavity. In the light, when photosynthesis takes place, carbon dioxide is consumed; in the dark, carbon dioxide is produced in respiration. Therefore it would be expected that the guard cells would be relatively more acid in dark and more alkaline in light. It follows that acidity should result in closure and alkalinity in opening. This has been observed experimentally by Sayre[133] and

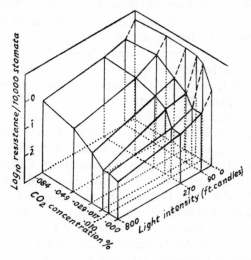

Fig. 9.4. *The relationship between light intensity concentration of carbon dioxide and the resistance of the stomata (i.e. the reciprocal of stomatal aperture). (After O. V. S. Heath and J. Russell[65])*

by Scarth,[134] who compared the stomatal aperture, the sugar content, the starch content, and the pH of the guard cells over a range of conditions. They showed that closure was related to an acid pH and opening to an alkaline one, and that corresponding changes in sugar and starch took place. This explanation was claimed to be substantiated by the subsequent discovery of the enzyme phosphorylase which catalyses the condensation of glucose-1-phosphate to form starch and phosphate. The equilibrium position of this is more towards the formation of starch in more acid systems. The more acid the system the more starch is present relative to sugar, hence the lower the osmotic pressure of the guard cells and closure takes place. The guard cells of some plants, e.g. the onion, contain no starch, but

147

here it is argued that the effect of pH is on the balance between hexoses and some form of condensed product such as sucrose.

The classical theory assumes that closure is the normal state of the stomata and that opening takes place as a consequence of a change in pH induced by some external factor such as light. Williams[157] put forward the alternative view that stomata are normally open and that factors influencing stomatal aperture operate by causing them to close. He has postulated that active water movement is necessary to keep the stomata closed and that in light, processes must take place which partially overcome this active movement. Since in general there is little real evidence for active water movement in plant cells (see Chapter 8), this must be regarded at the present time only as one possible hypothesis. There are certain points which make it difficult to believe that the classical theory is wholly adequate. The first of these is the well established fact that on certain plants grown under normal conditions the stomata undergo a diurnal rhythm. If the plants are placed under reasonably constant conditions the diurnal rhythm of opening and closing persists for some days.[100, 58] No biochemical explanation of this or indeed of rhythmic behaviour patterns in plants in general is yet available.[28] Williams claimed that whereas opening takes place quickly in the light, closure in the dark is relatively slow. Furthermore, once closure has begun it is relatively difficult to stop, whereas opening can be suppressed whilst it is taking place. Closure can be prevented by adding poisons or maltreating the cell. All the factors which influence stomatal movement are not yet adequately explained by any theory.

WATER BALANCE OF THE PLANT

The factors which influence the uptake of water by the root are not the same as those which influence the loss of water from the leaves and shoot by transpiration. During the day when the temperature rises, the transpiration rate increases, and there will be an increased tension on the water in the xylem which will tend to result in an increase in water uptake. However, the increase in water uptake may lag in time behind the increased transpiration, and there will be a period of net loss of water from the plant as a whole. Indeed, the rate of water uptake may reach a maximum value which is less than the maximum rate of transpiration, when there will be a continual loss in net water content of the plant and the plant will wilt. The plant is said to be in a state of negative water balance. When conditions change during the evening and the rate of transpiration falls, the rate of water uptake may remain at its earlier value so that during this period there is an excess water uptake compared with water loss. This restores the plant to a state of water balance, allowing it to make a net gain equal to the net loss of water during the day (see Fig. 9.5). It may be said that all plants are to a less or greater extent in a potential state of wilting during the day when conditions favour high transpiration. When water loss exceeds uptake by the leaves the water menisci will retreat within the pores of the mesophyll cell wall. This will lower the vapour

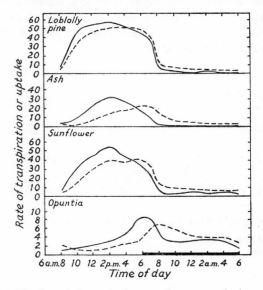

Fig. 9.5. The diurnal change in the rate of water uptake (- - - - - -) compared with that in the rate of transpiration (————) for four plants. (After P. J. Kramer[83])

pressure and hence the rate of transpiration. At this stage the leaf may not show any visible signs of wilting and it is referred to as being in a state of incipient wilting. Further water loss leads to a change in external appearance with drooping of the leaves. If the plant recovers when conditions are changed so as to reduce transpiration, the plant is said to be in a state of temporary wilting. If the plant can only be revived by supplying water to the roots, the state is one of permanent wilting and may lead ultimately to irreversible wilting and the death of the plant.

The onset of drought is determined by a relative deficiency of soil moisture under atmospheric conditions which favour high rates of transpiration. Its appearance will be delayed the larger the root absorbing surface and the smaller the leaf area of the plant. Ultimately, continued water loss results in dehydration of the protoplasm; the degree of dehydration which is irreversible varying appreciably between different species. These considerations determine the degree of drought resistance of a plant.

The phenomena of root pressure and stomatal movement are examples of physiological responses which are dependent on metabolism. But the precise explanation of these in metabolic terms is still not known. Other phenomena discussed in this chapter, e.g. the movement of water through a living tree, are probably fully understandable in biophysical terms.

GENERAL REFERENCES

H. H. DIXON (1914) *Transpiration and the Ascent of Sap in Plants.* Macmillan

K. N. H. GREENIDGE (1957) 'Ascent of sap'. *Ann. Rev. Pl. Phys.* **8,** 237

O. V. S. HEATH (1959) 'Light and carbon dioxide in stomatal movements'. *Encycl. Pl. Physiol.* **17/2,** 415

P. J. KRAMER (1949) *Plant and Soil Water Relationships.* McGraw-Hill

N. A. MAXIMOV (1929) *The Plant in Relation to Water*, trs. R. H. Yapp. Allen & Unwin

CHAPTER TEN

Translocation

The preceding chapters have considered the movement of water and salts into the root and thence through the plant. Of equal importance is the movement of the products of photosynthesis from the leaf to the shoot, root, or developing fruit. The growth and development of the mature plant is dependent on the movement or translocation of organic substances from one part of a plant to another. The manner in which this takes place has been discussed since the early seventeenth century. At that time Harvey discovered the circulation of the blood in animals and a similar circulation of sap in plants, up through the wood and down through the bark, was suggested by Meritt in 1664. By the middle of the nineteenth century the structure of the phloem and, in particular, of the sieve tubes was known and a movement of food substances through sieve tubes was postulated. The mass movement of food substances through the plant is of a magnitude approaching that of the movement of water. For example, measurements of the growth of a potato tuber show rates of accumulation of 50 g of sucrose in 100 days; if this substance is transported in a solution of a concentration of the order of 1 per cent, 5 litres of solution must move into the tuber.

MEASUREMENT OF TRANSLOCATION

Translocation is most easily measured by determining the loss of carbohydrate from the leaf. Sachs compared the loss of dry weight from a darkened attached leaf with that from a darkened detached leaf and attributed the difference to translocation loss. Other observers have determined the change in dry weight of different portions of the plant; then, from the gain in root and stem weight as compared with the total incorporation of material by the leaves as measured by photosynthesis, the percentage of assimilate which has been translocated can be calculated. Measurements show that in certain plants translocation from the leaves takes place equally in the day and at night, whereas in other plants translocation may take place relatively more in the day than at night.

THE ANATOMY OF PHLOEM

The phloem is now known to be the tissue mainly concerned in the movement of organic substances. The phloem of higher plants (Fig. 10.1) contains sieve tubes, each consisting of a longitudinal series of elongated elements, termed sieve tube segments, joined linearly together and having their end walls perforated by many pores to form sieve plates. This arrangement is most readily seen in

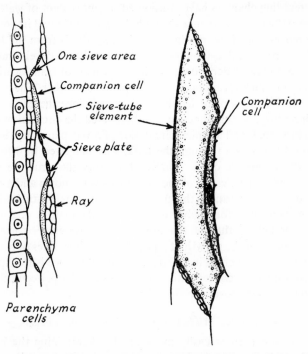

Fig. 10.1. The tissue elements of phloem. (After K. Esau)

many herbaceous dicotyledons in which the common end wall between contiguous sieve tube segments is approximately transverse, while the pores may be relatively coarse, so that strands of cytoplasm passing through them may be distinguished. In gymnosperms a less highly developed structural element, the sieve cell, is present. In the angiosperms, the sieve tubes are accompanied by specialized cells which have dense contents and an active metabolism, the companion cells. As the sieve tube segment approaches maturity the nucleus disappears, and often about the same time the cytoplasm changes its structure to a colloidal slime. None of these changes occurs in the associated companion cells in which the nucleus remains intact. A glucosan substance, called callose, is sometimes deposited around the pores of the sieve plate and later over the whole of it but some now believe that this is a consequence of damage resulting from injury. In the mature state the sieve tube still retains protoplasmic continuity from one element to the adjacent one, but the cross-sectional area of connecting threads may become very small. It is probable that the sieve tube segment can still be plasmolysed in its mature state, plasmolysis taking place more easily from the side walls than from the sieve plate, whereas in the young sieve element plasmolysis takes place equally from all walls.[48] During later development the walls of the cell also thicken appreciably.

THE PATH OF MOVEMENT

Malpighi first showed that removal of a ring of bark inhibited the growth of roots but did not suppress the development of branches above the ring. This was also observed by Stephen Hales, who noted a greater growth of tissue on the upper side of the ring than the lower. The use of ringing to interrupt the movement of substances in the phloem has been considerably extended in later work.

Mason and Maskell[102] made an extensive study of translocation in the cotton plant. They showed that normally there was a decrease in sugar concentration from the leaves through the petiole and down the phloem and xylem of the stem. The gradient changed in magnitude during the day; the concentration increased in the leaf lamina by noon and this rise in concentration was gradually reflected in an increased concentration shortly after in the petiole, later still in the bark, but with only a small change in the wood. After part of the bark was removed from the stem (and the terminal bud also, to ensure that the main movement of carbohydrates was from the leaves down to the root), Mason and Maskell were able to show an accumulation of sugar in the bark above the ring and a depletion below. The removal of a ring of phloem had no appreciable effect on the transpiration of the part of the plant above the ring, and it was considered that no secondary effects had been introduced. In other experiments a plant with a maturing fruit was chosen, and then by a suitably placed ring it was possible to demonstrate accumulation below the ring and depletion above, demonstrating transport from leaves up to the fruit, i.e. in the direction of a decrease in concentration. In all cases, major changes in concentration were found in the phloem tissue with only minor changes in the xylem, from which it was concluded that the movement of sugar was largely through the phloem and was non-polar, taking place in the direction of decreasing concentration.

In these experiments analyses were made both for sucrose and reducing sugars, and it was shown that the diurnal fluctuations in concentration were larger for sucrose. Ringing also resulted in a greater

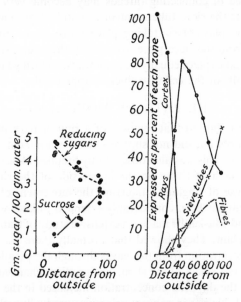

Fig. 10.2. The radial distribution of tissue elements in cotton and the change in concentration of sugars suggesting that sucrose is largely concentrated and moves in the sieve tubes. (The apparent overlap between increasing cortex and decreasing ray tissue is due to sampling; in any one piece of tissue the cortex begins where the rays end.) (After E. J. Maskell and T. G. Mason[101])

change in the concentration of sucrose than of reducing sugars. Mason and Maskell concluded that sucrose was the form in which carbohydrate was moved through the plant. When phloem tissue is cut the sap exudate can be collected and analysed. In a number of plants relatively little hexose is present. In cotton the carbohydrate is largely sucrose, but in other plants raffinose and stachyose have been shown to be the main sugars present.[165]

Further experiments have attempted to define the particular tissue of the phloem concerned. Schumacher[135] observed that the rate of translocation was greatly decreased in plants treated with eosin. Examination with a microscope showed that callose plugs had been formed on the sieve plates, and this suggested that the sieve tubes might be important in translocation. Fluorescein and other fluorescent dyes, whose location in plant tissue is easy to observe, have been used as indicators of movement and shown to move through the sieve tubes. Such experiments are not conclusive. The added substances may move in a different manner from food substances, and furthermore may be toxic and affect not only the sieve tube but also the metabolic activity of the companion cells.

Mason and Maskell[102] found that the concentration gradient of sucrose in bark was greater in the inner than outer phloem tissue. They correlated this with the presence of more sieve tubes towards the inner region of the tissue (Fig. 10.2). Since they had shown that sucrose was the mobile form of carbohydrate they deduced that its movement was largely confined to the sieve tubes. They were also able to show that the efficiency of a ring increased not proportionately with its depth but proportionate to the number of sieve tubes which had been removed by the ring. Weatherley and his co-workers[152] have been able to analyse the sap from single sieve tubes of willow by the use of aphids which feed upon them. By cutting the aphid in position on the plant it is possible to use the aphid stylet as a micro-pipette and collect the contents of a single sieve tube.[108] Analysis shows that the sieve tubes largely contain sucrose, and further that the concentration and rate of exudate from the sieve tube are consistent with those required from the observed rates of mass transfer.

The movement of other food substances

With the advent of radioactive tracers considerable work has been done on the movement of phosphate and of potassium through the plant, since both of these are readily obtainable in a radioactive form. When a plant is placed with its roots in a solution containing radioactive potassium an upward movement of radioactivity can be readily demonstrated which appears to be distributed equally between the phloem and the xylem. But if the phloem and the xylem are separated over a portion of the stem by making appropriate cuts and then placing a waxed paper between them, the radioactivity is now found to be concentrated in the xylem.[141] This indicates that the movement of inorganic ions from the root to the leaves takes place largely in the xylem but that lateral diffusion from xylem to phloem also occurs. Removal of a phloem ring does not appreciably affect the upward movement of minerals into the leaves. Hence inorganic materials move from the root hairs in which they are accumulated from the soil through the xylem and into the leaves. In the leaf they are often incorporated into organic compounds and then move down in the phloem.

The movement of nitrogen and nitrogenous compounds is more complex. Maskell and Mason[101] made measurements of the concentration gradients of nitrogen compounds in the cotton plant and the effect of ringing upon them. They found that there was a downward movement of nitrogen against a non-protein organic nitrogen concentration gradient, largely consisting of amide and amino compounds. They considered that there must be a mobile organic form moving along a positive concentration gradient, but that this gradient was concealed by the still greater negative gradient of amide and amino nitrogen. Nitrogen compounds are readily interconvertible and no single compound could be definitely identified as the mobile form either from its concentration gradient or as the substance which accumulated to the greatest extent near a ring. The sap-exudate from bark contains both amides, amino acids, and peptides.[165] In the apple tree, and probably trees in general, a large part of the nitrogen moving up the trunk is organic since, generally, reduction to the amino form takes place largely in the root and then organic nitrogen is moved up to the leaves. From the results of ringing experiments it would appear that this movement is not confined to either the phloem or the xylem, but that both tissues take part in the upward movement of nitrogen. In other plants and probably in cotton, nitrogen is largely moved from the root to the leaves in the form of inorganic nitrogen. In this case it is believed to move largely in the xylem. In the leaf it is converted to an organic form and then moves down the phloem to the other parts of the plant.

THE RATE OF TRANSLOCATION[32]

The rate of translocation may be considered with respect to the movement of some solution which flows through the bark tissue. From mass movements, which take place during the accumulation of dry material in fruits and tubers, it has been possible to measure the net mass transfer. If an assumption is then made about the average concentration in the phloem sap, one can deduce the rate of mass movement of the solution. Analyses of the phloem sap, obtained by the use of aphids, show concentrations of the order of 10 per cent for sucrose, indicating a rate of movement through the phloem of the order of 50 to 100 cm/hr (for movement of the order of something like 20 gm of sucrose per sq. cm of estimated sieve tube area per hour). This is the same rate at which dyes have been observed to move after injection into the plant. In plants in which there is a marked diurnal fluctuation in sugar concentration in the phloem tissue one can observe the rate of movement from the time of appearance of the maximum concentration in different tissues down the plant.[164] This again gives a value of the order of 60 cm per hour. More recently, estimates have been made of the rate of movement of radioactive isotopes injected into the plant.[38] Again, these measurements suggest a rate of the same order of magnitude although the absolute value is not well established. Alternatively, the rate of movement can be expressed in terms of the equivalent of a diffusion constant, if the concentration at two points a known distance apart is determined. Mason and Maskell deduced a coefficient for movement of sucrose in cotton of $6 \cdot 9 \ 10^{-2}/cm^2/sec$; for sucrose diffusing through water the corresponding coefficient is of the order of $10^{-6}/cm^2/sec$. Thus the rate of movement of substances through the phloem is of the order of ten thousand times what it would be if the substances were moving by free diffusion through an aqueous medium.

MECHANISM OF PHLOEM TRANSPORT

Several features of phloem transport are important in any considera-tion of the mechanism involved. First, it is a process associated with living cells. Anaesthetics, such as chloroform, decrease the rate of movement, and removal of oxygen from a portion of a stem will appreciably slow down the rate of movement. The rate of movement is more temperature sensitive than that of a simple physical diffusion process. The movement of carbohydrate and probably nitrogen (unlike that of IAA discussed in Chapter 11) is non-polar, taking place, according to the concentration gradient, from leaves to roots or from leaves to growing apex.

It has been suggested that substances are moved in the cytoplasm by virtue of protoplasmic streaming. The main objection to this is that direct observation shows that protoplasmic streaming only takes place in sieve tubes which are relatively immature; even so the rate of movement is too slow. A second theory due to Münch[113] is that dissolved substances are moved in a mass flow of an aqueous solu-tion from a place in the plant with a high suction pressure to a place with a low suction pressure. Hence the movement of dissolved sub-stances between two parts of the plant depends on the maintenance of a difference in turgor pressure. Such a mechanism can be shown to work in a simple physical model. It remains to be established that in living plants there are sufficient turgor pressure gradients to allow rates of the magnitude actually observed in translocation. It also remains to be shown that there is a free path of sufficient cross-sectional area through the sieve tubes to allow for mass flow. The hypothesis further implies that all substances in a given tissue must move in the same direction. Claims have been made that with the simultaneous injection of two tracers the tracers generally move at the same rate. Numerous experiments have attempted to demonstrate whether movement of two substances can take place simultaneously in opposite directions in the plant. For example, nitrogen might be transported from the lower leaves up to the higher leaves and growing point, whilst at the same time carbohydrate is being transported from the younger leaves down to the root. In order to refute the mass flow hypothesis, it would, however, be necessary to show that a movement in opposite directions took place in the same tissue element, for otherwise certain sieve tubes might operate for upward movement and others for downward movement. A third hypothesis is that movement is by a process similar to diffusion but that the rate of movement is far greater than that of diffusion in a physical system because of the structure and functioning of the plant. This type of movement has been referred to as activated diffusion, and one possibility suggested by van der Honert[73] is that it does not take place through the bulk of a liquid phase but rather along an interface. In non-living systems it has been shown that the movement of substances takes place at a faster rate across an interfacial surface than by diffusion through the bulk of the solution. It is suggested that a sufficient interfacial area is available within the fine structure of the cytoplasm of the sieve tube, that movement takes place across this, and that the interfacial surface is maintained in a suitable state by metabolic activity. Critical experiments have not been made which will permit a clear distinction between the theories of mass flow and activated diffusion. Further, the precise way in which diffusion can be activated by metabolism is not clear. Another theory due to Spanner[139] proposes that movement of sucrose across the sieve plate is accelerated by a mass water flow which results from electro-osmosis. (Electro-osmosis is the flow of water induced across a charged membrane when an electrical potential is applied across it.) An unequal distribution of potassium ions might be maintained across the sieve plate due to the metabolic activity of the companion cells, water

158

movement thus taking place by electro-osmosis and resulting in a movement of sucrose with the water. Again, there is no evidence that sufficient gradients in potassium ions can be maintained in this way.

As yet no single theory of the mechanism of translocation is firmly established. Renewed interest in this problem has been aroused by the possibility of using radioactive tracers. Unfortunately these experiments have not yet led to any new unequivocal conclusions concerning the mechanism involved.

GENERAL REFERENCES

O. F. CURTIS (1933) *The Translocation of Solutes in Plants.* McGraw-Hill

CHAPTER ELEVEN

Growth

The ultimate result of the uptake, movement, and metabolism of substances within the plant is growth. In the development of living
organisms there is progressive growth from the juvenile to the mature
stage and often continued existence after maturity. This implies that
in broad terms the growth of all organisms follows an essentially

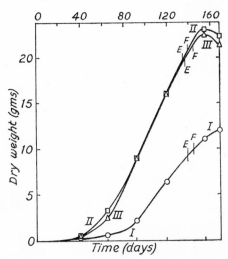

Fig. 11.1. *The growth of oats showing the 'S'-shaped curve of
development. Three levels of phosphorous fertilizer were used
(III > II > I). E indicates the time of exsertion of inflorescences
and F the time of flowering. (After R. F. Williams*[155])

similar pattern. If any attribute of a plant such as height, or weight,
or leaf area is plotted against time there is a period of increasing
growth rate, followed by a longer period of constant rate, and finally
a period of decreasing growth rate. This gives rise to an 'S'-shaped
curve for growth (Fig. 11.1). Departures from this general curve
result from the influence of the environment. Hence the growth of a
plant is determined both by internal and external factors.

Differentiation as well as a simple increase in cellular material occurs during the growth of a higher plant. Thus we have to consider not only the factors which influence an increase in size but also those which determine development as, for example, the transition from a vegetative to a flowering state. In an annual species this generally results in cessation of growth, whereas in other plants this change may be associated with a change in growth form from a dwarf rosette habit to a form characterized by marked shoot extension. In addition, there are other features of plant development which markedly affect the growth cycle – for example, the length of period during which seeds remain dormant, which varies appreciably from species to species.

The problems of plant growth can be separated into three categories: (i) the quantitative expression of increase in cellular material, (ii) the effect of certain chemicals which influence the growth and development of the plant, and (iii) the effect of the environment on the plant with special reference to its morphogenetic effect on plant development. Relatively few of the complex problems of growth can as yet be expressed in biochemical terms.

Quantitative Growth Curves

UNICELLULAR ORGANISMS

In the growth of a unicellular organism the characteristics of an individual cell such as length or volume follow the 'S' type of time course, ending with the division of the cell to form two cells. Such measurements have been made with single bacterial cells.

Similar considerations apply to the growth of a colony of unicellular organisms whose growth can be measured in terms of cell number, total cell volume, or total dry weight of the culture. In a closed system, the growth curve for the population as a whole may be divided into three stages; an initial period, a period of continued growth at a constant rate and a final period of decreasing growth called senescence (Fig. 11.2). It has been observed that during the middle period the increase in cell number is directly proportional to the number of cells, i.e. the growth of the colony is comparable with the growth of a capital sum invested at compound interest. It follows that if the logarithm of cell number is plotted against time a linear relationship is obtained, and this period of growth is often referred to as the phase of exponential or logarithmic growth. If cells are transferred in this phase to a new sub-culture under the same nutritional conditions they continue to grow at a constant rate (i.e. in the logarithmic phase). As the culture ages it becomes senescent and the growth rate falls. Kinetic studies indicate that this is because certain of the cells in the colony cease to divide, whereas others continue to divide at the same rate as was characteristic of the culture in the logarithmic phase. It is important at this stage to distinguish between the growth rate of individual cells and the growth rate of the colony. If cells are transferred from this senescent stage to a new culture they show a marked lag phase, i.e. the growth rate of the colony is considerably less than that characteristic of cells in the logarithmic phase.

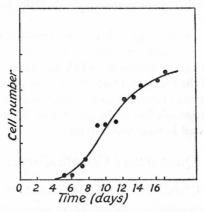

Fig. 11.2. The increase in cell number with time showing a 'S'-shaped growth curve for a culture of Chlorella vulgaris. *(After W. H. Pearsall and L. Loose[121])*

The growth rate progressively increases with time until the new population enters upon the logarithmic phase. In the lag phase it is believed that certain cells do not divide at all in the first place, but later begin to do so with the growth rate characteristic of the logarithmic phase. Thus the growth rate of the colony as a whole is lower, but that of individual cells in the colony may be the same as that in the logarithmic phase. Quantitative expressions have been deduced which relate the growth rate of the colony and that of individual cells in the form of growth equations.[109]

HIGHER PLANTS

In higher plant growth, differentiation is a notable feature of development. Ignoring this complication, the simplest assumption would be that the growth of a higher plant takes place at a rate proportional to its present size, i.e. the increase in dry weight (dW) is directly proportional to the existing dry weight (W).[15] The interest rate for increase in dry weight is called the *relative growth rate* (r), and is given by the expression d$W = We^{rt}$. The relative growth rate can only remain constant for a limited period since otherwise the plant would continue to grow to an infinite size (Fig. 11.3). One modification that has been suggested is that the growth rate is determined not only by the

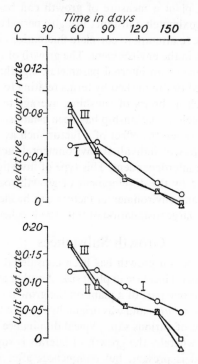

Fig. 11.3. The relative growth rate and unit leaf rate (or net assimilation rate) for oat seedlings for which the growth curve is given in Fig. 11.1. (After R. F. Williams[155])

present weight but also by the difference between the present and the final weight to be attained at maturity. On this basis a number of empirical growth equations have been proposed.

Differentiation of a plant results in the formation of dead tissue, e.g. heart wood, and it is obvious that such dead tissue cannot directly contribute to the formation of new material in growth. It has therefore been suggested that the growth of a plant should be referred not to its total weight but to the total weight of photosynthetically active material. This can be conveniently measured, approximately at least, by the total leaf area or the total leaf weight.[24] The change in dry weight per unit time expressed per unit leaf area or leaf weight is called the *unit leaf rate* or the *net assimilation rate*. Experimentally, it is found to remain approximately constant for sunflower and maize if both the initial early period of seedling growth and the final flowering period are excluded, but it is not so constant for oats (Fig. 11.3).

If for a given plant a measure of growth can be experimentally shown to be approximately constant through a period of development, then it is possible to attempt to correlate fluctuations in that quantity with fluctuations in the environment. The growth of the plant can be expressed in terms of an internal parameter, e.g. the unit leaf rate, which is enhanced or diminished by terms relating to variables in the environment such as hours of sunshine, average temperature, and rainfall. When such a relationship has been established it is possible to distinguish between the effect of a factor such as manurial treatment and the effect of individual environmental factors and to see how far they are interdependent. This type of investigation has been greatly facilitated by the development of growth rooms and chambers in which many environmental factors can be closely controlled and regulated. A large installation of this type is called a 'phytotron'.

Growth Substances

In the previous section growth has been considered from the point of view of the general increase in plant size. Another aspect of growth is the influence of one part of a plant on the growth of another. This is spoken of as *correlation* and was originally thought to be controlled by the movement of various saps. Apical dominance is one example of a correlation whereby the growth of laterals is suppressed whilst the terminal bud is present, but commences after its removal. In 1880 Sachs postulated the existence of specific root- and flower-forming substances, although Darwin in 1881 was the first to demonstrate experimentally that the growth of one part of a plant could be influenced by a stimulus travelling from another. Darwin showed that the presence of the tip of the root or shoot was essential for growth by elongation, for the perception of gravity, and of light, but that a different region showed the growth response. If the tip of a growing plant was removed and then replaced to one side, unequal growth of the two sides resulted in curvature. It became clear that the root and shoot tip were the centres of production of some growth-regulating substance, and in 1919 Páal postulated that such a substance was formed, internally secreted and distributed downwards through the living tissue. If the movement of this correlation carrier, as he called it, was disturbed on one side, then growth was decreased on that side, thus giving rise to a curvature. In 1926 Went finally obtained this substance as a diffusate into agar blocks. Kôgl in 1933 claimed to have isolated three specific chemical substances from urine which would affect the growth of elongating plant tissue. Subsequent work confirmed the growth activity of one of these substances which Kôgl called heteroauxin and is now known to be 3-indoleacetic acid (IAA). The other two substances isolated at that time and called auxin A and auxin B have never been obtained by subsequent workers. In addition to IAA a number of substances are now known

$NH_3^+ Cl^-$

Cl^-

$CH_2 - N^+$ — CH_3

CH_3 N

N

S

$CH_2 \cdot CH_2OH$

Thiamine hydrochloride
(vitamin B_1)

CH_2OH

HO—

—CH_2OH

H_3C—

N

Pyridoxine
(vitamin B_6)

—COOH

N

Nicotinic acid

which affect the growth of plants. The resulting growth and differentiation of a plant must be related to the balance resulting from the interaction of all these substances.[136] It is convenient to classify the substances which affect growth in the following way:

(a) *Vitamins*: growth substances that can be shown to be co-factors of known enzyme systems such as thiamine, pyridoxine, or nicotinic acid. These are synthesized in the leaves and translocated to other parts of the plant such as the roots. Isolated root segments grown in tissue culture show a requirement for these substances, and for full growth they must be added to the nutrient medium. Similarly, the development of buds on isolated stems grown in tissue culture requires the addition of adenine to the growth medium.

(b) *Auxins*: growth substances of known chemical structure but unknown biochemical significance which induce cell enlargement at low concentrations, i.e. promote extension growth. The effect of applied auxin may only be apparent if the tissue has been deprived of endogeneous auxin, e.g. by removal of the apex. Indoleacetic acid is the best characterized of the naturally occurring auxins.

(c) *Gibberellins*, which promote shoot growth in intact plants (but not in isolated tissues as do auxins) and most markedly in some dwarf varieties.

(d) *Kinins*, of which kinetin (6-furfuryl adenine) is the best known example, which are essential to maintain continued cell division in certain stem tissue cultures.

(e) *Growth inhibitors*: substances which occur naturally and are characterized by their ability to inhibit rather than promote growth.

(f) Substances which have been postulated to affect growth but which have been demonstrated only by indirect evidence and have so far eluded isolation and chemical identification. The substance which is thought to be responsible for the induction of flower primordia, florigen, is an example.

The word hormone was originally used to describe an organic substance which was produced in one part of an organism, translocated, and then at low concentration influenced the growth of some other part. Before the discovery of gibberellins the word auxin was used synonymously with 'growth hormone'. The term growth regulator is now generally used to include both naturally occurring and synthetic growth active substances.

The isolation and extraction of auxin from a plant
In the earliest experiments the tip was removed from a root, or shoot, placed on an agar block and the growth substances allowed to diffuse out from the tip into the agar block. The growth substances could then be transferred with the agar block and their effect observed on another plant whose growing tip had been removed. Alternatively, growth substances can be extracted with organic solvents such as methanol or diethyl ether. With short-term extraction slightly more auxin is obtained than by diffusion into an agar block, probably because some is lightly bound in the tissue and some broken down at the cut tissue surface. The auxin extracted by organic solvents in 1–2 hours at 0°C is called the 'free' auxin of the tissue. With long-continued extraction a further supply of auxin can be obtained, and this has been called 'bound' auxin. It is presumed to come from auxin precursors present in the tissue or by breakdown of auxin-protein complexes. After concentration, the auxin extract can be separated

into individual constituents, using paper chromatography.[11] The chromatogram is cut into strips, each substance is then eluted and the presence or absence of auxin activity in each sample determined by bioassay. Separation of the extract on paper, using a solvent containing isopropanol and ammonia, results in two main areas on the chromatogram. These represent indoleacetic acid and indoleacetonitrile. In addition, other compounds may be found such as indole-3-butyric acid and 3-indole-ethylacetate. In addition to the separation on the chromatogram of a number of growth-promoting substances, including some non-indole auxins, it is also found that a number of substances which inhibit growth are isolated.

Bioassay

The estimation of auxins at concentrations similar to those occurring *in vivo* can only be conveniently made in terms of their biological effects. The classical test is the *Avena* coleoptile growth test.

Avena coleoptiles must be grown under standard conditions and the material to be tested placed eccentrically on a decapitated coleoptile. In the presence of auxins the subsequent growth of the coleoptile will be curved, and from the angle of curvature the concentration of auxin can be estimated. If this is to be done accurately the naturally occurring auxins in the coleoptile must be first removed by decapitating the growing coleoptile, and subsequently removing a second piece of the tip after 2 or 3 hours to remove any residual auxin. The coleoptile must be grown at a constant temperature, exposed only to red light (since light of other wavelengths can be shown to have a destructive effect on auxins), and the humidity must be maintained constant. Under suitably controlled conditions there is a linear relationship between the degrees of curvature produced and the logarithmic concentration of auxin.

The most frequently used test depends on the effect of auxins on the linear straight growth of an isolated coleoptile or oat mesocotyl placed in buffered sucrose solution. The increase in length is compared with that of a control after a fixed period of further growth under standard conditions. The method is extremely sensitive. With IAA the growth of both roots and shoots is promoted up to an optimal concentration and then subsequently inhibited as shown in Fig. 11.4. The optimal concentration for the extension growth of roots is of the order of 10^{-10} M, whereas that for shoots is 10^{-5} M.

The split pea test is based on the fact that when an etiolated pea stem is split the epidermal cells respond to auxins more than the inner cortical cells. Hence growth of a split pea stem in a solution containing auxin is characterized by an increase in curvature. Over a limited range there is again a linear relationship between the curvature and the logarithm of the auxin concentration. The latter two tests have the advantage that the auxin can be tested in solution.

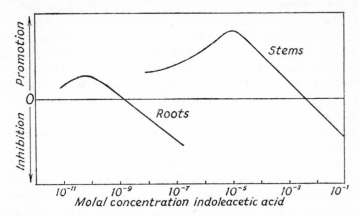

Fig. 11.4. The effect of concentration of auxin on the growth of roots and stems. (After A. C. Leopold and K. V. Thimann[92])

The presence of indoleacetic acid can be demonstrated chemically by a colorimetric reaction with ferric chloride. This may be useful for identification, but is too insensitive for determination of concentrations that have biological significance.

THE OCCURRENCE, FORMATION AND MOVEMENT OF AUXINS *IN VIVO*

Auxins occur predominantly in the meristematic regions of the plant such as the growing tip, or the cambium, or the intercalary meristem of grasses, and are present in lower concentration in leaves, fruits, and flowers. Definitive evidence for the presence of IAA has been obtained only for maize seeds and cabbage, but the very low concentration present *in vivo* makes characterization difficult. The auxin concentration is greatest at the tip of the plant, falls progressively through the stem and root, and then rises again a little in the root tip. In general, as the tissue approaches maturity the auxin concentration falls. In green tissue, light is generally necessary for its formation, but in excised tissue, grown in synthetic medium, auxin formation may occur in the dark. Seasonal changes in auxin occur. For example, dormant buds have a lower concentration than spring buds. Simi-

168

larly, when some seeds are soaked there is such an abundant production of auxin prior to germination that it is liberated into the external solution.

Indoleacetic acid is chemically related to tryptophane, and an enzyme has been obtained from spinach leaves which is able to synthesize auxin from tryptophane. In the plant the distribution of

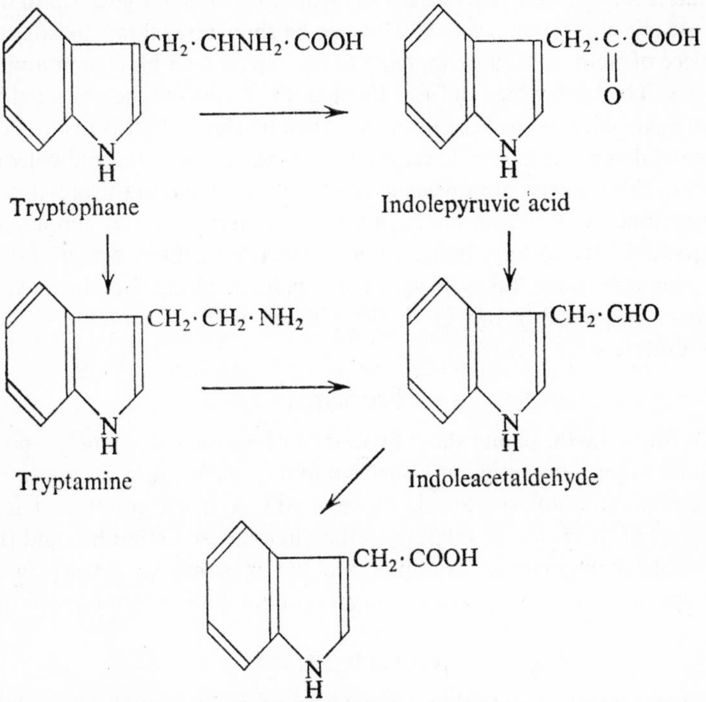

Fig. 11.5. Routes of biosynthesis of IAA

the enzyme can be shown to be closely correlated with the distribution of free auxin. It has been suggested that tryptophane is converted to indoleacetaldehyde, which is then converted to indoleacetic acid. Indoleacetaldehyde itself has no auxin action.[89] Another possible method of synthesis is via indoleacetylnitrile (which has been extracted from cabbage), with the subsequent removal of ammonia (Fig. 11.5). It has been shown that certain zinc-deficient plants fail to show elongation but undergo elongation in a normal way if auxin or tryptophane or serine are supplied. This is consistent with the suggestion that serine condenses with indole to form tryptophane prior to the formation of auxin. Indoleacetic acid is also destroyed by enzyme action in the plant. An adaptive enzyme system, IAA oxidase, catalysing the oxidation of IAA with the liberation of carbon dioxide, has been found particularly in roots.[145]

The most striking feature of the movement of IAA in the plant is that it is polar and takes place only from the morphological tip to the base of young stem tissue.[153] This can be shown by taking an isolated piece of stem tissue and applying to the top an agar block containing IAA. The IAA which diffuses through the tissue can be collected in an agar block at the bottom. It can then be shown that transmission only takes place in one direction, at least in young stems and coleoptiles. This polarity of movement may well be related to the previously mentioned correlation effect in which the terminal bud suppresses growth of the axillary buds. So far, there is no definite evidence that auxin movement takes place in the phloem alone, but in mature stems it probably moves in the phloem with the soluble carbohydrates.

Tropisms

During growth, plants show two kinds of movement, namely, spontaneous (or automatic) movements and movements in response to an external stimulus (paratonic movements). A tropic movement is a paratonic response in relation to the direction of a stimulus, and the two best understood examples are the response to gravity (geotropism) and the response to unilateral illumination (phototropism).

GEOTROPISM

If a plant stem is placed in a horizontal position, growth takes place with an upward curvature in such a way that the growing tip is returned to the vertical. In roots, the opposite curvature takes place so that the growing tip grows downwards to the vertical. Hence stems are referred to as negatively geotropic and roots as positively geotropic. The Cholodny–Went hypothesis proposed that the unequal growth on the two sides of a horizontally placed organ results from an unequal distribution of auxin within the organ. They suggested that owing to gravity auxin becomes concentrated on the lower side of a horizontally placed tissue. Within a concentration range of 0·001 to 1 mg/l, IAA, increase of auxin results in a decrease in growth rate of roots but an increase in growth rate of stems. Thus, within this range, the increased auxin concentration on the lower side of the organ will result in an increased growth and upward curvature in stems but a decreased growth and a downward curvature in roots.

If auxin is collected by placing agar blocks in contact with the upper and lower halves of a horizontally placed organ, it can be demonstrated experimentally that the concentration of auxin is greater in the lower than in the upper half. In the case of shoots the Cholodny–Went hypothesis offers a satisfactory explanation.

However, with roots it is necessary to suppose that the concentration of natural auxin is so high that an increase necessarily causes inhibition of growth. This does not appear to be always true. Furthermore, it is questionable whether the observed difference in concentration of auxin on the upper and lower side of roots is of sufficient magnitude to explain the growth response. Exposure of a decapitated root, and subsequent treatment with auxin after removal of the geotropic stimulus, has been claimed to result in a response. Furthermore, rhizomes which normally grow horizontally have been shown to contain IAA; yet there is no resulting growth curvature. If a rhizome is turned upside down its subsequent growth can show curvatures both up and down. It has been suggested that roots may contain an auxin inhibitor which is either produced as a response to gravity or whose distribution is altered by gravity.[11] The presence of several growth-promoting substances and of at least one growth inhibitor has been demonstrated by chromatographic analysis of root extracts. Analysis of rhizomes has shown an unequal distribution not only of auxin but also of sugars and certain cations. It is therefore not yet established how far the curvature of roots in response to gravity is directly a consequence of an unequal distribution in a single growth-promoting substance or as the result of a complex pattern involving many growth substances and growth inhibitors.

Furthermore, the problem remains as to how gravity induces an unequal distribution of auxin or auxin inhibitor in both stems and roots. The movement of statoliths, whose distribution can be definitely shown to be affected by gravity, has been suggested as responsible for the movement of auxin. The theory is by no means established, but the alternative suggestion that a 'geoelectric' effect is responsible has little experimental evidence to support it.

PHOTOTROPISM

According to the Cholodny–Went hypothesis the phototropic response must result from the presence of less auxin on the side of the tissue which is more highly illuminated. This would result in a bending towards the light by stems (positive phototropism) and away from light by roots (negative phototropism).

If a piece of stem tissue is supplied with IAA from an agar block placed on top, the auxin diffusing through can be collected separately in two agar blocks placed on the two halves of the bottom end separated by a mica strip. When this was done and the stem illuminated from one side, less auxin diffused to the bottom of the illuminated side. There was also a total loss of auxin in passing through the tissue. Thus light causes a redistribution of auxin and also a destruction of auxin.

Within a limited range of intensities the degree of phototropic curvature produced in the *Avena* coleoptile varies as the product of

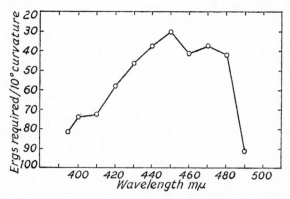

Fig. 11.6. The action spectrum for curvature of an Avena *coleoptile ('tip effect'). (After E. S. Johnston[77])*

the time and intensity of illumination. If the curvature resulting from equal incident intensities of different wavelengths is measured, an action spectrum for phototropism is obtained (Fig. 11.6). Light of wavelengths 445 mμ and 470 mμ produces the maximum response: and there is a region of less effectiveness in the near ultra-violet. Essentially the same action spectrum has been found for the phototropic response of *Phycomyces* sporangiophores.[40] This indicates the presence of a substance in the tissue whose absorption spectrum has maxima at these wavelengths and which sensitizes the destruction of auxin by light. Experiments show that the destruction of IAA by IAA oxidase *in vitro* is greatly increased in the presence of blue light. Two groups of substances predominantly absorb light in this wavelength region – carotenoids and flavoproteins. Flavoproteins are known to catalyse oxido-reduction reactions in respiration, and it is consistent with this to postulate that flavoproteins photosensitize the oxidation of auxin. Certain mutants of fungi and albino mutants of higher plants which show phototropic response have been claimed to be free of carotene, and it has been suggested that this supports the view that riboflavins are responsible for phototropism. Those who believe that carotenoids sensitize the system argue that mutants cannot be known to be entirely free of carotenoids. From our general knowledge of biochemistry, flavoproteins would appear to be the more probable.[146] If riboflavin photosensitizes the oxidation of IAA, the presence of carotene absorbing at similar wavelengths will act as a light filter and increase the relative destruction of IAA on the two sides of a unilaterally illuminated tissue.

Photodestruction of IAA will result in a maximum difference in auxin content between the two sides of a coleoptile equal to the auxin loss. Most theories have postulated that unequal illumination produces a greater difference than can be attributed to auxin loss, and postulate a lateral migration of auxin or of auxin precursor. Some have proposed that this migration results from the induction by light of a bioelectric potential. Migration of a precursor might also result if light inhibited the enzyme system synthesizing IAA in the tip. The relative importance of these effects cannot be critically assessed without further work.

With relatively low light intensities perception is at the tip of the coleoptile whilst response takes place a little below the tip. In addition to the positive response of the *Avena* coleoptile to relatively low light intensities, a second type of response which may be opposite in sign has been observed with higher intensities.[41] Unlike the low intensity response, the high energy curvature is distributed along the whole length of the coleoptile and after prolonged illumination appears mainly at the base. It has therefore been called 'base' response. In this case the action spectrum in the ultra-violet is unlike that of flavin or carotenoids, but has some similarity to the absorption spectrum of indole compounds. Thus it appears that there may be at least two different types of phototropic response in *Avena* coleoptile.

PHYSIOLOGICAL EFFECTS OF AUXINS AND THEIR APPLICATION IN HORTICULTURE[4]

The effects of IAA discussed so far depend on its ability to induce cell elongation. It also has marked effects on plant meristems. When applied to a cut stem IAA stimulates the formation of roots at the morphological base and hence may be used for the purpose of encouraging the rooting of cuttings. A number of chemical compounds related to IAA have been produced synthetically and found particularly suitable for this purpose, e.g. 3-indolebutyric acid and β-naphthoxyacetic acid. These substances also suppress the development of the meristem in the axils of the leaves. Normally, growth of the lateral buds is suppressed by the terminal bud (apical dominance), and if the terminal bud is removed the lateral buds develop into branches. However, replacement of the terminal bud by an agar block containing IAA keeps the lateral buds dormant.

Auxins affect not only cell division but also tissue differentiation. Cambial activity can be induced by treating seedlings with IAA, and it has been suggested that the seasonal activity of the cambium in woody plants is controlled by variations in natural auxin level. When isolated plant tissues are cultured *in vitro*, application of IAA may result in callus growth, i.e. the production of a large number of undifferentiated cells.

Leaf- and fruit-fall at maturity is generally preceded by the formation of an abscission layer. The application of IAA or related substances delays or prevents the formation of this abscission layer and thus can prevent leaf or fruit fall. This again has an important application in horticulture in preventing the premature drop of fruits owing to unfavourable windy conditions following fruit set. The compound 2:4 dichlorophenoxy-acetic acid (2:4:D) has been found to be extremely effective in the reduction of fruit drop. The growth of fruits can also be stimulated by auxin. In the tomato, for example, failure of fertilization results in the cessation of growth of the young fruit. If, however, tomato flowers are treated with auxin, normal fruits (which are seedless) will develop even in the absence of pollination. β-naphthoxyacetic acid has been used widely for the encouragement of fruit set.

A further important application of auxins in horticulture resulted from the observation that if a cereal crop containing dicotyledonous weed species was sprayed with a dilute solution of auxin the weeds were killed and the cereal was not. A whole variety of synthetic compounds has been developed which are particularly suitable for the treatment of certain specific crops and associated weeds. 2:4:D has been widely used for this purpose. An important difference between synthetic compounds such as 2:4:D and IAA is that synthetic compounds are not attacked in the plant by IAA oxidase. Because of their increased stability, synthetic compounds often prove more effective with respect to particular processes. Further discussion of the uses of auxins can be found in horticultural textbooks.

CHEMICAL NATURE OF AUXIN SUBSTANCES AND THE MECHANISM OF THEIR ACTION

Almost all the synthetic substances produced which affect the growth of plants are derivatives of indole or naphthalene or phenoxyacetic acids. Attempts have been made to designate the features of a molecule essential for auxin activity. The active molecules all have: (i) a ring structure containing an unsaturated ring, (ii) an acid side chain, and (iii) a particular special relationship between the acid side chain and the unsaturated ring. With respect to the side chain, it has been shown that if it contains an even number of carbon atoms the auxin is active, but an odd number results in little activity. This is because the side chain is degraded in the plant (like a fatty acid) by the removal of two carbon units and an initial odd number results in a side chain without the necessary carboxyl group. It has been suggested that these three essential features of the molecule are necessary for the attachment of auxin to some structure or enzyme in the plant. The first theory suggested a two-point attachment with the carboxyl and the unsaturated ring attached at two separate points on an enzyme. More recently, the importance of an intermediate grouping between the carboxyl and the ring (either a hydrogen atom or some other radical) has been emphasized as providing a three-point attachment to some important surface structure (possibly protein-aceous) in the cell.

The range of substances which have been synthesized or isolated from plants and shown to cause growth responses includes substances which accelerate or stimulate the activity of an auxin. In addition, substances have been found which competitively inhibit auxin activity, the anti-auxins, e.g. α(l-naphthyl methyl sulphide)-propionic acid. These are believed to attach themselves to the postulated structure in such a way as to prevent the attachment of the auxin. Other substances have been shown to inhibit auxin action which have no similarity in structure to the auxin molecules and do not act as competitive inhibitors. They decrease growth in general, and such a growth inhibitor is maleic hydrazide.

Attempts have been made to determine the mode of action of indoleacetic acid on the metabolism of the cell. In moderate concentration IAA stimulates respiration, but at higher concentrations it is inhibitory. The region in which stimulation takes place is the region in which growth by elongation is also stimulated. On the other hand, an inhibitor, such as iodoacetate, can completely inhibit growth at a concentration which inhibits respiration to only a small extent. In general, there is no quantitative relationship between inhibition of growth and inhibition of respiration. The particular part of the metabolic system which IAA affects is still not known, though it has been suggested that IAA is the coenzyme of an unknown enzyme which in some way controls growth. Over a limited concentration range the effect of increasing concentration of auxin on growth rate can be shown to follow a Michaelis–Menten relationship typical of an enzyme catalysed reaction.[50] Many have considered this approach too simple in analysing such a complex phenomenon as growth; they consider the stimulation of respiration by auxin to be a secondary effect. Several auxins when applied to a plant result in the disappearance of the —SH groups of coenzyme A and the more active auxins are more effective in this respect. Hence it has been suggested that auxin forms a thiol ester with coenzyme A, a reaction which may well be facilitated by the presence of ATP. This would result in an indirect effect on respiration. IAA also affects cell wall structure, increasing both its flexibility and extensibility, probably by affecting the synthesis and structure of the pectin substances.[35, 124] Whereas inhibition of root growth by IAA may result from a reduction in mean cell length at low concentration, at high concentration there is an inhibition of cell division; on the other hand IAN primarily has its effect at all concentrations by causing a reduction in the number of cell divisions. It is clear that no single mechanism of auxin action is likely to explain the whole range of phenomena.

Gibberellins[21]

Gibberellic acid, a substance first obtained from a fungus which causes the 'Bakanae' disease of rice, has been shown to have a marked effect on the growth of a variety of plants. It can be obtained as a crystalline substance and is effective in a concentration of one part per million. Increased growth is only maintained if gibberellic acid is given in successive doses. When applied to the leaves of certain dwarf species of plants it results in rapid growth by elongation of the internodes. There is generally no change in the number of internodes in the plant, but only in their length.

Root growth of intact plants is not stimulated by gibberellic acid, but at high concentrations it may prove inhibitory. Again, unlike indoleacetic acid, it has no effect on the rooting of cuttings. Gibberellins stimulate elongation in excised stem sections, e.g. pea

176

epicotyls, but do not result in growth curvatures when applied to one side only of a stem. Gibberellins will stimulate expansion of bean leaf discs, which IAA does not. If a terminal bud is removed, application of gibberellic acid does not suppress the growth of laterals; in some plants it stimulates the development of lateral shoots, in others, such as rice and cereals, gibberellins may reduce the number of tillers so that in this case apical dominance is enhanced. This is generally true in plants which normally branch, but exceptions have been observed. In the dwarf French bean the apical bud normally aborts, but after treatment with gibberellic acid the apical bud fails to abort and growth is no longer branching but confined to the main axis. Gibberellins also break dormancy in the potato tuber, in lettuce seed germination, and in resting buds of some trees. They are more effective than IAA in inducing parthenocarpic fruit formation.

Gibberellins have been obtained in methanolic extract from both seeds and seedlings and from fungi. Several different forms have been isolated and their chemical structure has been established. They differ in their order of effectiveness according to the particular biological response measured.

On the basis of studies of normal and dwarf varieties of maize and pea it has been suggested that the response to externally applied gibberellins is dependent on the level of native gibberellins already in the plant. Gibberellins have been shown to induce a normal growth response in a number of single-gene dwarf mutants of maize, indicating that a number of steps in the synthesis of gibberellins are probably genetically controlled and different mutants are blocked in different reaction steps. It has also been suggested that certain dwarf mutants result from the formation of inhibitors of, rather than specific enzyme blocks in, gibberellin synthesis.

Another effect of gibberellic acid is that plants which have a rosette habit when grown in long days or in the absence of vernalization (see later) can be induced to elongate and flower. In *Hyoscyamus* a quantitative difference in gibberellin-like substances has been found between the rosette and elongated upright forms. Only long day plants that have the rosette habit can be induced to bolt and flower with gibberellin treatment; flowering may therefore be a consequence of bolting, and this latter development may represent the effect primarily induced by the gibberellins.

The manner in which gibberellins result in this variety of responses is still unknown.

Kinins[105]

In order to culture isolated plant tissue in sterile medium it is frequently necessary to add certain plant extracts to maintain continued growth. Skoog[137] found that tobacco pith tissue would grow for only a limited time in a medium fully supplied with nutrients and vitamins unless coconut milk was added to the medium. The active compound in the coconut milk has now been shown to be kinetin (6-furfuryl adenine) and other 6-substituted aminopurines act similarly. Kinetin has also been shown to stimulate cell enlargement in leaf discs, root initiation and growth in cuttings, and bud initiation and growth in stem cuttings. The mechanism of its biochemical action is still unknown.

Effect of Specific Environmental Factors

THE CONTROL OF FLOWERING IN PLANTS

In the middle of the nineteenth century Henfrey had already proposed that variation in the day length with change in latitude might be an important factor in controlling plant distribution. In 1920 Garner and Allard[54] were the first to demonstrate clearly that flowering was not controlled by the total hours of light and darkness but by the relative duration of the dark and light periods. Tobacco plants of variety Maryland Mammoth, varieties of soya beans and *Xanthium* were all found to flower only in short days. The length of the night seemed to be most critical, the plants requiring dark periods of some 14 hours for flowering to occur. It became clear that some plants could be classified as long day plants, including spinach, lettuce, radish, oats, and timothy grass, which need a day length greater than 13–14 hours; or as short day plants, including soya bean and chrysanthemum, which need a relatively short day with less than 14–16 hours' light. Other plants were found to be day neutral. In long day plants flowering is frequently associated with a change from a rosette growth habit to one with marked stem extension ('bolting'). The conditions which result in the initiation of flower primordia may not necessarily result in the formation of mature flowers. Only the conditions for the formation of primordia are discussed here.

Klebs in 1918 realized that all plants can only be induced to flower after they have obtained a certain degree of maturity called 'ripeness to flower'; prior to this the plant is in a juvenile state. It is often necessary for the plant to produce a certain minimum number of leaves before any external factor can induce flowering.

178

It was found that plants need not be exposed to a continuous alternation of light and dark of the required duration for flowering to take place. For example, after a soya bean plant had been exposed to ten short days it could then be placed under conditions of longer days and would still flower. *Xanthium* has been reported to respond to only one cycle of a short day, flowering resulting even if growth is in long days, before and after the one short day period. Whilst single or relatively few short day periods may initiate flower formation, often a period of longer treatment will result in the formation of more flowers more quickly.

The whole of the plant need not be exposed to the photoperiodic stimulus. It has been shown that exposure of a very small portion of the surface of one mature leaf is enough to produce flower formation in the whole plant. Generally, immature leaves do not respond to treatment, but exposure of any portion of a mature leaf results in flower formation. Removal of the leaves after treatment abolishes any induction. It is postulated that a particular substance is produced in the leaf translocated into the rest of the plant and results, by its effect on the meristem, in flower formation. This substance was given the name *florigen*. If a plant is subjected to a stimulus causing flower formation and part of that plant grafted on to another untreated plant, the second plant will be induced to flower. Thus the substance florigen can move from a treated portion of one plant into an untreated plant. It can be shown that if the leaf midrib is cut, or the petiole killed, preventing transport from a treated leaf, flowers do not form. So far as is known, the substance florigen moves in the phloem rather than the xylem. It has also been demonstrated that during the period of photoinduction carbon dioxide is necessary and is taken up by the plant. When the compounds formed were investigated using radioactive carbon dioxide, no particular compounds peculiar to photoinduced plants could be detected.

If the inducing dark period for a short-day plant is interrupted, even by light of extremely low intensity and for only a very brief period, floral induction will not take place. A brief flash of light of an intensity of only a few tenths of a foot-candle is sufficient to break a dark period and reduce its effective duration. On the other hand, there must be a relatively high light intensity during the photoperiod, since during this time the plant must produce photosynthetic products for its subsequent development.

The action spectrum of the photoinducing light has been determined and it has been shown that absorption in the blue and far-red is most effective.[66] The action spectrum is not identical with the absorption spectrum of chlorophyll. Furthermore, it has been shown that irradiation with red light, that is, in the region of 620 to 680 mμ, will prevent flowering if given immediately after a photoinducing period (Fig. 11.7). Thus far-red light can undo the effect of red light, and a sequence of alternating near-red and far-red illumination will result in an effect which takes account of the last type of treatment alone. The pigment which is responsible for absorbing the light and activating the flower inducing system must exist in two forms.

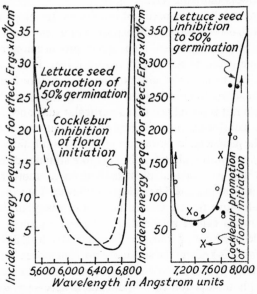

Fig. 11.7. The action spectrum for floral initiation in Xanthium pensylvanicum. The action spectrum for the germination of lettuce seeds is also shown. Irradiation at 735 mμ reverses the effect of radiation at 655 mμ. (After S. B. Hendricks[66])

It has now been isolated from several plants and called phytochrome.[30] When exposed to red light of relatively low intensity it is converted to a form which absorbs far-red (maximum 730 mμ), and this in turn when exposed to far-red light is converted to a form which absorbs red light (maximum 660 mμ). Only the far-red absorbing form is capable of causing floral induction.

A similar red/far-red system has been shown to operate with respect to the breaking of dormancy by light in some seeds, e.g. certain lettuce varieties, and in the effect of light on stem elongation (i.e. in suppressing etiolation). With respect to all these photo-morphogenetic effects there is evidence for an additional effect of blue light at high intensity (the 'high energy' reaction), suggesting that there may be more than one pigment concerned in different photoreactions.

The chemical nature of florigen is still not known. Both indole-acetic acid and gibberellic acid affect flowering, but florigen is thought to be identical with neither. In short day plants, when indoleacetic acid is applied to the cut leaf surface of a photoinduced plant, it will prevent the formation of flowers. It will also induce flowering in long day plants if the photo-periodic conditions are almost inductive. Short day plants grown under photoinducing periods have a lower auxin content than normal. From these facts it has been suggested that auxin is a flower inhibitor. Treatment of short day plants with gibberellic acid may prevent flowering in short days (e.g. in *Xanthium*) but will not cause flowering in long days. Many long day plants flower in short days after treatment with gibberellic acid, and in certain cases gibberellic acid can also substitute for vernalization (see next section).

In addition to floral induction, day length influences a number of other phenomena. Bulbing is often dependent on long days as in the onion, runner formation in strawberries is promoted by long days, whilst abscission of leaves and winter dormancy of buds can be induced by short days.

VERNALIZATION

In addition to day length as a factor in determining flower induction, temperature is often also of great importance. Thus the plant *Poinsettia*, a short day plant, will flower only if the night temperature is 12°C or higher. *Hyoscyamus* shows a linear relationship between the critical day length and the environmental temperature. Certain varieties of plants such as the winter varieties of cereals will not flower unless the plant has been exposed to a period of day lengths greater than 11–12 hours. If winter varieties of cereals are allowed to germinate at 1° to 2°C and the seedlings then planted out, it is found that the time to flowering has been considerably reduced. In spring varieties there is no corresponding effect of temperature, so that the change induced by cold temperature treatment is not due to an effect on growth rate but is the induction of a state of flowering. In cereals the age of the material is not important. Seeds of any age both immediately after they are formed and after a period of storage can be

PLANT PROCESSES

vernalized, provided they have begun to germinate at the time of treatment. In other plants, e.g. cabbage, the plant must pass through a juvenile phase before there is a flowering response to low temperature. Winter rye which has been vernalized was found to flower in a shorter period if exposed to long days, whereas another variety was found to flower in a short period if exposed to short days. Thus there may be an interaction between day length and low temperature on the effect of flowering.

The problems of growth have only just begun to be approachable from the biochemical point of view. The early chemical isolation of IAA and the more recent isolation of phytochrome are beginnings. The nature of florigen and the biochemical mechanisms by which IAA or gibberellic acid affect the overall metabolism of the plant are still unknown. These and other problems of growth are likely to attract the attention of the plant biochemist in the future.

GENERAL REFERENCES

L. J. AUDUS (1959) *Plant Growth*. 2nd ed. L. Hill
A. C. LEOPOLD (1955) *Auxins and Plant Growth*. C.U.P.
R. E. WITHROW (ed.) (1959) *Photoperiodism and Related Phenomena in Plants and Animals*. AAAS, Washington, D.C.

APPENDIX

The Chemistry of the Constituents of Living Organisms

Carbon, hydrogen, oxygen, and nitrogen are the basic elements out of which the living cell is made, but phosphorus, sulphur, and a large number of other elements, including metals, are also present. In this appendix a brief discussion of the main types of compound which exist in the cell is given, but for a detailed account a textbook of organic chemistry should be consulted.

Carbohydrates

SUGARS

The monosaccharides are molecules containing carbon, hydrogen, and oxygen of the general formula $C_n(H_2O)_n$. They are characterized by the number of carbon atoms they contain: $n = 3$ in the trioses, $n = 4$ in the tetroses, $n = 5$ in the pentoses, $n = 6$ in the hexoses, and $n = 7$ in the heptoses.

The most common sugars in the plant are those containing six carbon atoms – the hexoses. When written as a straight chain the sugars can be classified as aldo- or keto-hexoses, these groups being responsible for the reducing properties of the sugars (Fig. A.1). X-ray studies and a study of the chemical properties of glucose indicate that five of the six carbon atoms form a ring in a single plane – the pyranose ring form. The ring is joined between the first and fifth carbon atoms by an oxygen atom and the sixth carbon atom stands above the plane of the ring. Two series exist by virtue of the fact that two configurations are possible about the fifth carbon atom. These give rise to the D and L series; the L series having the configuration of laevo-glyceraldehyde and the D series that of dextro-glyceraldehyde. The D sugars predominate in nature. The symbols D and L represent structural configuration and do not indicate whether the substance causes rotation of the plane of polarized light to the right (shown by a + symbol) or to the left (shown by a − symbol). The configuration about carbon atom 1 (C_1) in aldoses and C_2

183

in ketoses results in two forms, according to whether the hydroxyl group stands on the opposite side of the planar ring as the sixth carbon atom or on the same side. The two forms are referred to as the α and β forms respectively. They can be distinguished by the

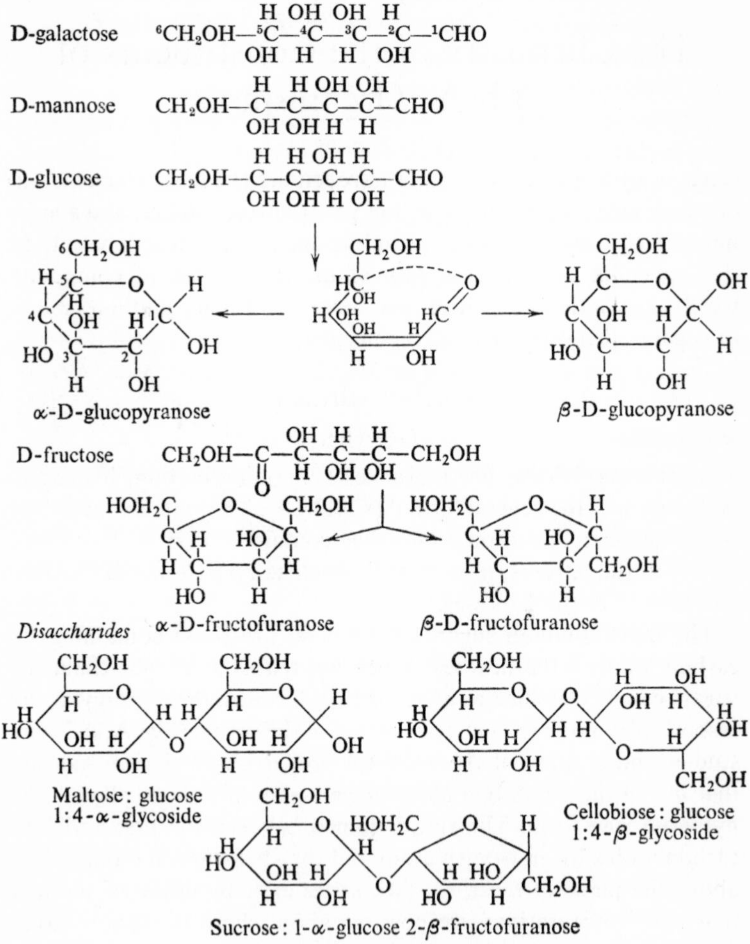

D-galactose $\quad ^6CH_2OH-^5C-^4C-^3C-^2C-^1CHO$ (with H OH OH H above and OH H H OH below)

D-mannose $\quad CH_2OH-C-C-C-C-CHO$ (with H H OH OH above and OH OH H H below)

D-glucose $\quad CH_2OH-C-C-C-C-CHO$ (with H H OH H above and OH OH H OH below)

α-D-glucopyranose

β-D-glucopyranose

D-fructose $\quad CH_2OH-C-C-C-C-CH_2OH$ (with OH H H above and H OH OH below, and O double bond)

Disaccharides $\quad$ α-D-fructofuranose $\quad$ β-D-fructofuranose

Maltose: glucose
1:4-α-glycoside

Cellobiose: glucose
1:4-β-glycoside

Sucrose: 1-α-glucose 2-β-fructofuranose

Fig. A.1. Structure of sugars: straight chain representation and ring formation

degree to which the molecule rotates polarized light. α-glucose rotates the plane of polarized light $110°$, whereas β glucose rotates it only $19°$. In solution the forms are slowly interconverted (mutarotation) to form an equilibrium mixture. The sugars containing six carbon atoms can exist in an alternative form in which the ring is reduced to a five-membered ring with two carbons out of the ring. For example, glucose can exist, although not in nature, as a five-membered ring. This ring, containing four carbon atoms and one oxygen atom, is referred to as the furanose as distinct from the normal pyranose form. Fructose can exist with a six-membered ring, when it is referred to as in the pyranose form, but normally occurs with a five-membered ring in the furanose form.

There are several naturally occurring sugars containing five carbon atoms including D-ribose, D-ribulose, D-xylose, and L-arabinose. Ribose, and 2-deoxy-D-ribose derived from it, will be considered later with reference to the structure of the nucleic acids. The four-carbon sugar, erythrose, the three-carbon triose (glyceraldehyde), the five-carbon ribulose, and the seven-carbon sedoheptulose play an important part in the metabolism of the cell, and their roles are discussed in connexion with photosynthesis and respiration in Chapters 4 and 6. Xylose and arabinose occur as polymers in the cell wall.

Disaccharides

Two monosaccharides can join together with the elimination of water, i.e. condense to form a disaccharide. The disaccharide is characterized by the nature of the two sugars which have joined together and by the linkage which joins them. For example, two molecules of glucose can join together with condensation between the C_1 of one molecule and C_4 of the other. This can result in two different types of molecule since the first sugar molecule may have an α or a β configuration. Two molecules of glucose condensing in the α position give rise to a $1:4$-α-linked disaccharide called maltose. If the C_1 in the first glucose molecule is in the β position, then the disaccharide cellobiose is produced with a $1:4$-β-link. The commonest disaccharide, sucrose, is formed by condensation between a molecule at 1-α-glucose with 2-β-fructofuranose. Since sucrose does not contain a free aldehydic or keto group it is not a reducing sugar.

The process of condensation can continue and give rise to oligosaccharides and polysaccharides. The best known polysaccharide in plants is starch formed by the condensation of a chain of glucose molecules mainly with $1:4$-α-links between them. In this case all the C_6 attached to the pyranose rings will appear on the same side of the chain. By contrast, cellulose, formed by a chain of $1:4$-β-linked glucose molecules, will have C_6 on alternate sides of the plane of the rings of the condensed sugars.

Polysaccharides

Starch

Starch is the principal seed reserve of most plants, particularly cereals. In the living plant it is often laid down in winter, in the xylem parenchyma of woody plants, or in the parenchyma of storage organs such as the potato tuber, and then in the spring hydrolysed and utilized. Its basic structure is a long chain of 1:4-α-glucose linked units. This chain does not stay in one plane but forms a spiral. Along the spiral there are points in which the chain branches and the linkage here is a 1:6 linkage, not a 1:4 linkage. When natural starch is examined it can be separated chemically into two fractions, one fraction which is relatively more soluble in water called amylose, and a second fraction which is less-soluble amylopectin. Amylopectin is characterized by a greater number of branched chains. Two well-known enzymes catalyse the hydrolysis of starch. β-amylase almost completely degrades the amylose chain by removing two glucose residues at a time as maltose, whilst α-amylase degrades the amylose or amylopectin chains to units consisting of 6–12 glucose residues called dextrins. α-amylase (sometimes called endo-amylase), unlike β-amylase (or exo-amylase), is able to attack 1:4 glucose linkages between two branching points; β-amylase can attack only the open chain ends. A third enzyme, R enzyme, hydrolyses the 1:6 linkage in amylopectin. The synthesis of starch is discussed in Chapter 5.

Cellulose

Cellulose is a major constituent of the mature plant cell wall. It is formed of a 1:4-β-linked chain of glucose residues; a structure which does not tend to a spiral form but lies in a plane. It has of the order of one thousand or more glucose residues per chain. The chains of cellulose tend to align themselves side by side, forming regions of relatively closely organized crystalline structure. These are referred to as micelles. A large assembly of micelles will give rise to a microfibril. These features of cellulose fibre structure have been observed by impregnating the fibres with gold when the gold derivative fills the cavity between the ordered regions of the micelles. X-ray studies have shown the cavities to be of the same order of size (100 Å diameter) as the micellar regions.

Other polysaccharides are formed from different monosaccharides. *Inulin* is a food reserve in members of the *Compositae* and is composed of 1:2 linked fructose residues. *Galactan* formed from β-1:4 linked galactose molecules, and *pentosans* derived from the pentoses xylose and arabinose called *xylan* and *araban* are present in the cell wall.

Other long chain carbohydrate derivatives present in the cell wall are formed from the oxidation product of sugars, the corresponding acids. The *hemicelluloses* contain both sugars and acids derived from sugars. *Pectin* contains long chains formed from galacturonic acid derived from galactan with methyl substitution. Pectic acid contains galacturonic acid chains with no methyl substitution. Protopectin is considered to be that fraction which consists of long chains of pectin molecules. The class of hemicelluloses, mucilages, gums, and pectins have branched and often irregularly branched chains. They contain a number of carboxyl groups which give these polysaccharides a high affinity for water, but they remain insoluble because of the length and branching nature of the chain structure.

Interconversion of sugars

Many of the simpler sugars are interconvertible in the plant through their phosphate derivatives. Phosphoric acid can condense with the —OH group either at C1 and/or C6 and the commonest derivatives are glucose 1P, glucose 6P, fructose 6P and fructose 1:6-diP. Their interconversion and the enzymes which catalyse these reactions are shown in Fig. 4.1. A discussion of the factors which control the formation and breakdown of the phosphate derivatives is given in Chapters 4 and 5.

NITROGENOUS COMPOUNDS

Chemical composition

The amino acids which occur in proteins have an amino group in the α position, i.e. adjacent to the carboxyl group. Those in higher plants have the same spatial configuration about the α carbon atom as L serine and belong to the L series. The formulæ of some common amino acids is shown in Fig. A.2. A further amino group can be substituted in the carboxyl group of dicarboxylic amino acids forming an amide with the —$CONH_2$ grouping. If two amino acids condense between the carboxyl group of one and the amino group of the other, a peptide link is formed and the resulting compound is a dipeptide. When this process is repeated to form a long chain a protein is produced. The constituent amino acid residues form side chains attached to the main polypeptide chain. Both the sequence and the nature of amino acid residues along the chain determine the properties of the protein. Since a protein contains at least one free carboxyl group, which can ionize with a negative charge, and one amino group, which can ionize positively, proteins can exist with either a net positive, negative, or neutral charge, i.e. they are amphoteric.

Simple proteins may combine with other nonproteinaceous compounds to form conjugate proteins. For example, conjugation with nucleic acid will form a nucleoprotein and with flavin a flavoprotein.

Amino acids

Glycine	$CH_2(NH_2)COOH$
Alanine	$CH_3.CH(NH_2)COOH$
Serine	$CH_2OH.CH(NH_2)COOH$ }Pyruvic Acid $CH_3.CO.COOH$
Cysteine	$HS.CH_2CH(NH_2)COOH$
Aspartic Acid	$COOH.CH_2.CH(NH_2)COOH$

Oxaloacetic Acid $COOH.CH_2.CO.COOH$

Glutamic Acid $COOH.CH_2.CH_2.CH(NH_2).COOH$

Ketoglutaric Acid $COOH.CH_2.CH_2.CO.COOH$

Tryptophane

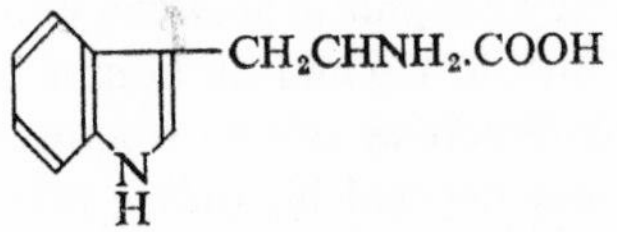

$-CH_2CHNH_2.COOH$

Amides

Asparagine $CONH_2.CH_2.CH(NH_2).COOH$

Glutamine $CONH_2.CH_2.CH_2.CH(NH_2).COOH$

Dipeptide formation

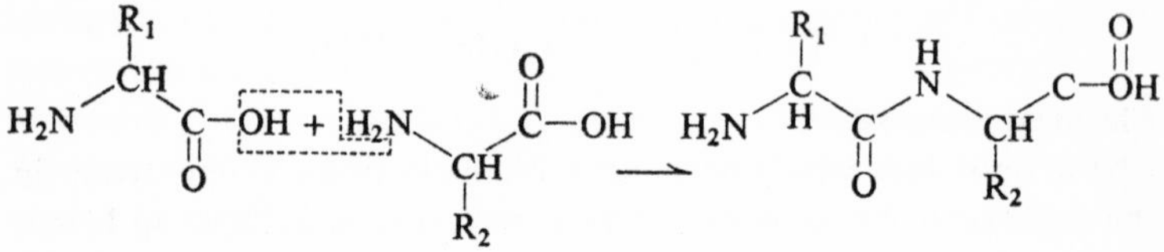

Polypeptide chain

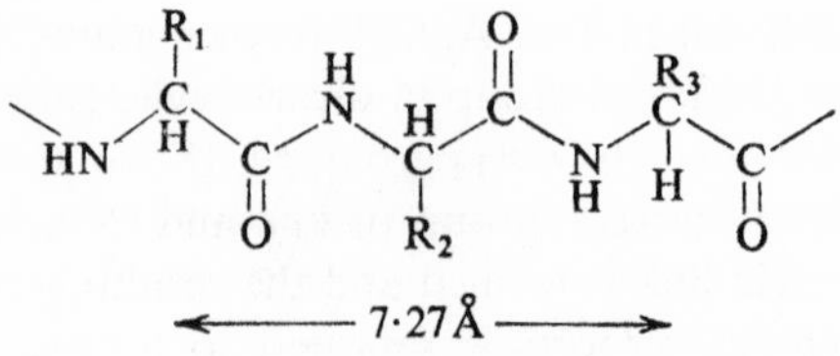

$\longleftarrow 7.27\text{Å} \longrightarrow$

Fig. A.2. Amino Acids and related compounds

The physical properties of proteins

Simple proteins have been classified on the basis of their solubility. Albumins are soluble in water, dilute acids, and alkalis and can be precipitated with saturated ammonium sulphate. Globulins are soluble in salt solutions, acids, and alkalis and are precipitated with half-saturated ammonium sulphate. Both of these forms occur in protoplasm and are widespread as seed reserves. Glutelins, soluble in weak bases, and gliadins, soluble only in 70 to 80 per cent alcohol, occur as reserves in cereal seeds.

The polypeptide chain which is the basic backbone of the protein can exist in various forms. It occurs in stretched fibres of animal origin as, for example, in wool in the fully extended β form (Fig. A.2). Alternatively, whilst still in an extended form the backbone can fall into the α position in the form of a helix with just less than four amino acids per turn. The helix is maintained by hydrogen bonding between adjacent chains and the coiling of the helix adds rigidity to the normal flexible polypeptide chain. In proteins the helix is right-handed. Fibres can change their configuration from the β to the α form. A third type of fibre structure is derived by the twisting together of three polypeptide helices. Proteins which exist in the globular form have individual polypeptide chains which are in part in the helical form and are cross-connected to form a network. A change in pH can result in transition from the helical to a random coil arrangement, and vice versa.

The molecular weight of a protein can be determined from the diffusion constant and represents the average weight of the whole molecule. The number of chain ends can be determined by a method of end group assay, i.e. by determining the number of free amino and carboxyl groups which, after allowing for diamino and dicarboxylic acids, must represent the number of chain ends. In this way the average chain length is determined and may be as little as twenty amino acid units between branching points.

The formation of cross-linkages between adjacent polypeptide chains will largely depend on the chemical nature of the side chains which represent the radicals of the constituent amino acids. These may ionize and form ionic linkages between adjacent chains, or they may form chemical links as in the formation of a disulphide between two adjacent —SH groups. These covalent bonds will be considerably stronger than the weaker physical links which will occur due to hydrogen bonds formed between adjacent polypeptide chains. When the molecule is heated the cross bonds are ruptured and the molecule uncoils and unfolds. This is referred to as denaturation and may take place to a greater or smaller extent; it is an irreversible process.

Nitrogenous organic bases

The important nitrogen bases from the point of view of metabolic activity are derivatives of purine and pyrimidine. The most important purines are xanthine, guanine, and adenine, of which the latter two are amino purines. The most important pyrimidines are uracil, cytosine, and thymine (Fig. A.3). Some alkaloids are related to these compounds; caffein, the alkaloid occurring in coffee and tea, and theobromine, which occurs in cocoa, are methylated derivatives of

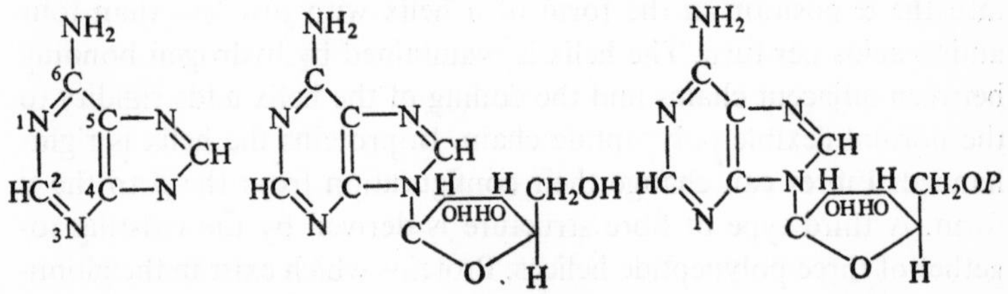

Adenine	Adenosine	Adenosine-5'-Phosphate
(6-amino purine)	(9-D-ribofuranoside-adenine)	(AMP)

In ADP and ATP one and two additional phosphorylations occur at the same carbon atom as in AMP. Note in nucleotides obtained from nucleic acids the phosphate is at the 2 or 3 position in the ribose:

Guanine = 2-amino-6-oxypurine
Uracil = 2,6-dioxypyrimidine
Thymine = 2,6-dioxy-5-methylpyrimidine
Cytosine = 2-oxy-6-aminopyrimidine

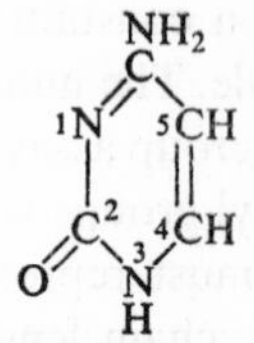

Cytosine
(2-oxy-6-amino-pyrimidine)

Fig. A.3. The structure of purines and pyrimidines

xanthine. On the other hand, the alkaloids, nicotine, quinine, and morphine, are not directly related to the purines or pyrimidines.

The purines and pyrimidines can condense with a pentose sugar and phosphoric acid to form a nucleotide, e.g. adenylic acid (or adenosine 3'-monophosphate). Two nucleotides can condense together between the phosphate group of one and the sugar of the other; a long chain polymer formed in this way constitutes nucleic acid. There are two main nucleic acids; one in which D-ribose is the sugar called ribonucleic acid (RNA) and the other with deoxyribose called deoxyribonucleic acid (DNA). RNA is formed from nucleotides containing adenine, guanine, cytosine, and uracil; in DNA adenine, guanine, cytosine, and thymine are present. RNA is found principally in the cytoplasm and DNA in the nucleus. Both acids conjugate with protein to form nucleoproteins. It is generally believed that the DNA of the nucleus determines the genetic character of the organism.

X-ray studies have shown that DNA consists of a double helix containing two spiral phosphate sugar chains winding round the same axis. The two backbones are joined by cross-linkages between the bases of one chain and the bases of the other. Guanine pairs only with cytosine and adenine with thymine, so that the sequence of bases on one chain determines the sequence on the other. The bases along the backbone do not follow a regular sequence, but their arrangement is thought to contain a code of information which determines the gene structure and hence the biological activity of the cell. It is believed that RNA consists of a single chain, but its structure is less clearly understood.

Adenylic acid (adenosine-5'-monophosphate, AMP) also plays an important part in the phosphate metabolism of the cell in that it can add on a second molecule of phosphate to form adenosine diphosphate (ADP) (or adenylic phosphate) and a third to form adenosine triphosphate (ATP). The function of these compounds is discussed in Chapters 4 and 5.

LIPIDS

The lipids which occur naturally can be separated into three groups. These are the true fats, which result from the esterification of fatty acids with glycerol, the waxes, which result from esterification of fatty acids with long chain alcohols, and the phospholipids, which are derivatives of fat-containing phosphate groups.

The fats predominantly occur as reserve food materials. They are formed during the development of the seed and broken down during germination and growth of the seedling. The fats which occur most commonly are those formed by the condensation of glycerol with fatty acids containing 12 to 18 carbon atoms. The character of the fat is determined by the carbon chain of the fatty acid; this may be fully saturated or it may contain double bonds and be unsaturated. Glycerol contains three hydroxyl groups so that the fat molecule contains three fatty acid residues (see Fig. A.4). The three fatty acids are in general different, so that the possible variety of fats is very considerable. The enzyme lipase catalyses the hydrolysis of fats to

191

glycerol and the constituent fatty acids. Further discussion of the synthesis and breakdown of fats is dealt with in Chapter 4.

Waxes occur principally in cell walls and in the cuticle. Phospholipids occur in the cytoplasm and in many structural units such as the chloroplast and plant membranes. The simplest phospholipids are similar to fats, except that one of the three fatty acids is replaced

Acids

Acetic acid	CH_3COOH
Butyric acid	$CH_3(CH_2)_2COOH$
Palmitic acid	$CH_3(CH_2)_{14}COOH$
Stearic acid	$CH_3(CH_2)_{16}COOH$
Linoleic acid	$CH_3(CH_2)_4CH{=}CH{-}CH_2{-}CH{=}CH(CH_2)_7COOH$

The formation of a true fat

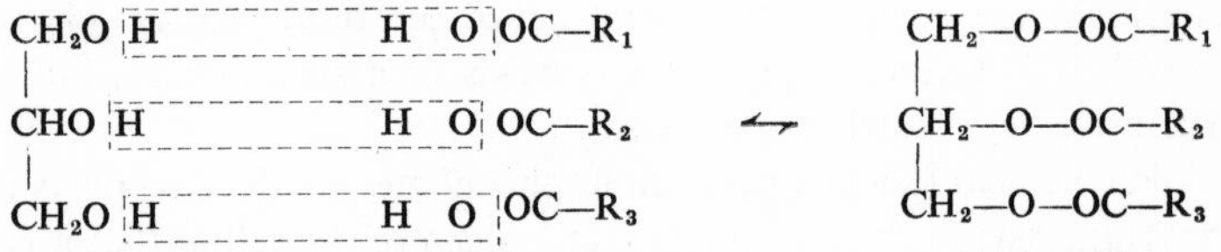

$$
\begin{array}{ccc}
CH_2O{\mid}H & H\ O{\mid}OC{-}R_1 & CH_2{-}O{-}OC{-}R_1\\
CHO{\mid}H & H\ O{\mid}OC{-}R_2 & CH_2{-}O{-}OC{-}R_2\\
CH_2O{\mid}H & H\ O{\mid}OC{-}R_3 & CH_2{-}O{-}OC{-}R_3\\
\end{array}
$$

Glycerol + fatty acid   Triglyceride

Phospholipid

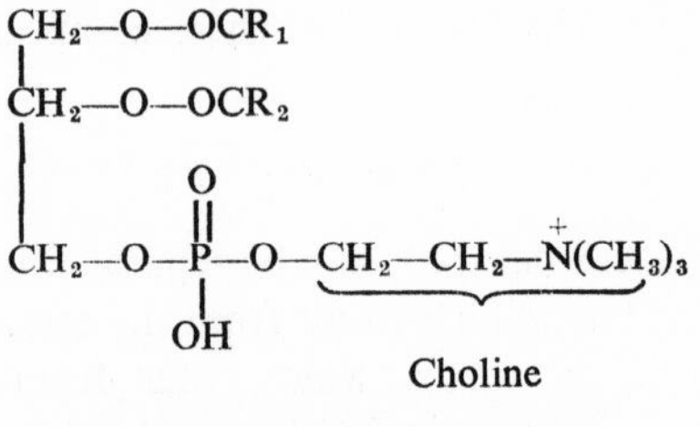

$$
\begin{array}{l}
CH_2{-}O{-}OCR_1\\
CH_2{-}O{-}OCR_2\\
\ \ \ \ \ \ \ \ \ \ \ \ O\\
\ \ \ \ \ \ \ \ \ \ \ \ \|\\
CH_2{-}O{-}P{-}O{-}CH_2{-}CH_2{-}\overset{+}{N}(CH_3)_3\\
\ \ \ \ \ \ \ \ \ \ \ \ OH
\end{array}
$$

Choline

Lecithin: an important phospholipid
of plant cells

Fig. A.4. Fatty acids and fats

by phosphoric acid; in more complex derivatives the third fatty acid is replaced by an organic nitrogenous phosphate derivative (Fig. A.4). Thus phospholipids have a hydrophobic group in the fatty acid and a hydrophilic group in the phosphate radical. They are therefore well suited to occupy an interface separating two phases. Alternatively, they may form a bimolecular layer with the hydrophobic groups inwards and the polar groups outwards, associating with proteins in an aqueous phase.

Colloids

Proteins and other high molecular weight organic substances are capable of forming colloidal solutions in water. Such a solution, containing dispersed aggregates of molecules, is stable indefinitely and is intermediate between a true solution and a suspension. It exhibits such characteristic properties as: (i) the Tyndall Effect – the scattering of light at right-angles to an incident beam indicating the presence of particles of appreciable dimension. (ii) Relatively low osmotic pressures – since for constant volume and constant quantity of material a higher molecular weight species will have a smaller number of particles. (iii) Electrophoresis – migration of the dispersed particles (which in general are charged) in an electric field. (iv) The inability of the dispersed particles to pass through a suitable porous membrane (i.e. with pores less than 1μ diameter) into an external aqueous phase (dialysis).

Two types of colloidal solutions are distinguished.

(i) *Lyophobic* – the particles show no affinity for molecules of the solvent. If water is the solvent the colloid is referred to as *hydrophobic*.

(ii) *Lyophilic* – in which the particles show an affinity for solvent molecules and are, therefore, solvated. If water is the solvent the colloid is referred to as *hydrophilic*.

All colloidal particles tend to absorb an excess of either positive or negative ions and thus acquire a net charge. Similar particles consequently repel each other and thus prevent combination which would result in precipitation of the dispersed material. The stability of hydrophobic colloids, as opposed to that of hydrophilic colloids, is dependent only upon the net charge on the particle. Precipitation results from addition of an appropriately charged ion. In the case of hydrophilic colloids, in addition to the net charge on the particle there is an additional factor of hydration. It is, therefore, to be expected that the precipitation of hydrophilic colloids will be more difficult. Precipitation of a hydrophilic colloid can be effected only by simultaneous dehydration with alcohol and compression of the diffuse double charge layer by the addition of a sufficient concentration of an appropriately charged ion. A hydrophilic colloid solution may change its physical state as the concentration is increased or as the temperature is lowered from the *sol* state when it has little rigidity to the *gel* state which has greater rigidity.

If two colloids, both hydrophilic and oppositely charged, are

APPENDIX

mixed, a phenomenon quite different from ordinary coagulation is observed. The phenomenon has been called 'coacervation', and is characterized by the separation of the colloidal solutions into two distinct phases in equilibrium with each other. One phase is a fluid sediment rich in colloidal substance and the other phase is the liquid relatively free from colloid. This phenomenon may be concerned in the formation of vacuoles in plant cells.

GENERAL REFERENCES

L. F. FIESER and M. FIESER (1956) *Organic Chemistry*. 3rd ed. Harrap

J. S. FRUTON and S. SIMMONDS (1953) *General Biochemistry*. Wiley

References

1 ARNOLD, W., & SHERWOOD, H. K. (1957) 'Are chloroplasts semi-conductors?' *Proc. Nat. Sci. U.S.* **43**, 105

2 ARNON, D. I. (1959) 'Conversion of light into chemical energy in photosynthesis'. *Nature* **184**, 10

3 ARNON, D. I., ALLEN, M. B., & WHATLEY, F. R. (1956) 'Photosynthesis by isolated chloroplasts'. *Biochim. Biophys. Acta* **20**, 449

4 AUDUS, L. J. (1959) *Plant Growth Substances.* 2nd ed. L. Hill, London

5 BARKER, J., & EL SAIFI, A. F. (1952) 'Studies in the respiratory and carbohydrate metabolism of plant tissues. I'. *Proc. Roy. Soc.* B **140**, 362

6 BARKER, J., & MAPSON, L. W. (1955) 'Studies in respiratory and carbohydrate metabolism of plant tissues'. *Proc. Roy. Soc.* B **143**, 523

7 BASHAM, J. A., BENSON, A. A., KAY, L. D., HARRIS, A. Z., WILSON, A. T., & CALVIN, M. (1954) 'The path of carbon in photosynthesis. XXI. The cyclic regeneration of carbon dioxide acceptor'. *J. Amer. Chem. Soc.* **76**, 1760

8 BENDALL, D. S. (1958) 'Cytochromes and some respiratory enzymes in mitochondria from the spadix of *Arum maculatum*'. *Biochem. J.* **70**, 381

9 BENNET CLARK, T. A., & BEXON, D. (1940) 'Water relations of plant cells. II'. *New Phytol.* **39**, 337

10 BENNET CLARK, T. A., GREEN, A. D., & BARKER, J. W. (1936) 'Water relations of osmotic pressures of plant cells'. *New Phytol.* **35**, 277

11 BENNET CLARK, T. A., YOUNIS, A. F., & ESNAULT, R. (1959) 'Geotropic behaviour of roots'. *J. exp. Bot.* **10**, 69

12 BIRKBECK, M. S. C., & MERCER, E. H. (1961) 'Cytology of cells which synthesize protein'. *Nature* **189**, 558

13 BLACKMAN, F. F. (1895) 'Experimental researches on vegetable assimilation and respiration. II'. *Proc. Roy. Soc. Phil.*, trans. B **186**, 503

14 BLACKMAN, F. F. (1905) 'Optima and limiting factors'. *Ann. Bot.* **19**, 281

15 BLACKMAN, V. H. (1919) 'The compound interest law and plant growth'. *Ann. Bot.* **33**, 353

16 BOLLARD, E. G. (1956) 'Nitrogenous constituents of xylem sap'. *Amer. Soc. Pl. Physiol. Proc.* **31**, 9

17 BOND, G. (1953) 'An isotopic study of the fixation of nitrogen associated with nodulated plants of *Alnus, Myrica* and *Hippophae*'. *J. exp. Bot.* **6**, 303

18 BONNER, J., BANDURSKI, R. S., & MILLERD, A. (1953) 'Linkage of respiration to auxin-induced water uptake'. *Physiol. Plantar.* **6**, 511

19 BRADBEER, C., & STUMPH, P. K. (1959) 'The conversion of fat into carbohydrate in peanut and sunflower seedlings'. *J. biol. Chem.* **234**, 498

20 BRENNER, S., JACOB, F., & MESELSON, M. (1961) 'An unstable intermediate carrying information from genes to ribosomes for protein synthesis'. *Nature* **190**, 576

21 BRIAN, P. W. (1959) 'Effects of gibberellins on plant growth and development'. *Biol. Rev. Camb. Philos. Soc.* **34**, 37

22 BRIGGS, G. E. (1922) 'The characteristics of subnormal photosynthetic activity resulting from deficiency of nutrient salts'. *Proc. Roy. Soc.* B **94**, 20

23 BRIGGS, G. E., & HALDANE, J. B. S. (1925) A note on the kinetics of enzyme action'. *Biochem. J.* **19**, 338

24 BRIGGS, G. E., KIDD, F., & WEST, C. (1920) 'A quantitative analysis of plant growth'. *Ann. app. Biol.* **7**, 103

25 BRIGGS, G. E., & ROBERTSON, R. N. (1957) 'Apparent free space'. *Ann. Rev. Pl. Physiol.* **8**, 11

26 BROWN, A. H. (1953) 'The effects of light on respiration using isotopically enriched oxygen'. *Amer. J. Bot.* **40**, 719

27 BROWN, H. T., & ESCOMBE, F. (1905) 'Researches on some physiological processes of green leaves'. *Proc. Roy. Soc.* B **76**, 29

28 BUNNING, E. (1956) 'Endogenous rhythms in plants'. *Ann. Rev. Pl. Physiol.* **7**, 1

29 BURTON, K., & KREBS, H. A. (1953) 'Free energy changes associated with the individual steps of the tricarboxylic acid cycle, glycolysis and alcoholic fermentation and with the hydrolysis of pyrophosphate groups of adenosine triphosphate'. *Biochem. J.* **54**, 94

30 BUTLER, W. L., NORRIS, K. H., SIEGELMAN, H. W., & HENDRICKS, S. B. (1959) 'Detection, assay and preliminary

purification of the pigment controlling photoresponsive developments in plants'. *Proc. Nat. Acad. Sci.*, **45**, 1703

31 BUVAT, R. (1958) 'Recherches sur les infrastructures du cytoplasme, dans les cellules du meristeme apical, des ebauches foliaires et des feuilles développées'. *Ann. des Sci. Nat. Bot.* **19** (11e seree), 121

32 CANNY, M. J. (1960) 'The rate of translocation'. *Biol. Revs. Camb. Philos. Soc.* **35**, 507

33 CHANCE, B. (1951) 'Enzyme substrate compounds'. *Adv. Enzymol.* **12**, 153

34 CHANCE, B., & SMITH, L. (1957) *Research in Photosynthesis.* Interscience

35 CLELAND, R. & BONNER, J. (1956) 'The residual effect of auxin on the cell wall'. *Plant Physiol.* **31**, 350

36 COLLANDER, R. (1957) 'Permeability of plant cells'. *Ann. Rev. Pl. Physiol.* **8**, 335

37 COLLANDER, R., & BÄRLUND, H. (1933) 'Permeabilitätsstudien *Chara ceratophylla*'. *Acta Botan. Fennica* **11**, 1

38 CRAFTS, A. S. (1956) 'The mechanism of translocation'. *Hilgardia* **26**, 287

39 CURRIER, H. B. (1944) 'Water relations of root cells of *Beta*'. *Amer. J. Bot.* **31**, 378

40 CURRY, G. M., & GRUEN, H. E. (1959) 'Action spectra for the positive and negative phototropism of *Phycomyces* sporangiophores'. *Proc. Nat. Acad. Sci. U.S.* **45**, 797

41 CURRY, G. M., THIMAN, K. V., & RAY, P. M. (1956) 'The base curvature response of *Avena* seedlings to the ultraviolet'. *Physiol. Plantar.* **9**, 429

42 DAVENPORT, H. E. (1959) 'Coenzyme reduction by illuminated chloroplasts'. *Biochem. J.* **73**, 45

43 DAVIES, D. D. (1953) 'The Krebs cycle enzyme system of pea seedlings'. *J. exp. Bot.* **4**, 173

44 DUYSENS, L. N. M. (1954) 'Reversible photo-oxidation of a cytochrome pigment in photosynthesising Rhodospirillum'. *Nature* **173**, 692

45 EMERSON, R., & ARNOLD, W. (1932) 'A separation of the reactions in photosynthesis by means of intermittent light'. *J. gen. Physiol.* **15**, 391

46 EMERSON, R., & LEWIS, C. S. (1942) 'The photosynthetic efficiency of phycocyanin in *Chroococcus*'. *J. gen. Physiol.* **25**, 579

47 EPSTEIN, E., & LEGGETT, J. L. (1954) 'The absorption of alkaline earth cations by barley roots: kinetics and mechanism'. *Amer. J. Bot.* **41,** 785

48 ESAU, K., CURRIER, H. B., & CHEADLE, V. I. (1957) 'Physiology of phloem'. *Ann. Rev. Pl. Physiol.* **8,** 349

49 FARMER, J. B. (1918) 'On the quantitative differences in the water conductivity of the wood in trees and shrubs'. *Proc. Roy. Soc.* B **90,** 232

50 FOSTER, R. J., MCRAE, D. H., & BONNER, J. (1952) 'Auxin induced growth inhibition a natural consequence of two-point attachment'. *Proc. Nat. Acad. Sci.* **38,** 1014

51 FRENCH, C. S. (1961) 'Light pigments and photosynthesis'. *Light and Life* ed. W. D. McElroy and B. Glass. Johns Hopkins Press

52 GAFFRON, H. (1960) 'Energy storage: Photosynthesis', *Plant Physiol.* vol. 1B, ed. F. C. Steward. Acad. Press

53 GALE, E. F., & FOLKES, J. P. (1955) 'The assimilation of amino acids by bacteria 20: the incorporation of labelled amino acids by disrupted staphylococcal cells'. *Biochem. J.* **59,** 661

54 GARNER, W. W., & ALLARD, H. A. (1920) 'Effect of the relative length of day and night on plants'. *J. Agric. Res.* **18,** 553

55 GIBBS, M., & BEEVERS, H. (1955) 'Glucose dissimilation in the higher plant; effect of age of tissue'. *Plant Physiol.* **30,** 343

56 GIBBS, M., & HORECKER, B. L. (1954) 'The mechanism of pentose phosphate conversion to hexose phosphate with pea leaf and pea root preparations'. *J. biol. Chem.* **208,** 813

57 GRANICK, S. (1955) 'Plastid structure development and inheritance'. *Encycl. Pl. Physiol.* **1,** 507

58 GREGORY, F. G. & PEASE, H. L. (1937) 'The effect on the behaviour of stomata of alternating periods of light and dark'. *Ann. Bot.* N.S. **1,** 3

59 HACKETT, D. P., & THIMANN, K. V. (1950) 'The action of inhibitors on water uptake by potato tissue'. *Plant Physiol.* **25,** 648

60 HALDANE, J. B. S. (1930) *The Enzymes.* Longmans Green

61 HANES, C. S. (1940) 'The reversible formation of starch from glucose 1 phosphate'. *Proc. Roy. Soc.* B **129,** 174

62 HAXO, F. T., & BLINKS, L. R. (1950) 'Photosynthetic action spectra of marine algae'. *J. gen. Physiol.* **33,** 389

63 HEATH, O. V. S. (1938) 'An experimental investigation of the mechanism of stomatal movement'. *New Phytol.* **37,** 385

64 HEATH, O. V. S., & MILTHORPE, F. L. (1950) 'Studies in stomatal behaviour. V'. *J. exp. Bot.* **1**, 227

65 HEATH, O. V. S., & RUSSELL, J. (1954) 'Studies in stomatal behaviour. VI'. *J. exp. Bot.* **5**, 269

66 HENDRICKS, S. B. (1960) 'Photoreactions in Photoperiodism'. *Comparative Biochemistry of Photoreaction Systems* chap. 19, ed. M. B. Allen. Acad. Press

67 HILL, R. (1939) 'Oxygen produced by isolated chloroplasts'. *Proc. Roy. Soc.* B **127**, 192

68 HILL, R., & BENDALL, F. (1960) 'Function of two cytochrome components in chloroplasts: a working hypothesis'. *Nature* **186**, 136

69 HILL, R., & HARTREE, E. F. (1953) 'Hematin compounds in plants'. *Ann. Rev. Pl. Physiol.* **4**, 115

70 HILL, R. & WHITTINGHAM, C. P. (1957) *Photosynthesis* 2nd ed. Methuen

71 HODGE, A. J., MCLEAN, J. D., & MERCER, F. W. (1955) 'Ultrastructure of the lamellae and grana in the chloroplasts of *Zea mays*'. *J. Biophys. Biochem. Cytol.* **1**, 605

72 HOFLER, K. (1920) 'Ein schema für die osmatische Leistung der Pflanzenselle'. *Ber. dent. bot. Gesell.* **35**, 706

73 VAN DEN HONERT, T. H. (1932) 'On the mechanism of transport of organic materials in plants'. *Proc. Acad. Sci. Amst.* **35**, 1104

74 JAMES, W. O. (1953) 'The terminal oxidases of plant respiration'. *Biol. Rev. Camb. Philos. Soc.* **28**, 245

75 JAMES, W. O., & BEEVERS, H. (1950) 'The respiration of *Arum spadix*'. *New Phytol.* **49**, 353

76 JAMES, W. O., & LUNDEGÅRDH, H. (1959) 'The cytochrome system of young barley roots'. *Proc. Roy. Soc.* B **150**, 7

77 JOHNSTONE, E. S. (1934) 'Phototropic sensitivity in relation to wavelength'. *Smith. Misc. Coll.* **92**, 11

78 KANDLER, O., & GIBBS, M. (1956) 'Asymmetric distribution of C^{14} in the glucose phosphates formed during photosynthesis'. *Plant Physiol.* **31**, 411

79 KEILIN, D. (1925) 'On cytochrome: a respiratory pigment common to animals, yeast and higher plants'. *Proc. Roy. Soc.* B **98**, 312

80 KIDD, F., & WEST, G. (1945) 'Respiratory activities and duration of life of apples gathered at different stages of development'. *Plant Physiol.* **20**, 476

81 KORNBERG, H. L., & KREBS, H. A. (1957) 'Synthesis of cell constituents from C_2 units by a modified tricarboxylic acid cycle'. *Nature* **179**, 988

82 KOSTYCHEV, S. (1927) *Plant respiration* trs. C. L. Lyons. Blakiston, Phil., Pa.

83 KRAMER, P. J. (1937) 'The relation between rate of transpiration and rate of absorption of water in plants'. *Amer. J. Bot.* **24**, 10

84 KRAMER, P. J. (1956) 'The uptake of water by plant cells'. *Encycl. Pl. Physiol.* **2**, 316 ed.

85 KRAMER, P. J. (1956) 'Root pressure'. *Encycl. Pl. Physiol.* **3**, 188

86 KRASNOVSKY, A. A. (1948) 'Reversible photochemical reduction of chlorophyll by ascorbic acid'. *Dok. Akad. Nauk. SSSR* **60**, 421

87 KUHN, W. (1923) 'Ü. Saccharase und Raffinasewirkung des Invertins'. *Z. physiol. Chem.* **125**, 28

88 LANDMAN, O. E., & SPIGELMAN, S. (1955) 'Enzyme formation in protoplasts of *Bacillus megatherium*'. *Proc. Nat. Acad. Sci.* **41**, 698

89 LARSEN, R. (1949) 'Conversion of indole acetaldehyde to indoleacetic acid in excised coleoptiles and coleoptile juice'. *Amer. J. Bot.* **36**, 32

90 LATIES, G. G. (1949) 'The oxidative formation of succinate in higher plants'. *Arch. Biochem.* **22**, 8

91 LELOIR, L. F., & CARDINI, C. E. (1955) 'The biosynthesis of sucrose phosphate'. *J. biol. Chem.* **214**, 157

92 LEOPOLD, A. C., & THIMAN, K. V. (1949) 'The effect of auxin on flower initiation'. *Amer. J. Bot.* **36**, 342.

93 LEVITT, J. (1957) 'The significance of apparent free space in ion absorption'. *Physiol. Planta.* **10**, 882

94 LINNEWEAVER, H., & BURK, D. (1934) 'The determination of enzyme dissociation constants'. *J. Amer. Chem. Soc.* **56**, 658

95 LINSBAUER, K. (1927) 'Weitere Beobachtung an Spaltöffnungen'. *Planta* **3**, 527

96 LIPMANN, F. (1941) 'Metabolic generation and utilization of phosphate bond energy'. *Adv. in Enzymol.* **1**, 99

97 LIVINGSTONE, R. (1960) 'The photochemistry of chlorophyll'. *Encycl. Pl. Physiol.* **5**, 1, ed W. Ruhland. Springer

98 LUNDEGÅRDH, H. (1954) 'Anion respiration'. *Soc. Emp. Biol. Symp.* no. **8**, 262

99 LUNDEGÅRDH, H. (1956) 'Spectrophotometrical investigations on enzyme systems in living objects'. *Biochim. Biophys. Acta* **20,** 469.

100 MASKELL, E. J. (1928) 'The relation between stomatal opening and assimilation'. *Proc. Roy. Soc.* B **102,** 488

101 MASKELL, E. J., & MASON, T. G. (1929) 'Studies on the transport of nitrogenous substances in the cotton plant'. *Ann. Bot.* **43,** 615

102 MASON, T. G., & MASKELL, E. J. (1928) 'A study of diurnal variation in the carbohydrates of leaf bark and wood and of the effects of ringing'. *Ann. Bot.* **42,** 188

103 MERCER, F. V. (1960) 'The submicroscopic structure of the cell'. *Ann. Rev. Pl. Physiol.* **11,** 1

104 MICHAELIS, L., & MENTEN, M. L. (1913) 'Die Kinetik der Invertinwirkung'. *Biochem. Z.* **49,** 333

105 MILLER, C. O. (1961) 'Kinetin and related compounds in plant growth'. *Ann. Rev. Pl. Physiol.* **12,** 395

106 MILLERD, A., BONNER, J., AXELROD, B., & BANDURSKI, R. S. (1951) 'Oxidative and phosphorylative activity of plant mitochondria'. *Proc. Nat. Acad. Sci. U.S.* **37,** 855

107 MILTHORPE, F. L. (1955) 'The significance of the measurement made by the cobalt paper method'. *J. exp. Bot.* **6,** 17

108 MITTLER, T. E. (1953) 'Amino acids in the phloem sap and their extraction by aphids'. *Nature* **172,** 207

109 MONOD, J. (1949) 'The growth of bacterial cultures'. *Ann. Rev. Microbiol.* **3,** 371

110 MONOD, J., COHEN-BAZIRE, G., & COHN, E. (1951) 'Sur la biosynthese de la galactoside chez *Escherichia coli*'. *Biochim. Biophys. Acta* **7,** 585

111 MOTHES, K. (1931) 'Zur Zenntniss des N Stoffwechsels Höherer Pflanzen'. *Planta* **12,** 686

112 MÜHLETHALER, K. (1950) 'Electron microscopy of developing plant cell walls'. *Biochim. Biophys. Acta* **5,** 1

113 MÜNCH, E. (1926) 'Dynamik der Saftströmung'. *Ber. deut. bot. Ges.* **44,** 68

114 NICHOLAS, D. J. D. (1957) 'Role of metals in enzymes with special reference to flavoproteins'. *Nature* **179,** 800

115 NICHOLAS, D. J. D., NASON, A., & McELROY, W. D. (1954) 'Molybdenum and nitrate reductase'. *J. biol. Chem.* **207,** 341

116 NORTHCOTE, D. H. (1958) 'The cell walls of higher plants'. *Biol. Rev. Camb. Philos. Soc.* **33,** 53

117 OLSEN, J. M., & CHANCE, S. (1958) 'Cytochrome reactions in *chromatium*'. *Biochim. Biophys. Acta* **3**, 227

118 PALADE, G. E. (1953) 'An electron microscope study of the mitochondrial structure'. *J. histochem. Cytochem.* **1**, 188

119 PARDEE, A. B. (1954) 'Nucleic acid precursors and protein synthesis'. *Proc. Nat. Acad. Sci.* **40**, 263

120 PEARSALL, W. H., & BILLIMORIA, M. C. (1938) 'Effects of age and of season upon protein synthesis in detached leaves'. *Ann. Bot.* **2**, 317

121 PEARSALL, W. H., & LOOSE, L. (1937) 'The growth of *Chlorella vulgaris* in pure culture'. *Proc. Roy. Soc.* B **121**, 451

122 PRESTON, R. D. (1946) 'The fine structure of the wall of the conifer tracheid I. The X-ray diagram'. *Proc. Roy. Soc.* B **133**, 327

123 PRESTON, R. D. (1959) 'Wall organisation in plant cells'. *Int. Rev. Cytol.* **8**

124 PRESTON, R. D., & HEPTON, J. (1960) 'The effect of IAA on cell wall extensibility in *Avena* coleoptiles'. *J. exp. Bot.* **11**, 13

125 PRITCHARD, G. G., GRIFFIN, W., & WHITTINGHAM, C. P. (1962) 'The photosynthetic production of glycollic acid by *Chlorella*'. *J. exp. Bot.* **13**, 176

126 RACKER, E. (1955) 'Synthesis of carbohydrates from carbon dioxide and hydrogen in a cell-free system'. *Nature* **175**, 249

127 REES, A. P. T., & BEEVERS, H. (1960) 'Pathways of glucose dissimilation in carrot slices'. *Plant Physiol.* **35**, 830

128 RICHMOND, A. E., & LANG, A. (1957) 'Effect of kinetin on protein content and survival of detached *Xanthium* leaves'. *Science* **125**, 651

129 ROBERTSON, J. D. (1959) 'On the ultrastructure of cell membranes and their derivatives'. *Biochem. Soc. Symp.* **16**, 3

130 ROBERTSON, R. N., & WILKINS, M. J. (1948) 'Quantitative relation between salt accumulation and salt respiration in plant cells'. *Nature* **161**, 101

131 ROBERTSON, R. N. (1960) 'Ion transport and respiration'. *Biol. Rev. Camb. Philos. Soc.* **35**, 231

132 SAN PIETRO, A., & LANG, H. M. (1958) 'Photosynthetic pyridine nucleotide reductase'. *J. biol. Chem.* **231**, 211

133 SAYRE, J. D. (1926) 'Physiology of stomata of *Rumex patienta*'. *Ohio J. Sci.* **26**, 233

134 SCARTH, G. W. (1932) 'Mechanism of the action of light and other factors on stomatal movement'. *Plant Physiol.* **7**, 481

135 SCHUMACHER, W. (1933) 'Untersuchungen über die Wanderung des Fluoreszeins in den Siebröhen'. *Jahrb. wiss Bot.* **77**, 685

136 SCOTT, F. M., HAMMER, K. C., BAKER, E., & BOWLER, E. (1956) 'Electron microscope studies of cell wall growth in the onion root'. *Amer. J. Bot.* **43**, 313

137 SKÖG, F., & MILLER, C. O. (1957) 'Chemical regulation of growth and organ formation'. *Soc. Expt. Biol. Symp.* **9**, 118

138 SIMON, E. W., & CHAPMAN, J. A. (1961) 'The development of mitochondria in *Arum spadix*'. *J. exp. Bot.* **12**, 414

139 SPANNER, D. C. (1958) 'The translocation of sugar in sieve tubes'. *J. exp. Bot.* **9**, 332

140 STALFELT, M. G. (1932) 'Der stomatäre Regulator in der pflanzlichen Transpiration'. *Planta.* **17**, 22

141 STUMPF, P. K., & BARBER, G. A. (1956) 'Oxidation of fatty acids by peanut mitochondria'. *Plant Physiol.* **31**, 304

142 SUTCLIFFE, J. F. (1959) 'Salt uptake in plants'. *Biol. Rev. Camb. Philos. Soc.* **34**, 159

143 SVEDBERG, T., & KATSURAI, T. (1929) 'The molecular weights of phycocyanin and phyerythrin from *Porphyra tenera* and of phycocyanin from *Aphanizomenom flos aquae*'. *J. Amer. Chem. Soc.* **51**, 3573

144 TAGAWA, K., & ARNON, D. I. (1962) 'Ferredoxins as electron carriers in photosynthesis'. *Nature* **195**, 537

145 TANG, Y. W., & BONNER, J. (1947) 'The enzymatic inactivation of indoleacetic acid'. *Arch. Biochem.* **13**, 11

146 THIMANN, K. V., & CURRY, G. M. (1961) 'Phototropism'. *Light and Life* ed. W. D. McElroy and B. Glass. Johns Hopkins Press

147 ULRICH, A. (1942) 'Metabolism of organic acids in excised barley roots as influenced by temperature, oxygen tension and salt concentration'. *Amer. J. Bot.* **29**, 220

148 NIEL, VAN C. P. (1941) 'The bacterial photosynthesis and their importance for the general problems of photosynthesis'. *Adv. Enzymol.* **1**, 263

149 VICKERY, H. B., PUCHER, G. W., SCHOENHEIMER, R., & RITTENBERG, D. (1940) 'The assimilation of ammonia nitrogen by the tobacco plant'. *J. biol. Chem.* **135**, 531

150 VISHNIAC, W., & ROSE, I. A. (1959) 'Mechanism of chlorophyll action in photosynthesis'. *Nature* **182**, 1089

151 WARBURG, O., & NEGELEIN, E. (1928) 'Über den Einfluss der Wellenlange auf die Verteilung des Atmungsferments'. *Biochem. Z.* **193**, 339

152 WEATHERLEY, P. E., PEEL, A. J., & HILL, G. P. (1950) 'The physiology of the sieve tube'. *J. exp. Bot.* **10,** 1

153 WENT, F. W., & WHITE, R. (1939) 'Experiments on the transport of auxin'. *Bot. Gaz.* **100,** 465

154 WHITTINGHAM, C. P., & BISHOP, P. M. (1961) 'Thermal reaction between two light reactions in photosynthesis'. *Nature* **192,** 426

155 WILLIAMS, R. F. (1936) 'Physiological ontogency in plants and its relation to nutrition. 2. The effect of phosphorous supply'. *Austr. J. exp. Biol. and Med. Sci.* **14,** 165

156 WILLIAMS, W. T. (1953) 'The role of starch in the light response of stomata'. *J. exp. Bot.* **3,** 110

157 WILLIAMS, W. T. (1954) 'A new theory of the mechanism of stomatal movement'. *J. exp. Bot.* **5,** 343

158 WILLSTATTER, R., & STOLL, A. (1928) *Investigations on Chlorophyll* trs. F. M. Schertz and A. R. Merz. Science Press, Pancaster, Pa.

159 WILSON, A. T., & CALVIN, M. (1955) 'The photosynthetic cycle. CO_2 dependent transients'. *J. Amer. Chem. Soc.* **77,** 5948

160 WITT, H. T. (1955) 'Zum primarprozess der Photosynthese'. *Z. physikal. Chem.* **4,** 120

161 WOLKEN, J. J., & SCHWERTZ, F. A. (1953) 'Chlorophyll monolayers in chloroplasts'. *J. gen. Physiol.* **37,** 111

162 YEMM, E. W. (1937) 'Respiration of barley plants. III. Protein catabolism in starving leaves'. *Proc. Roy. Soc.* B **123,** 243

163 ZELITCH, I., ROSENBLUM, E. D., BURRIS, R. H., & WILSON, P. W. (1946) 'Isolation of the key intermediate in biological nitrogen fixation by Clostridium'. *J. biol. Chem.* **191,** 295

164 ZIMMERMAN, M. H. (1957) 'Translocation of organic substances in trees. II'. *Plant Physiol.* **32,** 299

165 ZIMMERMAN, M. H. (1958) 'Translocation of organic substances in trees. III'. *Plant Physiol.* **33,** 213

166 ZSCHEILE, F. P., & COMMAR, C. L. (1941) 'Influence of preparative procedure on the purity of chlorophyll components is shown by absorption spectra'. *Bot. Gaz.* **102,** 463

167 ZSCHEILE, F. P., WHITE, J. W., BEADLE, B. W., & ROACH, J. R. (1942) 'The preparation and absorption spectra of five pure carotenoid pigments'. *Plant Physiol.* **17,** 331

Index

Abscission layer, 174
Absorption spectrum, barley root, 55
  carotenoid, 92
  chlorophyll, 91
  coenzyme I, 51
  cytochrome c, 54
  phycobilin, 93
  red alga, 98
Acetaldehyde, 42
Acetyl CoA, 47, 60
Acetyl phosphate, 67
Aconitase, 48
Action spectrum, cytochrome oxida-
    tion, 100
  floral induction, 180
  phototropism, 172
  red alga, 98
Activation energy, 27, 64
Active uptake, water, 124, 148
  salts, 128
Adenosine 5' triphosphate, 43, 67,
    132
Adenosine formula, 190
Alanine, 80, 107, 188
Alcohol dehydrogenase, 40
Alcoholic fermentation, 36
Aldehyde dehydrogenase, 51
Aldolase, 38
Amidase, 110
Amide, breakdown and synthesis, 67,
    108
  formula, 188
Amination, reductive, 106
Amino acid formation, 106
Ammonia as intermediate, 105
Amylase, 25, 67
Amylopectin, 38, 186
Amylose, 38, 69, 186
  synthetase, 69
Antiauxin, 175
Antibiotics, 14
Aphids as phloem feeders, 155
Apical dominance, 174, 177
Arsenate, 43, 59
Ascorbic acid oxidase, 56
Asparagine, 109
Aspartase, 26, 107
Assimilation number, 76
Auxin, 165
  bioassay, 167
  bound, 166
  chemical structure, 175

  extraction, 166
  inhibitors, 166, 171
Azide, 125

Bacteria, photosynthetic, 85
Bacterial chromatophores, 87
Bacteriochlorophyll, 73
Base response, 173
Bioelectric effects, 171, 173
Bioluminescence, 102
Birefringence, 20
Bisulphite, 40
Bond, disulphide, 20, 47, 189

Callose, 153, 155
Calvin cycle, 81
Carbohydrates, chemistry of, 183–187
  metabolism, 36–45
  formation in photosynthesis, 79–82
Carbon dioxide fixation, dark, 62
  photosynthetic, 79–84
Carbon monoxide, 57
Carotenoids, 89, 91
  absorption spectrum, 92
Carrier, electron, 51
  mechanism, 131
Catalase, 25, 50, 56
Catalysis, enzyme, 25, 27
Cell wall, structure, 18
  permeability, 119
Cellulose, 18, 186
Chlorophyll, absorption spectrum, 91
  content, 77
  fluorescence, 73
  formation, 77
  formula, 90
  in chloroplast, 21
  long wave, 101
  photobleaching, 94
Cholodny-Went hypothesis, 170
Classification, plant, 11
Cobalt chloride method, 144
Co-carboxylase, 40
Code for amino acids, 113
Coenzyme A, 47, 57, 60, 176
Coenzyme 1, absorption curve, 51
  formula, 35
  in electron transfer, 50, 57, 71
  in fermentation, 40
  in phosphorylation, 65
  redox potential, 65
  redox reagent, 26

205

Coenzyme 2, formula, 35
  in electron transport, 50
  in pentose shunt, 44
  in photosynthesis, 84
  redox reagent, 26
Coenzymes, 25, 40
Colloidal solution, 193
Companion cell, 152
Condensing enzyme, 48
Control mechanisms, 27, 70
Correlation, growth, 164
Coupled reactions, 65, 86
Cross linkage, 20, 173, 189
Cyanide, 57, 68, 76, 129, 136
Cytochrome a, b_6, f, 54
Cytochrome b_3, 53
Cytochrome b_7, 57
Cytochrome c, absorption curve, 54
Cytochrome oxidase, absorption curve,
  53
Cytochrome reductase, 51, 53
Cytochromes, in photosynthesis, 88,
  94, 102
  in respiration, 31, 50, 51
  in salt uptake, 129
Cytoplasm, properties of, 20
  structure, 18, 20
Cutin, 18

Dark fixation of carbon dioxide, 62
Dark reaction of photosynthesis, 79
Dehydrogenases, 26, 50, 106
  aerobic, 56
Denaturation, 32, 34, 127
Deoxyribonucleic acid (DNA), 112, 190
Derivative spectrum, 99, 100
Differentiation, 162
  and auxin, 174
Diffusion, 26, 31, 76, 117, 118, 126,
  139, 141, 157
  activated, 158
Diffusion pressure deficit (see suction
  pressure)
Dinitrophenol, 125, 130
Dipeptide, 188
Diphosphopyridine nucleotide (see
  coenzyme 1)
Disaccharides, 185
Diurnal rhythm, 148
Diurnal sugar fluctuation, 154
Donnan equilibrium, 128
Dormant buds, 168
Dormant seeds, 161, 180
Dormant tissue, 70

Double charge layer, 193
Dynamic equilibrium, 68, 111

Efficiency energy utilization, 22, 66, 74,
  99
Electron transport systems, 50–57
  and phosphorylation, 58, 64–65
  in photosynthesis, 87, 89
Electro-osmosis, 158
Embden Meyerhof Parnas path, 38, 40,
  45
Endodermis, 135
Endoplasmic reticulum, 20, 21
Energy of activation, 27, 64
Enolase, 38, 43
Enzymes, 25–34
  additive, 26
  classification, 26
  inductive, 27
  localization, 23, 132
  mechanism catalysis, 27–30
  oxidative, 22
  specificity, 26
  substrate complex, 29, 32
Equilibrium constant, 63
Erythrose 4 phosphate, 46
Esterases, 36
Extinction point, 43

Fat oxidation, 60
Fat structure, 192
Fat synthesis, 61
Fatty acid oxidation, 60
Fatty acid structure, 191
Feedback, 71
Fermentation, 36–43
Fibre structure, 189
Flavoprotein, 51–53, 57, 65, 106, 172
Floral induction, 178–82
Florigen, 166, 179
Fluorescence, 73, 97
Fluoride, 39, 40, 43
Free energy, 22, 63–65
  of phosphorylation, 66
  of photosynthesis, 73
Free radicals in photosynthesis, 102
Free space, 119, 125, 135
Freezing point lowering, 118, 124
Fructose, 184
  6 phosphate, 46
  1·6 diphosphate, 38, 46, 58, 83
Fucoxanthol, 101
Fumarase, 48
Furanose sugar, 185

Galactan, 186
Galactose, 184, 186
Gas laws, 118
Geoelectric effect, 171
Geotropism, 170
Germination seeds, 17, 42, 60, 108, 191
Gibberellin, 166, 176, 181
α-glucosidase, 26
Glucose, 184
Glucose 1 phosphate, 38, 67, 147
Glucose 6 phosphate, 38, 46
Glutamic dehydrogenase, 107
Glutamine, 109
Glutathione, 56, 110
Glyceraldehyde 3 phosphate (see triose phosphate)
Glycine, 84, 107, 188
Glycollic acid, 84
  oxidase, 56
Glyoxylate cycle, 61
Grana, 21, 96
Growth curves, 160, 164
  relative rate of, 163
Guanosine 5′ triphosphate, 113
Guttation, 136
Gymnosperms, 91, 136, 138, 152

Haem, 25, 54
Hales, S., 12, 153
Heat of reaction, 63
van Helmont, J. B., 12, 13
Herbals, 11
Herbicides, 14, 174
Hexokinase, 38
Hill reaction, 85
Hydrogen bonds, 20
Hydrolases, 26
Hydroxylamine, as inhibitor, 76
  as intermediate, 105

Indoleacetaldehyde, 167
Indoleacetic acid, 125, 136, 165–70, 171, 173, 174, 181
Indoleacetonitrile, 167, 169
Inductive enzymes, 27
Inductive resonance, 99
Ingenhousz, J., 13
Inhibition, competitive, 33
  non-competitive, 33
Initial rates, 31
Invertase, 26
Iodoacetate, 39, 43, 44, 68, 176
Ion flux, 132
Iron in cytochrome, 50

Isocitric dehydrogenase, 48, 52, 58
Isocitritase, 61
Isoelectric point, 32
Isonicotinyl hydrozide, 84
Isotonic coefficient, 119

Juvenility, 178, 182

Keilin, D., 50
Kinins, 166, 178
Krebs cycle, 45–48, 57
Krebs-Kornberg cycle, 61

Labelling sequence in photosynthesis, 80
Lactic acid, 37, 41
Lactic dehydrogenase, 40, 52
Lag phase, 162
Leghaemoglobin, 105
Limiting factor, 74
Lipase, 26, 191
Lipids, structure, 191
  formation and breakdown, 60
Lipoic acid, 47
Logarithmic growth, 161
Long day plant, 178

Malic dehydrogenase, 48, 52
Malic enzyme, 31
Malic synthetase, 61
Malonate inhibition, 47
Maltase, 67
Maltose, 38, 184
Mannose, 38, 184
Mass flow, 118, 135, 157
Mass transfer, 155
Membranes, 19, 21, 22, 132
  semipermeable, 117
Meristematic cells, 20, 21
Methylene blue, 129
Michaelis constant, 29, 31, 76, 176
Microfibrils, 18
Microscope electron, 17, 19
Microscope, phase contrast, 17
Microsome, 113
Middle lamella, 18
Mitochondria, 21, 22, 48, 58, 67 74, 89, 130
Monosaccharides, 183
Mutarotation, 184

Net assimilation rate (unit leaf rate), 164
Nicotinamide adenine dinucleotide (see Coenzyme 1)
Nicotinamide adenine dinucleotide phosphate (see Coenzyme 2)
Nicotinic acid, 165

Nitrate assimilation, 105
Nitrate reductase, 105
Nitrate reduction, 105–106
Nitrite reductase, 105
Nitrogen fixation, 104–105
Nitrogen movement, 156
Nucleic acids, 190
 (*see* also DNA, RNA)
Nucleotide, 190

Old yellow enzyme, 53
Optimum pH, 32
Optimum temperature, 34
Osmosis, 117, 135
Osmotic pressure, 117
Osmotic relationship of root, 134
Osmotic volume, 121
Oxidases, 53–57
Oxidation-reduction potential, 65
Oxidative phosphorylation, 57–59, 66
Oxidoreductases, 22
Oxygen as inhibitor, 43, 47

Pacemaker, 71
Pantothenic acid, 47
Pasteur effect, 70
Path carbon, in photosynthesis, 79–84
 in respiration, 44–49
Pectin, 18
Pentoses, structure, 185
Pentosans, 186
Pentose phosphate pathway, 44–46
Peptidases, 26, 108, 111
Peptide bond, structure, 188
 synthesis, 64, 108, 112
Permeability, 19, 21
 coefficient, 121, 126
Peroxidase, 32, 50, 56
Phloem, exudate, 155, 156
 ringing, 153
 transport, 154, 179
Phosphatase, 132
Phosphoenol pyruvic carboxylase, 62
Phosphoenol pyruvic carboxykinase, 62
Phosphoglucomutase, 38
Phosphogluconate, 45
Phosphoglyceric acid in photosynthesis, 80
Phospholipids, 192
Phosphorescence, 93
Phosphorylase, starch, 38, 69
 sucrose, 69
Phosphorylation, balance sheet, 58
 oxidaton, 22, 57

photosynthetic, 86
 substrate, 57
Photoconductivity, 102
Photolysis, 85
Photosynthesis, dark reaction in, 79–85
 light reaction in, 85–89
 rate of, 75–76
Phototropism, 171
Phycobilins, absorption spectrum, 93
 role in photosynthesis, 96, 99, 101
Phytochrome, 180
Phytol, 90
Phytotron, 164
Pits, 18
Plasmalemma, 19, 119, 120
Plasmodesmata, 19
Plasmolysis, 19, 20
 incipient, 119
Polar movement, 170
Polyphenol oxidase, 23, 55, 56
Polysaccharides, 186
Pool, metabolic, 23
Porometer, 142
Potometer, 137
Priestley, J., 13
Prosthetic groups, 25
Protein, as enzyme, 25
 breakdown, 61
 structure, 62, 64, 69
 synthesis, 189
Protochlorophyll, 91
Protoplasm, 18
 streaming, 157
Protoplast, 18
 isolated, 125
Pump, ion, 132
Purines, 190
Purple sulphur bacteria, 85
Pyranose sugar, 185
Pyridoxine, 165
Pyrimidines, 190
Pyrrole synthesis, 62
Pyruvic acid, in fermentation, 37, 41
 oxidation, 47

Quanta, definition, 73
Quantum efficiency, photosynthesis, 98, 100
Quinone, 85

Radioactive, carbon dioxide, 62, 79
 glucose, 45
 tracer movement, 155
Resistance of wood, 138

Respiration and oxidation, 22
Respiration, carbon path, 44–49
  salt, 129
Respiratory, carriers, 49–57
  quotient, 60
Response, plant, 170
Reticulum, endoplasmic, 20, 21
Rhizome, tropic response, 171
Ribonucleic acid (RNA), 20, 21, 112, 190
  soluble, 113
  transfer, 113
Ribose 5 phosphate, 46, 85
Ribosomes, 20, 113
Ribulose 5 phosphate, 46
Ribulose 1·5 diphosphate, 83
Ringing, phloem, 153
Root hairs, 134
Root pressure, 136, 150
Rosette habit, 161, 177, 178

S growth curve, 160
Salt accumulation, 129
Salt uptake, 128–133
  by root, 135
Sedoheptulose 7 phosphate, 83
Sedoheptulose 1·7 diphosphate, 83
Senescence, 162
Serine, 170, 188
Shearing layer, 140, 144
Short day plant, 178
Sieve tube, function, 155
  structure, 152
Soil moisture tension, 134
Soluble RNA, 113
Solute uptake, 126–33
Starch, in guard cell, 146
  structure, 186
  synthesis, 38, 68
Starch, sugar balance, 67–69
Statoliths, 171
Stomata function, 146
Stomata, measurement of, 141
Stomata structure, 146
Stroma, 21, 96
Structure, plant, 14, 15, 76
  cell, 17, 22
Suberin, 18
Substomatal cavity, 140, 143
Substrate phosphorylation, 57
Succinate as substrate, 62
Succinate dehydrogenase, 48, 51, 52
Sucrose, 38, 69, 184, 185
Suction pressure, 119, 123, 140

Sugar chemistry, 183–186
Symbiotic nitrogen fixation, 104

Temperature coefficient, enzyme catalysis, 34
  photosynthesis, 76
Terminal oxidase systems, 53–57
Thiamine, 165
Tonoplast, 20, 119, 120, 131
Trace elements, 13
Transaldolase, 44, 46, 81
Transaminases, 26, 107
Transfer RNA, 113
Transferases, 26
Transketolase, 44, 46, 81
Translocation rate, 156
Transpiration, as physical process, 139–45
  cuticular, 139
Tricarboxylic acid cycle (see Krebs cycle)
Triglyceride, 192
Triosephosphate, 38, 46, 83
  dehydrogenase, 38, 52
  isomerase, 38
Triplet state, 93
Tropisms, 170
Tryptophane, 169

Uncoupling, 59, 70
Uridine diphosphate glucose, 38, 69

Vacuole, 19, 20, 117
Vapour pressure lowering, 118
Vernalization, 181
Vitamin K, 87, 88
Vitamins, 165

Wall structure, 18
Wall growth, 19
Water balance of plant, 148
Waxes, 192
Wilting, 111, 149

X-ray methods, 17, 19
Xeromorphs, 146
Xerophytes, 146
Xylose 5 phosphate, 45

Yeast, 31, 36, 37, 53
  juice, 37, 41

Zinc deficiency, 169
Zonation seaweeds, 98